TALKING ANIMALS IN BRITISH CHILDREN'S FICTION, 1786–1914

For Nico and Bobbin

Talking Animals in British Children's Fiction, 1786–1914

TESS COSSLETT
Lancaster University, UK

ASHGATE

Published by
Ashgate Publishing Limited
Gower House
Croft Road
Aldershot
Hampshire GU11 3HR
England

Ashgate Publishing Company
Suite 420
101 Cherry Street
Burlington, VT 05401-4405
USA

Ashgate website: http://www.ashgate.com

British Library Cataloguing in Publication Data
Cosslett, Tess
    Talking animals in British children's fiction, 1786–1914. – (The Nineteenth Century Series)
    1.Animals in literature. 2.Children's stories, English – History and criticism. 3.English fiction – 19th century – History and criticism. I.Title
    823.8'09362

Library of Congress Cataloging-in-Publication Data
Cosslett, Tess
    Talking animals in British children's fiction, 1786–1914 / Tess Cosslett.
        p.   cm. – (The Nineteenth Century Series)
    Includes bibliographical references and index.
    1. Children's stories, English – History and criticism. 2. Animals in literature. 3. Anthropomorphism in literature. 4. English fiction – 19th century – History and criticism. 5. English fiction – 18th century – History and criticism. I. Title. II. Series: Nineteenth century (Aldershot, England)
    PR830.C513C67 2006
    823'.809362083–dc22   2005033638

ISBN-10: 0-7546-3656-9

This volume is printed on acid-free paper

Printed and bound in Great Britain by MPG Books Ltd, Bodmin, Cornwall.

Contents

List of Illustrations   vi
Acknowledgements   vii
General Editors' Preface   viii

Introduction   1

1   Animals in Eighteenth-Century Children's Books   9

2   Fabulous Histories and Papillonades   37

3   Animal Autobiography   63

4   Parables and Fairy-tales   93

5   Wild Animal Stories   123

6   Arcadias?   151

Afterword   181

Bibliography   185
Index   199

List of Illustrations

2.1   Illustration by William Mulready in William Roscoe,   52
       The Butterfly's Ball (1807). By permission of the British Library,
       shelfmark C.a.57.

2.2   Illustration by William Mulready in William Roscoe,   52
       The Butterfly's Ball (1807). By permission of the British Library,
       shelfmark C.a.57.

3.1   'Billy would take his ball and go off by himself.' Illustration   66
       in Marshall Saunders, *Beautiful Joe* (1901). Prize Collection,
       Senate House Library, University of London.

3.2   'Luath tells his story.' Illustration by Harrison Weir in   67
       Gordon Stables, *Sable and White* (1894). By permission
       of the British Library, shelfmark 012807 f.14.

6.1   Illustration from *The Tale of Peter Rabbit* by Beatrix Potter,   154
       copyright © Frederick Warne & Co., 1902, 2002. Reproduced
       by permission of Frederick Warne & Co.

6.2   Illustration from *The Tale of Peter Rabbit* by Beatrix Potter,   155
       copyright © Frederick Warne & Co., 1902, 2002. Reproduced
       by permission of Frederick Warne & Co.

Acknowledgements

Many thanks to the Arts and Humanities Research Board (now a Research Council) for time under the Research Leave scheme to complete this book. Versions of Chapters One, Two and Three were given as papers to conferences at Oxford and Hull organised by the British Society for Eighteenth Century Studies and the British Association for Victorian Studies, and to a seminar at the Centre for International Research on Children's Literature in Reading: I am grateful to everyone concerned for useful feedback. Thanks to Alison Easton for acting as 'research buddy' and listening to my tangled thoughts. Thanks as always to Greg and Alice.

The Nineteenth Century Series
General Editors' Preface

The aim of the series is to reflect, develop and extend the great burgeoning of interest in the nineteenth century that has been an inevitable feature of recent years, as that former epoch has come more sharply into focus as a locus for our understanding not only of the past but of the contours of our modernity. It centres primarily upon major authors and subjects within Romantic and Victorian literature. It also includes studies of other British writers and issues, where these are matters of current debate: for example, biography and autobiography, journalism, periodical literature, travel writing, book production, gender, non-canonical writing. We are dedicated principally to publishing original monographs and symposia; our policy is to embrace a broad scope in chronology, approach and range of concern, and both to recognize and cut innovatively across such parameters as those suggested by the designations 'Romantic' and 'Victorian'. We welcome new ideas and theories, while valuing traditional scholarship. It is hoped that the world which predates yet so forcibly predicts and engages our own will emerge in parts, in the wider sweep, and in the lively streams of disputation and change that are so manifest an aspect of its intellectual, artistic and social landscape.

Vincent Newey
Joanne Shattock

University of Leicester

'I am sure I shall never kill anything without first magnifying it in my mind, and thinking what it would say for itself if able to speak.' (Sarah Trimmer, *Fabulous Histories*, 1786)

> Birds, beasts and fishes, are so learned grown,
> They speak the English language as their own …
> (Anon., 'Madame Grimalkin's Party', 1808)

'No doubt … this cat could tell us some entertaining adventures, if she could speak.' (Elizabeth Sandham, *Poor Puss*, 1809)

Introduction

As the parent of a small child, I was often struck by the plethora of animal stories on offer to children: why, I wondered, were contemporary children's books populated with talking elephants, rabbits or pigs? Where has this genre come from, and why do we think it is so suitable for children? To answer these questions we must go back to the rise of children's literature in the mid-eighteenth century, when the talking animal story began its career as a genre specifically for children. Like the fairy story, the animal story has migrated down the hierarchy of literary genres from adults to children, in consequence of an increasing polarization between adults and children. Adults were more and more seen as rational and cultured, while children were imaginative and primitive. At the same time, Enlightenment educational thought differentiated between fairy stories and animal stories, the one encouraging fear and superstition, the other encouraging benevolence and knowledge. Animals, even when talking, were allied with science, ethics and truth. Animal stories could bridge the gap between child and adult, combining delight with instruction. There was still a connection between the modern animal story and the fantastic talking animals of fairy story, but where fairy story had a large influence – for instance in Charles Kingsley's *Water Babies* – it was modernised and made to carry scientific messages.

The eighteenth and nineteenth-century children's animal story, then, was not just a repetition of the Aesopian fable, but added either an anti-cruelty message and/or natural historical information to the fabular genre. A connection was always made to the treatment or the understanding of animals in the world outside the book, allowing issues of animal protection, conservation and what was later called ecology to be raised in a child-friendly manner. This is something that has been lost in most present-day versions of the genre: in this book, I am concerned both to trace the origins of the children's animal story, and to investigate its distinctive nineteenth-century form. Parents are often shocked to discover the violence depicted in such classics as *Black Beauty* or *Peter Rabbit* (where children are told that Peter's father was put into a pie), a violence which is part of their realistic project. Animal characters do not guarantee a cosy, protected space. Another distinctive feature of these stories was a self-consciousness about allowing the animal protagonists to talk. This anxiety could be expressed in an explanatory preface, that reassured child readers that animals could not in fact talk, or only through the presence of an 'editor' or 'translator' or other type of human mediator with special powers of understanding. Sometimes comedy or metafiction were used to point up the fictionality of the talking animal device, and sometimes the first-person narration of animal to reader was juxtaposed with a story in which the human characters cannot understand the animal, reminding the reader of the true state of affairs. These devices provide complex ways of presenting animals and animal consciousness, by being both anthropomorphic and not anthropomorphic at the same time.

One of the continuing themes of this book is the *variety* of different representational devices that are covered by the term 'anthropomorphic', involving degrees of animal speech, dress and thought. Too often, both literary and scientific representations of animals are dismissed as 'anthropomorphic'. Interestingly, however, anthropomorphism is now being revalued as a tool in the study of animal behaviour, and as a means to teach science, while other critics have shown its inevitability.[1] I will be expanding on this topic in Chapter Five. Nineteenth-century children's animal stories can show us ways of 'doing' anthropomorphism that are effective in animal advocacy and scientific education, while at the same time framing and questioning the practice. Another of my continuing themes is the relation of child and animal. The belief, differently expressed by Rousseau, the Romantics and Darwin, that children are somehow 'nearer' to nature and to animals than adults, means that these children's stories can explore the animal-human divide with more freedom and playfulness than literature directed at adults. Anthropomorphic animals meet theriomorphic children, often with the effect of blurring or questioning the difference between human and animal, and stopping in its tracks the 'anthropological machine' whose action Giorgio Agamben deplores in Western philosophy – a thought-machine that always reinstates the difference between *man* and animal.[2] *Child* and animal may not have the same distinction.

Another distinctively eighteenth and nineteenth-century feature of these stories is the inevitable framework of hierarchy on which they depend. This can be a religious hierarchy or an evolutionary hierarchy, and is nearly always an analogy for a social hierarchy. Margaret Gatty puts the concept at its starkest: 'Animals under man – servants under masters – children under parents – wives under husbands – men under authorities – nations under rulers – all under God'.[3] But stories for children about animals are implicitly taking a perspective from 'lower' down this hierarchy, and this can have the effect of upsetting its terms. Suffering or noble animals can seem 'higher' than cruel or degenerate men, and child-like vision can be truer than prideful grown-up science. At this point, ideas of carnival become relevant, as hierarchies are inverted, and animals usurp the place of humans, often to comic effect. However, hierarchical social ideas are often reinstated when we find there is a 'natural' hierarchy among the animals themselves, with different species standing for different classes. One question I ask in this book is just how subversive

---

1   Eileen Crist, *Images of Animals, Anthropomorphism and the Animal Mind* (Philadelphia, PA, 1999); J. S. Kennedy, *The New Anthropomorphism* (Cambridge, 1992); Kim A. McDonald, 'Scientists Rethink Anthropomorphism', *Chronicle of Higher Education* 41/24 (1995): A8–A9, A14; Robert W. Mitchell, Nicholas S. Thompson and H. Lyn Miles (eds), *Anthropomorphism, Anecdotes, and Animals* (New York, 1997); Anat Zohar and Shlomit Ginossar, 'Lifting the Taboo Regarding Teleology and Anthropomorphism', *Science Education*, 82/6 (1998): 679–99.

2   Giorgio Agamben, *The Open, Man and Animal* (Stanford, CA, 2004).

3   Margaret Gatty, *Parables from Nature* (London, 1907), p. 268.

these various carnivalesque inversions of hierarchy are. I am also concerned to show the variety of ways in which the concept of hierarchy is deployed. Just as with 'anthropomorphism', so the term 'hierarchy' covers a number of different moves, and can be used in unusual ways – for instance, Mary Wollstonecraft is concerned to stress the lowly position of children, perhaps in order to elevate the position of women. Gender is an important aspect of the hierarchies deployed in these books. In some cases, woman writers identify with small, powerless creatures, while male writers celebrate large, powerful carnivores. On the other hand, Beatrix Potter's domestic spaces are full of threat and violence, while Kenneth Grahame's all-male animal world celebrates the cosy, womb-like homes of small animals.

The political and scientific contexts for these stories, with their anti-cruelty messages and their natural historical dimensions, encompass the rise of the animal protection movements, and the advent of evolutionary theory. The story of animal protection, and its adult literature, has been skilfully told by a number of writers: Barbara Gates, Hilda Kean, Christine Kenyon-Jones, Douglas Perkins, Brian Turner.[4] Key dates are the founding of the SPCA (1824) which became the RSPCA in 1840, the first legislation to protect animals (1822), and the founding of Frances Power Cobbe's anti-vivisectionist Victoria League (1876). Chapter Three charts the contribution of the animal autobiography to these movements, and the effectiveness of animal 'voices' in testifying against human cruelty. There is a change towards the end of the period from a concern with animal protection to a concern with conservation, shown in Thompson Seton's work, and implicit in Potter's and Grahame's creation of separate animal 'worlds' worthy of conservation. Earlier texts too, however, use a natural theological framework to teach versions of what we would call ecological understanding. Natural theology uses the evidence of nature to demonstrate the existence and goodness of God. The scientific study of Nature was seen as part of this project.

The scientific framework of the stories moves from natural theology to a Darwinian evolutionary world, via some combinations of the two. Both natural theological and evolutionary frameworks, like anthropomorphism and hierarchical ordering, take a variety of forms in these books. Natural theology is investigated in Chapter One, and the impact of evolutionary thought in Chapters Four and Five. It is interesting that many of the writers were themselves naturalists: Margaret Gatty, Charles Kingsley, Ernest Thompson Seton, Beatrix Potter. The movement from natural theology to Darwinism does not produce as big a change as might be thought: writers still preserve some element of hierarchy, and they still cast the child as closer to nature than the adult. The 'red in tooth and claw' aspect of Nature was not discovered by evolutionists: both earlier and later writers are open about animal violence and suffering, and the exigencies of the food-chain. Similarly,

---

4   Barbara T. Gates, *Kindred Nature* (Chicago, IL and London, 1998); Hilda Kean, *Animals Rights* (London, 1998); Christine Kenyon-Jones, *Kindred Brutes* (Aldershot, 2001); David Perkins, *Romanticism and Animal Rights* (Cambridge, 2003); James Turner, *Reckoning with the Beast* (Baltimore, MD and London, 1980).

Romantic conceptions of Nature and childhood are not necessarily at variance with scientific evolutionism. Kingsley makes great use of Wordsworth in his synthesis of Darwinism and theology, and the impetus behind the Boy Scout movement, with its literary ties to the animal stories of both Kipling and Seton, has been characterised as a combination of Rousseauesque and Darwinian ideas. The implication of this combination of ideas in the ideologies of Empire and colonialism are investigated in Chapter Five.

These children's animal stories, then, engage with some of the big issues of their day – nature, class, gender, empire – casting a new light on them, from a different perspective. They also offer different ways of representing animals and their relation to human beings that are of great relevance to current debates about animal rights, ecology and anthropomorphism. As children's books, they illuminate the ways children and their literature have been constructed by our culture in the past, and might make us question the way we now construct childhood and our assumptions about what is suitable or not for children's reading.

The structure of this book is both chronological and generic. In Chapter One, I investigate the eighteenth-century context in which animals became a staple of an emerging children's literature. I consider a number of related topics: Lockean educational theory; the publishing history of children's books; the preceding traditions on which the earliest children's books drew; the natural theological context; attitudes to animals and children; ideas of sentimentalism and sensibility; Rousseau's ideas on education. Wherever possible I illustrate these ideas by reference to the many varied appearances of animals (not necessarily talking) in children's books of the time. John Newbery's *Goody Two-Shoes* combines Lockean educational ideas and entrepreneurship in the emergence of a separate children's literature, a development in which talking animals play a part. Samuel Pratt's *Pity's Gift* shows the structures and limits of sentimental attitudes to animals. Sarah Trimmer's *Easy Introduction* demonstrates the natural theological framework within which most children's animal stories took place. Thomas Day's *Sandford and Merton* combines Rousseauesque and Lockean approaches to animals and children, and foreshadows Kipling's *Jungle Books*. Mary Wollstonecraft's *Original Stories from Real Life* has a more conflicted attitude to Rousseau, and an interesting turn to the hierarchical scheme that usually accompanies animals in children's stories. Anna Barbauld and John Aikin's *Evenings at Home* exemplifies the range and eclecticism of children's animal stories at the end of the eighteenth century. The multi-faceted nature of Barbauld and Aikin's enterprise belies the Romantic critique of instructional children's literature, which Charles Lamb focuses on one of their dialogues about animals.

Chapter Two begins with a consideration of the founding text of this study, Sarah Trimmer's *Fabulous Histories*, later published as *The History of the Robins*. Trimmer inaugurates a tradition of talking animal stories that use the fabular to inculcate kindness to animals and to convey accurate natural historical information. At the same time, Trimmer and other writers in this tradition exhibit an anxiety that their child readers will be misled into thinking animals really can talk. This self-consciousness about animal language as a literary device continues to haunt most nineteenth-century animal stories. Trimmer uses the device partly in order to amuse her readers, but also as a way of educating them into sympathy with animal's-eye views. This sympathy is sometimes at odds with the hierarchical arrangement the book puts forward, by which human dominion over the animals is justified. The second part of the chapter deals with two sets of comic animal poems for children from the beginning of the nineteenth century, which have been characterised as purely entertaining, as opposed to instructional works like Trimmer's. I argue that these poems do nevertheless, in what may seem a very incongruous way, endeavour to teach children about natural history, or to educate them into being kind to animals. Their strange mixture of the fantastic and the scientific, the anthropomorphic and the natural, provides an 'ancestry' for later works such as Kingsley's *Water Babies* and Beatrix Potter's *Tales*. The two sets of poems come out of different carnivalesque traditions, the eighteenth-century masquerade and the more populist 'World-turned-upside down' chapbooks. Both raise questions about the relation between carnival and hierarchy, and the alleged liberating effects of carnival for those at the bottom of a hierarchy – children and animals in this case.

Chapter Three focuses on a popular and numerous genre, the animal autobiography, which spans the whole of the period I am concerned with in this book. Anna Sewell's *Black Beauty* is the only one of these texts remembered today, but it can usefully be seen as part of a long tradition. Mice, rats, donkeys, cats, dogs, all wrote their life stories. Explaining just how these come to be written, or 'translated', creates some problems for the human writers of these texts. The animal autobiography develops the anti-cruelty message of other eighteenth-century animal stories, inviting the reader to experience life from an animal's perspective. Children are addressed by these books, as they are considered effective agents in promoting the better treatment of animals, and at the same time they can learn lessons in good behaviour from the animals and their owners. In creating a subjectivity for their animal autobiographers, writers often draw on analogies with human types or classes: children, women, slaves and servants. The animal autobiography has much in common generically with the slave narrative, also an autobiographical account written as part of a campaign to change the law. Issues of testimony and witness are investigated here, in particular the courtroom analogy suggested by the phrase 'animal advocacy'. The analogy of animal and servant suggests a different way of reading these texts, not as testimony, but as testimonials to the respectability and faithful service of their animal speakers. In return, the animals are rewarded, like old servants, with a peaceful retirement.

The next chapter deals with Margaret Gatty's *Parables from Nature* and Charles Kingsley's *The Water Babies*. Both writers use children's animal stories to debate evolutionary issues, Gatty attacking Darwin and Kingsley promoting a synthesis of Darwinian and theological thought. Neither is particularly interested in animal protection, or creating animal subjectivity. Instead, they use talking animals to convey natural historical information. Both writers were serious amateur naturalists, who nevertheless deploy parable, analogy and fairytale to convey their scientific and theological messages. Their books derive from both the serious, moral, semi-realistic animal story, and the fantastic, grotesque, carnivalesque comic animal poem. Their stories are, however, not as rigorously child-directed as, for instance, Trimmer's *History of the Robins*. Writing for children provides them with the opportunity to debate momentous scientific issues of great interest to adults, and to deploy the attributes of the Romantic child to argue against materialistic science. They both engage with the Romantic and post-Romantic poetry of the time, Gatty striving to counteract the despair of Tennyson's *In Memoriam*, and Kingsley making use of Wordsworth, Coleridge and Longfellow in support of his own polemic. Gatty appears to be a fierce supporter of social and natural hierarchy, but the animal's-eye perspectives she takes sometimes upset her hierarchical scheme, and introduce a barely controlled carnivalesque element. Kingsley unsettles hierarchy in a different way, through his promotion of the concepts of evolution and degeneration. Human individuals and also whole species can move up or down an evolutionary ladder. Both writers place their talking animals within a strongly maternalist vision of Nature.

Chapter Five concerns stories about wild animals – not the small wild creatures of the English countryside that concern Trimmer and Potter, but large, destructive beasts in exotic foreign locations that offer scope for masculine adventure and violence. Kipling produces his *Jungle Books* in the context of Empire, while Ernest Thompson Seton's stories are set on a colonial 'Frontier'. Both writers reveal Darwinian affinities, and I begin the chapter by tracing the ways in which the Romantic child is reconstituted as the evolutionary child by Darwin and others. Kipling, with his use of myth and fable, might seem at first not to belong to the tradition I am concerned to trace. But he too insists that his animal stories are modern and not 'superstitious', as opposed to the degraded native Indian variety. A comparison of the *Jungle Books* to *Man and Beast in India*, a book by Kipling's father, reveals both Kiplings busy at a demystifying task, purifying native beliefs of inaccuracies and distortions, preserving the poetic and childlike qualities of the 'primitive', while discarding what they see as its superstitious and childish elements. Kipling plays with the talking animal convention, developing the idea of a 'translation', while Seton claims to be translating actual animal noises into their real meanings. Seton became embroiled in a controversy about the accuracy of his animal stories, which raises questions about the methods of animal behaviour as a study. His work has much in common with the anthropomorphic and anecdotal method of Darwin and his follower George Romanes, a method discredited by subsequent behaviourists, but now being revalued. What is 'scientific' and what is 'childish' is not so easily decided.

The final chapter deals with Beatrix Potter's *Tales* and Kenneth Grahame's *Wind in the Willows*. Potter has some interesting connections back to eighteenth-century animal stories. She also, like Gatty, Kingsley and Seton, combines natural history expertise with her story-telling. The natural historical element of her stories is largely carried by her illustrations, while the tales themselves play with different degrees of anthropomorphism, involving animal speech, dress and behaviour. The dividing line between humans and animals is not clear. The 'world' that Potter creates is by no means Arcadian, and her stories do not purvey conventional morals or hierarchical messages. They are, however, strongly identified with a particular Lake District location, which carries a conservationist implication. *The Wind in the Willows* takes the confusion of animals and humans even further, with animal characters who seem to change size in order to interact with the human world, driving cars, riding horses and catching trains, while at other times they are small creatures living in holes. Grahame is clearly influenced by the Romantic poets and their views of Nature: his animal speech emerges out of a 'talking', numinous landscape. The appearance of the god Pan not only helps to create this numinousness, but also represents an attempt at constructing a religion for and of animals. On another level, the story has been read as a political allegory, with the animals representing various classes. As such, it reinforces a hierarchical social structure, but it can also be read as a subversive hymn to pleasure, idleness and uselessness, in the face of mechanical efficiency and the destruction of the natural environment.

The Afterword concerns some recent discussions of anthropomorphism as a strategy for the animal rights movement, and as a teaching tool. In both cases, current concerns have been anticipated by the stories I investigate in this book.

Chapter One

Animals in Eighteenth-Century Children's Books

The animal story was central to the rise of a separate children's literature in the eighteenth century, and was intimately linked to the progressive attitudes that prevailed in enlightened educational circles at that time. In order to understand how animal stories became such a staple of children's fiction, we must look first at the eighteenth-century context in which they arose. This will involve a brief consideration of a number of related topics: Lockean educational theory; the publishing history of children's books; the preceding traditions on which the earliest children's books drew; the natural theological context; attitudes to animals and children; ideas of sentimentalism and sensibility; Rousseau's ideas on education; and finally the many varied appearances of animals (not necessarily talking) in children's books of the time by writers such as Thomas Day, Mary Wollstonecraft, Anna Barbauld and John Aitkin.

Samuel Pickering confesses he was at first surprised to find eighteenth-century literature for children permeated not by religion, as he had anticipated, but by the ideas and influence of the philosopher John Locke.[1] While Locke too had his predecessors and influences, he can be credited with initiating a liberalisation in the way children were treated, and a new interest in their education and reading matter. In his influential *Essay Concerning Human Understanding* (1689), Locke had argued that the mind was formed by the association of ideas through experience. He opposed the concept of innate ideas, and, famously, saw the infant mind as a 'tabula rasa', a blank sheet on which ideas and habits could be inscribed. Locke's arguments were later taken up by more radical thinkers, such as Godwin and Hartley, and the young Wordsworth and Coleridge, but initially they were not seen as threatening to the status quo, and were adopted by orthodox and unorthodox alike. His theories have several consequences for children: childhood becomes very important, as the stage when the mind is most malleable; if there are no innate ideas, children are freed from the notion of original sin; education becomes crucial, and parents have a new responsibility to provide it; children's reading matter becomes a vital part of the mind-formation process; and it is necessary to amuse and to respect children in order that the proper associations of ideas can be formed. If instruction is linked to pain or force, it will not succeed.

---

1 Samuel F. Pickering, *John Locke and Children's Books in Eighteenth-Century England* (Knoxville, TN, 1981).

In his *Thoughts Concerning Education* (1693), Locke followed up these implications of his theory, and, interestingly, animals and literature about animals are seen as crucial to children's development. The only suitable reading matter for children he can find to recommend, is *Aesop's Fables*:

> When by these gentle ways he begins to be able to *read,* some easy pleasant Book suited to his Capacity, should be put into his Hands, wherein the entertainment, that he finds, might draw him on, and reward his Pains in Reading, and yet not such as should fill his Head with perfectly useless trumpery, or lay the principles of Vice and Folly. To this purpose, I think, *Aesop's Fables* the best, which being Stories apt to delight and entertain a Child, may yet afford useful Reflections to a grown Man. Even better it has pictures – ; it will entertain him much the better, and encourage him to read, when it carries the increase of Knowledge with it.[2]

When Locke comes to consider the best way to learn Latin, he again recommends that 'the Fables of *Aesop*, the only Book almost that I know fit for Children, may afford them Matter for this Exercise of writing *English,* as well as for reading and translating to enter them in the *Latin* tongue.'[3] Locke himself published a version of Aesop, with English and Latin parallel texts.

As well as recommending Aesop, Locke also links this reading matter to the treatment of actual animals. A passage in his *Letters to Edward Clarke on Education* (1684–91) laments children's cruelty to animals, and suggests ways of preventing it:

> One thing I have observed in children, that when they have got possession of any poor creature, they are apt to use it ill, and they often torment and treat ill very young birds, butterflies, and such other poor things, which they get into their power, and that with a seeming of pleasure. This, I think, should be watched in them, and if they incline to any such cruelty they should be taught the contrary usage. For the custom of tormenting and killing of beasts will by degrees harden their minds even towards men, and they who accustom themselves to delight in the suffering and destruction of inferior creatures, will not be apt to be very compassionate or benign to those of their own kind ... I cannot but commend both the kindness and prudence of a mother I know, who was wont always to indulge her daughters when any of them desired dogs, squirrels, birds, or any such things, as young girls use to be delighted with. But then, when they had them, they must be sure to keep them well, and look well after them, that they want nothing, or were not ill-used.[4]

Here Locke uses what becomes a standard eighteenth-century argument against cruelty to animals: that it will lead on to cruelty to men. Animals provide a testing ground for benevolence and humanity. This passage in Locke is immediately followed by another recommendation of Aesop as reading matter, making the link

---

2 James L Axtell (ed.), *The Educational Writings of John Locke* (Cambridge, 1968), p. 259.

3 Ibid., p. 298.

4 Ibid., p. 349.

between animal fable and animals in the real world which is so much in evidence in texts like Fenn's *Fables* and Trimmer's *Fabulous Histories* (see pp. 37–39 below).

Why did Locke recommend Aesop so strongly? It seems that stories about animals, as natural beings, are to be preferred to superstitious fairy-tales, even if the animals do talk. The Fables also carry acceptable and useful morals about human life, combining instruction and delight. Locke, like many of the eighteenth-century writers for children, notes that children delight in animals, without speculating on why this might be so. Aesop was very popular – perhaps just because there was so little other reading matter for children. There were twenty-six English editions between 1647 and 1700.[5] Mary Jackson and David Whitley have traced the history of Aesops in the seventeenth and eighteenth centuries, noting an increased adaptation to a child audience.[6] As well as Locke's version, there is one by Samuel Richardson (1739), which Whitley calls 'a remarkable contribution to the emerging tradition of writing for children in its own terms', in the way it develops 'the potential of the fable to speak for and about children', by emphasising values of playfulness and curiosity in the morals drawn from the Fables.[7] Whitley also reminds us of the political uses to which the Fables were put by different translators and editors: as we will see, political implications are not absent in later animal stories for children. Jackson remarks on the existence of many 'multipurpose' books, 'for example, pictorial Aesops that are also language texts; emblem works that might have been used as encyclopaedic books of knowledge'.[8] This kind of heterogeneity is also very characteristic of later animal stories for children.

Jackson also points here to other traditional genres that contributed to the children's animal story: emblem books and bestiaries. Though the animals in these books do not talk, they are imbued with moral and religious meanings. The emblem books used pictures of animals to convey moral and religious allegories. They rest on a belief in the divine meanings encoded in natural phenomena: 'an Emblem is but a silent parable ... what are the heavens, the earth, nay, every creature, but Hieroglyphics and Emblems of his glory?' asks an address to the reader in a 1777 edition of Frances Quarles' *Emblems Divine and Moral* (1635). The editor worries about 'the pious education of youth' in an 'age of dissipation and levity'.[9] He clearly expects his book to be read by the young. Quarles was republished in the nineteenth century too, and influenced Margaret Gatty's *Parables from Nature* which I will be discussing in Chapter Four. Bestiaries were medieval forerunners of natural histories, consisting of 'illustrated catalogues or compendia of actual and fabulous beasts'.[10] Their purpose was not scientific description or categorisation,

---

5 Ibid., p. 271, footnote 2.

6 Mary V. Jackson, *Engines of Instruction, Mischief, and Magic* (Lincoln, NB, 1989); David Whitely, 'Samuel Richardson's Aesop', in Mary Hilton and Morag Styles, (eds), *Opening the Nursery Door* (London, 1997), pp. 65–79.

7 Whitely, pp. 66, 76.

8 Jackson, p. 36.

9 Frances Quarles, *Emblems Divine and Moral* (London, 1777), pp. 11, iii–iv.

10 Harriet Ritvo, 'Learning from Animals', *Children's Literature* 13 (1985): 73.

but a mixture of allegorical and fabulous information about each beast. Early natural histories imitated their form, and, according to Harriet Ritvo, still retained a tendency to describe the animals morally as well as scientifically, concentrating on their usefulness to man (evidence of Divine Providence), and their hierarchical relationships (evidence for the Divine ordering of human hierarchies). Interestingly, one of the first books published specifically for children by Thomas Boreman was *A Description of Three Hundred Animals* (1730). Both the emblem book and the bestiary emphasise illustration; pictures of animals are also given a new, secular purpose by Locke, as a reading and writing aid: 'as soon as he [the child] begins to spell, as many Pictures of Animals should be got him, as can be found, with the printed names to them.'[11] Alphabet books, as well as natural histories, made great use of animal illustrations: the humorous results of this are seen in Maria Edgeworth's story 'The Bee and the Cow' (1814), where a little girl confuses these two beasts, because the illustration for 'B' in her alphabet book was a Bull.[12]

While Boreman may have published his natural history for children in 1730, credit is usually given to John Newbery for initiating the children's book trade, when he published *A Little Pretty Pocket Book* in 1744. Newbery's shop was 'at the corner of St Paul's Churchyard', and a whole string of successors (F. Newbery, E. Newbery, J. Harris, Griffith and Farran) lay claim to the well-known address on the title pages of children's books well into the nineteenth century. The *Pocket Book* was a miscellany for children, which included several verse fables. Its motto was 'Delectando monemus' – we instruct by delighting, a very Lockean sentiment. Later, Newbery also published his own version of Aesop, *Fables in Verse for the Improvement of the Young and the Old; by Abraham Aesop, Esqu. To which are added, Fables in Verse and Prose; with the Conversation of Birds and Beasts, At their several Meetings, Routs, and Assemblies; by Woglog the great Giant* (1758). The title alone gives a flavour of the enticing playfulness of Newbery's productions, while the Preface promises 'virtue and instruction'.[13] Nor did Newbery neglect the natural history, publishing in 1752 his *Pretty Book of Pictures for Little Masters and Misses; or, Little Tommy Trip's History of Birds and Beasts*.

Several reasons have been put forward for Newbery's success. The eighteenth-century family had become increasingly child-centred, and parents began to invest more, emotionally and financially, in their children. J. H. Plumb comments that children had become 'luxury objects', and 'superior pets' – an interesting metaphor in this context.[14] At the same time, an ideology of social aspiration and betterment fuelled the desire to educate one's children out of their class. Locke's ideas chimed

---

11   Axtell, p. 259.

12   Mitzi Myers, 'Reading Rosamond Reading', in Elizabeth Goodenough, Mark Heberle and Naomi Sokoloff (eds), *Infant Tongues, The Voice of the Child in Literature* (Detroit, MI, 1994), pp. 57–79.

13   Pickering, p. 52.

14   J. H. Plumb. 'The New World of Children in Eighteenth-Century England', *Past and Present*, 67 (1975): 64–95.

in with this ideology, emphasising the potentially transformative effect of children's reading. Newbery's stories often involve social advancement through education – his most famous production, *The History of Little Goody Two-Shoes* (1765), is written for those 'Who from a State of Rags and Care, /And having Shoes but half a Pair; /Their Fortune and their Fame would fix, /And gallop in a Coach and Six.' The title of John Harris's later (1808) *Alphabet of Goody Two-Shoes, by learning of which she soon got rich*, makes the point more crudely. The message would not only be popular with purchasers, it would also encourage them to buy more books. All this was happening in an age of increasing consumerism and commercialisation. Children's books became another commodity to be purchased and consumed.

The canny way in which Newbery articulated these trends in his books can be seen in *Goody Two-Shoes*, which makes use of talking animals to further its project. The poor orphaned Margery Two-Shoes gains success and popularity through teaching the village children in her schoolroom. Eventually she marries a rich man. Animals, talking and otherwise, function in her story as a classroom aid, encouraging both play and instruction. They are also used to inculcate a message of kindness, to teach facts about animal instinct, to demystify ghost-stories and superstitions, to demonstrate God's goodness, and to provide Biblical instruction. Like Dickon, in Frances Hodgson Burnett's much later *Secret Garden*, Margery has a whole menagerie of pets: Ralph the raven, Tom the pigeon, Billy the lamb and Jumper the dog. A typical playtime involves the children 'all running about the school, and diverting themselves with the birds and the lamb'. But Ralph and Tom are also instrumental in the teaching of reading. Margery teaches Ralph 'to speak, to spell, and to read', and it is he who lays out the capital letters of the alphabet, which are then reproduced in the text as an aid to the child reader. Tom the pigeon takes care of the small letters – he has been taught 'to spell and read, though not to talk, and he performed all those extraordinary things which are recorded of the famous bird that was sometime since advertised in the Haymarket'.[15] It is clear here that the birds' ability to 'talk' or 'read' is to be seen as a performing trick, not a fiction or fable. At the same time, these performing animals effectively link the world of entertainment to the teaching of reading.

Both the birds have also been rescued from children's cruelty, circumstances which emphasise Margery's good qualities, and provide the opportunity for a message of kindness to animals:

Margery, you must know, was very humane and compassionate; and her tenderness extended not only to all mankind, but even to all animals that were not noxious, as yours ought to do if you would be happy here, and go to heaven hereafter. These are God Almighty's creatures as well as we ... How then can people dare to torture and wantonly destroy God Almighty's creatures? They, as well as you, are capable of feeling pain, and of receiving pleasure! And how can you, who want to be made happy yourself, delight in making your fellow-creatures miserable? Do you think the poor birds, whose nests and young ones that wicked boy, Dick Wilson, ran away with yesterday, do not feel as much

---

15 *The History of Little Goody Two-Shoes* (London, 1765), pp. 30, 38.

pain as your father and mother would feel, was any one to pull down their house and run away with you? To be sure they do.[16]

The message is reinforced here by two arguments that were to become standard in children's literature about animals: the religious appeal to the idea of 'fellow creatures', and the rhetorical device of reversing roles, translating animal pain into the equivalent human pain. The movement from the more generalised religious appeal to the particularity of 'that wicked boy, Dick Wilson', and the immediacy of 'yesterday', brings the message into the everyday, concrete world of the child reader, who is interpellated throughout by the familiar second-person address – 'you'. That the particular child reader may not know any 'Dick Wilson' only adds a dimension of metafictional play to the seriousness of the moral advice.

While the attribution of human emotions to animals here, and the human-like reading activities of Ralph the raven and Tom the pigeon, all anthropomorphise the animals, another incident in the book stresses instead the difference of animals from humans. Margery and her school children are all saved from death when the school building collapses, by the warning given by the little dog. The dog's 'sagacity and instinct' are attributed to God's plan:

> Though God Almighty has made man the lord of the creation, and endowed him with reason; yet, in many respects, he has been altogether as bountiful to other creatures of his forming. Some of the senses of the other animals are more acute than ours, as we find by daily experience.[17]

The incident in which humans are saved from disaster by animal instinct recurs up to *Black Beauty* and beyond. The supporting examples given next are not from daily life, but from the Bible: the ravens feeding Elijah in the desert, and the pigeon sent forth from Noah's ark. The moral drawn is to do with the way animals serve man, and so deserve good treatment:

> As these, and other animals, are so sensible and kind to us, we ought to be tender and good to them … Does not the horse and the ass carry you and your burdens? Does not the ox plough your ground, the cow give you milk, the sheep clothe your back, the dog watch your house, the goose find you in quills to write with, the hen bring eggs for your custards and puddings … [18]

Harriet Ritvo remarks on how Natural Histories of the time focus mainly on domestic animals, and their usefulness to man.[19] For her, this emphasis reinforces the social hierarchy, in which animals play the part of servants, and we will find this servant analogy pervasive in children's books about animals. But here the animals are rather characterised as acting out of kindness, and their activities given as another reason to

---

16 bid., pp. 36–7.
17 Ibid., p. 51.
18 Ibid.
19 Ritvo, 'Learning from Animals'.

treat them well. Newbery, with his message of social advancement through education and hard work, is not concerned to emphasise hierarchy in his portrayal of animals. Margery's pets appear as friends and helpers, not as her servants.

The educational use of animals in *Goody Two-Shoes* is very much in the spirit of Locke – their presence adds delight to instruction and inculcates kindness. The book is Lockean too in the way it counters superstitious associations with reason and nature. Margery is shut in the church overnight, and terrified when 'something very cold, as cold as marble, ay, as cold as ice, touched my neck.' The 'ghost' turns out to be a dog, and Margery concludes 'I am sure there are no ghosts to hurt or frighten them [good boys and girls] though anyone, possessed of fear, might have taken neighbour Sanderson's dog, with his cold nose, for a ghost.' The narrator emphasises the point here, in a separate section entitled 'Reflection': 'After this, my dear children, I hope you will not believe any foolish stories that ignorant, weak, or designing people may tell you about ghosts; for the tales of ghosts, witches, and fairies, are the frolics of a distempered brain.' These kinds of beliefs have dangerous consequences, when Margery is accused of witchcraft: 'People stuff children's heads with stories of ghosts, fairies, witches, and such nonsense, when they are young, and so they continue fools all their days.' [20]

What is interesting here is the way animals are identified with the natural and the rationally explicable, as opposed to witches, fairies and ghosts. The cold nose belongs to a dog, not a ghost. Margery's helpers are not fairies, but trained animals. They rescue her by natural instinct, not by supernatural powers. Their presence in the book is part of the enlightenment project. Animals are extremely useful to the children's writer, taking over the roles of ghosts and fairies in a new Lockean world. By their appeal to benevolence, they teach morality and social cohesion, and, as God's creatures, they can also teach a rational and natural form of religion. To explain these last two points more fully, I will now turn briefly to eighteenth-century ideas on sensibility and on natural theology.

The words 'sensibility' and 'sentiment' denoted a whole complex of overlapping ideas in the eighteenth century. They described a capacity to respond emotionally to suffering, which gave evidence of the refinement of the person responding. Markman Ellis locates the cult of sensibility among a series of discourses: 'theories of the moral sense in the history of moral philosophy; theories of benevolence in the history of theology; theories of sociability in the history of political economy; and theories of nervous sensibility in the history of science'. Sensibility could be conservative, or reformist. On the one hand, attention could be directed to the superior emotional qualities of the witness, and confirm the suffering as inevitable, 'voyeuristically focus[ing] on the powerless resigned to powerlessness'.[21] On the other, sensibility could be a force for change. Here, sensibility is linked to other important terms: 'benevolence' and 'humanity'. G. J. Barker-Benfield notes 'the coincidence of the

---

20 *Goody Two-Shoes*, pp. 30, 31, 60.
21 Markman Ellis, *The Politics of Sensibility* (Cambridge, 1996), pp. 22, 128.

rise of the culture of sensibility ... with the rise of humanitarianism', and Ellis insists on the 'reformative, morally instructive and virtuous' nature of sentimentalism.[22] The objects of sensibility's pity and benevolence were stereotypically women, children, animals and slaves – that is, all those lower down the hierarchy of power, who could be abused or oppressed. This is not to say that only men could be sentimental: women could feel for children, animals and slaves; children could feel for animals and slaves; slaves could feel for animals, and animals, in some of the stories I will be looking at, can feel for slaves. The more humane attitude to children, which was one of the causes of the growth of children's literature, can partly be ascribed to the cult of sensibility; and the arguments in children's books for kindness to animals belong to the same structure of humanitarian feeling. Literature in particular was seen as a vehicle for spreading sensibility and benevolence: 'In all forms of sentimental literature, there is an assumption that life and literature are directly linked, not through any notion of a mimetic depiction of reality but through the belief that the literary experience can intimately affect the living one.' Eighteenth-century literature for children about animals often makes this direct link to the treatment of animals in the world outside the book. Children's literature was especially suitable for cultivating sensibility and benevolence: 'the sensationalist assumptions of environmental psychology and the ductility of young and tender nerves made children's reading a logical route by which reform could be implemented.'[23]

Our present use of the word 'sentimentality' to mean mawkish and excessive displays of feeling can obscure what is happening in sentimental literature. Pickering labels as negatively 'sentimental' all children's books that argue too powerfully for the better treatment of animals, or allow this to become their main theme.[24] Ritvo labels all fiction about animals sentimental, bracketing together the fantastic with the reformist and the didactic: 'such sentimental favourites as Black Beauty, Toad of Toad Hall, and the Cowardly Lion'.[25] Pickering values 'all-round educational' texts, and Ritvo texts that give true information about animals as animals; one prioritises children, and the other animals. But there is no reason why children's literature should not be used with the explicit purpose of improving the lot of animals, with anthropomorphised ('sentimental') animal characters who nevertheless have an effect on human behaviour towards animals in the real world. The eighteenth-century children's text which does seem to lean most towards the maudlin and self-congratulatory variant of sentimentalism is perhaps *Pity's Gift, A Collection of Interesting Tales To Excite the Compassion of Youth for the Animal Creation* (1798), compiled from the works of Samuel Pratt. In 'The Hermit and His Dog', 'A heart too tender here from man retires, / A heart that aches, if but a *wren* expires.' A 'friend from Holland' writes, 'What pleasure there is in gentle offices, whether

---

22   G. J. Barker-Benfield, *The Culture of Sensibility* (Chicago, IL, 1992), p. 225; Ellis, p. 42.

23   Janet Todd, *Sensibility, An Introduction* (London, 1986), pp. 4, 236.

24   Pickering, pp. 33, 34, 96.

25   Ritvo, *Learning From Animals*, p. 90.

administered to bird, beast, or man! How it refreshes in warm, how it animates one in rigorous weather!' The story of Noah and the dove moves the narrator to exclaim: 'the eye melts at the simplicity, and the heart warms at the sentiment.'[26] The stories with actual child protagonists, however, are much more tough-minded: a family of children are punished for their cruel treatment of some robins, by being made to undergo similar treatment themselves; and some boys learn that a blackbird would prefer liberty to being kept as a pet. Most of the children's books that raise the issue of cruelty to animals do in fact emphasise action and rescue, as in *Goody Two-Shoes*, where Margery's 'humane and compassionate' nature leads her to buy and educate the persecuted birds. The didactic, educational aim of these books means there is no incentive to dwell on the fine feelings of child characters.

Natural Theology means using the evidence of nature to demonstrate the existence and goodness of God. In particular, natural theologians used the argument from design: the signs of purposeful contrivance in Nature lead us to infer a Divine Designer as its Creator. It is a form of theology that fits well with the Enlightenment emphasis on reason and nature: religion is not superstition, it can be proved. All eighteenth-century children's writers are writing within this framework, and some are trying to teach it as well. Natural religion was seen as a gentle and easy way to lead children towards the concept of God. This project can best be seen in Sarah Trimmer's *An Easy Introduction to the Knowledge of Nature, and Reading the Holy Scriptures, Adapted to the Capacities of Children* (1770). The Preface quotes Isaac Watts' *Treatise on Education*: 'Shew them the Birds, the Beasts, the Fishes, the Insects, Trees, Fruit, Herbs, and all the several parts and properties of the vegetable and Animals World ... Teach them that the Great God made all these.' Trimmer's book intends 'a general survey of the Works of providence', leading to 'knowledge of the Supreme Being. For we need only read the Volume of Nature, in order to discover his *Wisdom* and *Goodness*'. In order to achieve this survey, Harry and Catherine's mother takes them on nature walks through the countryside: 'for every object in Nature, when carefully examined, will fill us with admiration', and 'we shall find that nothing has been made in vain.' The story is told by the mother in the first person, and the present tense, in the everyday language of a parent speaking to children: 'Henry, fetch your hat.'[27]

During their walks, Mamma points out the usefulness of the grass, corn, fruit, flowers, sheep and cattle to man. She also draws attention to evidence of design: 'We have examined a variety of Flowers, Plants, Trees, &c, and find them all most wonderfully formed to answer the purposes they seem to have been designed for'. As well as demonstrating usefulness and intelligent design, she also justifies animal suffering in a world created by a benevolent God. The sheep, she maintains, are happy at present in the field. They have no relations who might grieve at their deaths, as their fondness for their mothers does not continue, and they are unaware of their

---

26 Samuel Pratt, *Pity's Gift* (London, 1798), pp. 16, 46–7, 59.
27 Sarah Trimmer, *An Easy Introduction* (London, 1770), pp. vi, vii–viii, 1, 2, 4.

coming fate: 'We must kill them, to preserve our own lives, but should never be cruel to them while they do live.' Usefulness to humans comes first in the scale of values she applies to animals, but kindness is a close second: God has provided the animals for our use, but He also wishes us to treat them well. As in other children's books of the time, children are encouraged to think themselves into the subjectivity of animals: 'never take pleasure in hurting anything that is less and weaker than yourself. Think how you should like to have a Man tie a string about you, and pull you along, whirl you about in the air till you lost your Senses, break your Limbs, and throw you down at last and tread upon you.' This reversal of animal and human roles, so violent and frightening here, can sometimes become comic. Urging Harry not to be afraid of spiders, Mamma says: 'I never heard that a Spider took a Broom and swept a little Boy away.'[28]

Mamma, then, encourages sympathy with animals, but she is not overly sentimental. In the end, man is superior to animals, because of his powers of learning, speaking and making. Of animals she says, 'You never see them conversing together, and telling their thought and opinions as mankind do.' Mamma is teaching differences and demarcations here, to children who need to learn to distinguish the human from the animal. Interestingly, she puts in here an anti-slavery point, insisting that 'Negroes' are men, though they are sometimes used worse than horses. Her emphasis on speech as one of the essential differences between man and animals explains her worries about the talking robins in her later book, *Fabulous Histories*, especially as here she assures the children, admirably, that 'I will never tell you anything but truth.' She ends this section of the book with a focus on man's unique ability to make things, for instance, a watch. This leads her seamlessly into the famous 'watch' analogy, later explained by William Paley in his influential *Natural Theology* (1802): 'for every indication of contrivance, every manifestation of design, which existed in the watch, exists in the works of nature' (35), testifying to the existence of a Creator. The natural theological framework is confirmed here, and the second part of the book takes the children into a reading of the Bible, for which they have been gently prepared by their reading of Nature.[29]

The consonance of the study of Nature with the study of religion is central to eighteenth-century Natural Theology, which was wholly in harmony with scientific pursuits. Not only did theologians use scientific evidence, but scientists investigated Nature with a religious reverence for the wonders of Divine design. Science is also part of what Mamma teaches her children. Her emphasis on 'carefully examining' natural objects is similar to scientific observation, and her references to the microscope confirm her scientific approach. At first, the power of the microscope is only something to be reported to the children: describing the powder on a butterfly's wings, Mamma says, 'I have seen some like it in a Microscope.' But then the instrument promises to become part of their experience: 'I shall shew you Parts of them in the Microscope'; finally 'Here is the Microscope', and they look at feathers

---

28 Ibid., pp. 7, 10–11, 12–13, 42, 46, 192, 49, 90–1, 82.
29 Ibid., pp. 202, 121, 157, 35.

and flies together. This hands-on approach becomes an essential part of later scientific books for children, such as Mrs Marcet's many *Conversations*, where an instructive governess or mother leads her charges to experience and understand the workings of nature, in a present-tense dialogue. Education was an area in which women could undertake scientific pursuits within the domestic role. These texts emphasise the scientific, and therefore divine, wonders hidden in the everyday – for Trimmer, the plants and animals the children encounter on their local walks. Scientific study is not cruel, but is linked to kindness: 'I am sure you will not take a Pleasure in tormenting Flies, now you have seen what Limbs they have.' [30]

So far I have been discussing eighteenth-century children's literature in a predominantly Lockean framework. The other great influence on contemporary educational theory was Jean Jacques Rousseau, especially his educational treatise, *Émile* (1762). The followers of Locke and Rousseau are sometimes set in opposition to each other, but there are plenty of children's books which show the influence of both thinkers. Both theorists posit the potential goodness of man, as opposed to ideas of original sin; for Locke, this means early education; for Rousseau, it means secluding the child to develop naturally, away from the corrupting elements of human civilisation. Christine Kenyon-Jones points out that Rousseau is not interested in animals as such, or in alleviating their suffering.[31] But animals become relevant to the child in his educational scheme in that the nearer the child is to the animal, the less corrupt he is. The famous opening of *Émile* makes this clear, comparing man's miseducation of children with his misshaping of both plants and animals:

> Everything is good as it comes from the hands of God; everything degenerates in the hands of man … He mutilates his horses, dogs and slaves … He is not content with anything as Nature made it, not even his fellow-man. Even his offspring must be trained up for him like a horse in his stable, and must grow after his fancy like a tree in his garden.[32]

While Locke's exemplary children's book is Aesop, the only book Rousseau allows Émile to read, and not till he is twelve years old, is *Robinson Crusoe*. Both texts are 'natural', rather than supernatural or fantastic, involving either animals and simple social morality, or the natural environment and man's basic ('natural') needs, rather than fairies, ghosts or magic. Nevertheless, there is an interesting difference here: Rousseau is suspicious of fables because their morals are too complicated for a child to understand, and they require an exercise of reason that is beyond a child's mind:

> How can we be so blind as to think fables a moral training for children, without reflecting that the moral, while amusing, only deceives them, and that, charmed by the fiction,

---

30 Ibid., pp. 79, 83, 88, 90.
31 Kenyon-Jones, p. 59.
32 Jean Jacques Rousseau, *Émile* (New York, 1964), p. 55.

they miss the underlying truth? Fables may instruct adults, but the naked truth must be presented to children. Men may be taught by fables; children require the naked truth.[33]

These strictures evidently made an impression on Eleanor Fenn. In the Preface to her *Fables*, she cites Rousseau's arguments:

> *Rousseau's* remarks upon Fables, as making a part of the Library for Children, seem to me just: most of his objections militate strongly against all the Fables I ever met with. If I did not hope that these are exempted from his charges I would not offer them to the public, still less would I have presented them to the dear little ones for whom they were written.[34]

A footnote dissociates her from the dangerous political implications of Rousseau's thought: 'However mistaken, however detestable, many notions of *Rousseau's* may be; there are useful maxims to be gleaned from his work respecting children. I wish the wheat were better separated from the chaff.' Presumably, Fenn feels her Fables are clearly and simply enough explained, and they rely for effect on a simple pragmatic morality: 'Fables are stories written to teach children what they should do by shewing them what may happen to them if they do not act as they ought to do.'[35] It is by this sort of direct physical consequence that Rousseau proposes to educate Émile, always teaching him only that which the boy can see as useful. For instance, Émile decides a knowledge of astronomy might be useful when he is lost in a wood, tired and hungry. Facts about North and South in relation to the position of the sun suddenly seem important and worthwhile.

Animals and their needs are often called into children's books that are influenced by Rousseau to function as the hard, physical, obvious reality which the child must come to terms with, just as Robinson Crusoe must come to terms with the demands of his environment and his physical needs. Far from giving a 'sentimental' picture of a benign nature, Rousseau uses it as a reality principle. The first lesson that the child must learn is to bear pain, a lesson which relates to its existence as an animal body in a physical world. The harshness and violence of the animal world depicted in much eighteenth-century children's literature is partly down to Rousseau. Also attributable to his influence is the 'nature walk' as a narrative device, as in Trimmer's *Easy Introduction*. Much of Émile's education takes place outside, and never in a classroom, as he learns by direct experience and observation. Trimmer's narrator's promise always to tell her charges the truth also conforms to Rousseau's exhortations to parents never to make mysteries for a child, and always to tell them the plain facts.

The most Rousseauesque children's writer is perhaps Thomas Day, whose *Sandford and Merton* (1783–89) was phenomenally successful, far into the nineteenth

---

33 Ibid., p. 115.
34 Lady Eleanor Fenn, *Fables in Monosyllables by Mrs Teachwell* (London, 1783), vol. 1, p. viii
35 Ibid., viii, vol. 2, p. 10.

century. The book concerns the education of Tommy Merton, a spoiled rich brat, by Mr Barlow, the perfect tutor. Mr Barlow is also educating Harry Sandford, a poor farmer's son, who possesses all the natural virtues. Animals are central to the book and to the project of educating Tommy. Tommy has been corrupted by his family's stay in Jamaica, and supposes wrongly that black people were made to serve him. Mr Barlow disabuses him of this and other assumptions of superiority, including the idea that he can treat animals badly. Cruelty to animals is one of the corruptions of an unnatural, 'civilised' society: Lockean and Rousseauesque motifs combine here.

Harry's goodness, in a typical eighteenth-century move, is attested by his kindness to animals:

> Once, indeed, Harry was caught twirling a cockchafer round, which he had fastened by a crooked pin to a long piece of thread: but this was through ignorance and want of thought; for as soon as his father told him that the poor helpless insect felt as much, or more, than he would do were a knife thrust through his hand, he burst into tears, and took the poor insect home, where he fed him a fortnight upon fresh leaves; and when perfectly recovered, he turned him out to enjoy liberty and the fresh air.[36]

Harry here is educated through sentiment: sympathetic crying is ubiquitous in novels of sensibility. It is his subsequent good behaviour towards animals that brings him to the attention of Mr Barlow. Mr Barlow's methods include physical labour, practical lessons in benevolence, and story-telling. The book is punctuated by a series of stories, supposed to be read out by Mr Barlow or one of the boys, many of which involve animals. The stories are followed by question-and-answer sections, in which Mr Barlow draws moral lessons from what they have just heard. The story of 'Androcles and the Lion', for instance, carries a message of kindness to animals and benevolence returned, but also gives the opportunity for Mr Barlow to impart information about the creature's habits, and to reduce Tommy's pride of rank: he has just mistreated a poor boy, giving as excuse, 'Sir, he was a ragged little boy, and I am a gentleman.' Mr Barlow concludes:

> So, now I see what constitutes a gentleman. A gentleman is one that, having abundance of everything, keeps it all to himself; beats poor people, if they will not serve him for nothing; and when they have done him the greatest favour, in spite of his insolence, never feels gratitude, or does them any good in return. I find that Androcles's lion was no gentleman.[37]

Animals here provide a levelling lesson for human behaviour, instead of reinforcing ideas of hierarchy.

One of the earliest stories concerns two dogs, one brought up in luxury, one in hardihood. These two are obvious parallels to the two boys. The dog brought up in country poverty, amidst danger from wild beasts, is 'hardy, active and diligent'; the rich town dog is cowardly and lazy. But when they exchange circumstances, their

---

36 Thomas Day, *Sandford and Merton* (London, n.d.), pp. 11–12.
37 Ibid., p. 90.

natures also reverse. There is a Lockean message about training and environment here, as well as a Rousseauesque one about the benefits of nature and the corruption of civilisation. Besides this contrast between the natural and the civilised boys, Harry and Tommy, there is also a similar contrast between the world in which the story takes place, in the 'civilised' English countryside, and the world of the stories, many of which are set in distant times or places, where there is more danger, more wilderness, more room for heroic action, and bigger, more dangerous animals. This contrast can best be seen in an episode about hunting. The local squire is indulging in the cruel and unnecessary sport of hare coursing. Harry is indignant: 'I wonder they are not ashamed to meddle with such a poor inoffensive creature, that cannot defend itself: if they have a mind to hunt, why don't they hunt lions and tigers, and such fierce mischievous creatures, as I have read they do in other countries?' The defence of the poor hare could be an intertextual reference to Cowper's poem, *The Task*. It is in keeping with Lockean strictures against cruelty to animals. Harry's excitement at the idea of lion hunting, however, brings in a different set of values: 'the men are accustomed in some places to go almost naked; and that makes them so prodigiously nimble, that they can run like deer; and when a lion or tiger comes into their neighbourhood, and devours their sheep or oxen, they go out six or seven together, armed with javelins.' The over-civilised Tommy is terrified by Harry's description: '"I should like to see it out of a window, where I was safe." – "So should not I," answered Harry; "for it must be a great pity to see such a noble animal tortured and killed; but the men are obliged to do it in their own defence."'[38]

Harry's comment neatly combines sympathy for animal suffering with an appreciation of the violence of nature. Many of the stories told by Mr Barlow involve explorers or savages in extremis, being forced to hunt and eat large wild animals, such as polar bears or reindeer. The danger involved is presented as good for the character, fostering courage and resourcefulness. It is harder for Day to provide instances of heroic responses to danger in the boys' everyday life: Tommy first becomes acquainted with Harry when the latter saves him from a poisonous snake. Later, Harry demonstrates his goodness to Tommy's sceptical family by saving his friend from a runaway bull, with the help of a grateful Negro he has aided. Mr Barlow gets a chance to demonstrate the way animals respond to courage and authority, by holding an escaped bear at bay with his stick. Both these animals, the bull, who is being baited, and the bear, who is forced to perform, have earlier been the objects of humanitarian sympathy. In the hare-hunting episode, Harry demonstrates his Spartan courage in refusing to tell the squire where the hare is, even when the squire lays into him with his whip. Here, the 'civilised' squire becomes the equivalent of the large, dangerous animals who must be resisted. Harry then demonstrates his benevolence, as well as his courage, when he rescues the very same Squire, who has been thrown by his horse. Harry, we are told, 'was always prepared to perform an act of humanity, even at the risk of his like, and, besides that, was a boy of extraordinary courage and

---

38 Ibid., pp. 54, 55.

agility.'[39] Sympathy and benevolence for animals and humans alike are removed from any associations with weakness and femininity, and linked to hardy masculine virtues.

Day's combination of kindness to animals with an appreciation of their danger and violence does not always work without contradiction. As I have said, bull-baiting is condemned in the book, as an 'inhuman sport', a 'persecution' of the bull. Bull-baiting was one of the earliest targets for legislation against cruelty to animals. But later in the book, the grateful Negro tells an exciting tale of a multiple bullfight, which Tommy, now completely reformed, describes as 'the most wonderful story I ever heard'.[40] There is a difference in the courage of the bulls' antagonists, but not much, one would think, in the experience of the bull. Another episode involves Tommy feeding and taming a robin who comes into his room. The tame robin has a long history, as Mitzi Myers points out, and forms the basis of Trimmer's tale of talking birds.[41] But Tommy's robin is torn to pieces by his cat. Tommy is very upset, and wants the cat killed, but Mr Barlow points out that it was only following its nature, and Tommy is at fault for leaving the door open, and not protecting his robin. He also shows Tommy that robins feed on worms: the cat is not uniquely cruel. Mr Barlow is educating his charges in reality – people eat animals, and animals eat each other. There is no sentimental evasion here: Mr Barlow goes on to offer to train the cat not to attack tame birds. His attitude to nature does not preclude the training of animals, though he usually advocates kindness as the most effective method, assuring Tommy that even crocodiles can be tamed by kindness. Thomas Day himself was almost too emblematically killed while trying to train a colt using this method. But in the case of Tommy's cat, the method seems extremely cruel: a hot grid-iron is placed before a cage with a bird in it, and when the cat pounces, she throws herself against the grid-iron, and is 'burned in several parts of her body; and retired from the field of battle mewing dreadfully and full of pain'.[42] This incident throws into relief the contradiction in the book between the value put onto kindness and benevolence, and the equal value given to pain, violence and danger as educative agents.

Animals in *Sandford and Merton,* then, are trainable, like children; they are objects of pity and rescue; they are beneficially dangerous antagonists; they are both hunters and prey; they are objects to be understood, in their habits and natures. They have multiple roles in Mr Barlow's educational project, which could hardly work without them. There is no question of these animals talking, because of their function as the 'reality' into which Mr Barlow is educating his charges. But the animals and the ethos of *Sandford and Merton* must surely have influenced a later famous series of children's stories featuring talking animals: Kipling's *Jungle Books.* Sandford, the 'natural' boy, has affinities with Mowgli, and the jungle world of big dangerous

---

39 Ibid., p. 59.

40 Ibid., p. 426.

41 Mitzi Myers, 'Portrait of the Female Artist as a Young Robin', *Lion and Unicorn*, 20/2 (1996): 230–63.

42 Day, p. 150.

carnivores engaging in exciting fights bears a distinct relation to the world of Mr Barlow's stories. This relation is strengthened by the fact that Thomas Day also wrote a short story, 'The History of Little Jack' (1788), in which the hero is suckled by a goat, whom he comes to regard as his mother. This childhood is similar to Mowgli's upbringing by the wolves, except that Jack has a human adoptive father, who owns the goat. Both stories have an earlier common source, in the story of Romulus and Remus, and Kenyon-Jones also points to the story of the baby Jupiter being fed on goat's milk by shepherds, as a possible source for Day's story.[43] Jack's natural upbringing fits him to rise in human society, despite initial prejudice against him. His story takes him across the world, and includes a phase of Robinson Crusoe-like solitude on an African island, and a stay with a wild Tartar tribe. Like Goody Two-Shoes, his story ends with riches – he becomes owner of a foundry back home – but the means are the natural upbringing symbolised by the goat, rather than a formal education. Rousseau's influence is again evident here.

Mary Wollstonecraft's relation to Rousseau is more conflicted, as she was deeply opposed to his plans for female education, as set out in *Emile*. Sophie, Emile's female counterpart, is educated only to please men:

> The first and most important attribute to a woman is good temper: formed to obey so imperfect a being as man ... she ought to learn betimes to submit even to injustice, and to bear oppression ... a man needs knowledge, a woman needs taste ... All the reflexions of women on subjects not immediately connected with their duties ought to be directed to the study of man or to the recreative arts.[44]

In her children's book, *Original Stories from Real Life* (1788), Wollstonecraft counters Rousseau's scheme by enacting her own educational project for girls, designed to produce women as rational, moral, even heroic, agents, using some of the methods recommended by Rousseau for his male protagonist's education. The narrative centres on two girls on the verge of womanhood, Mary and Caroline, aged twelve and fourteen. Their ages are significant: it is not till he is twelve that Emile's education begins. Before that, the plan has been to preserve him from bad habits and let him find out things for himself. Mary and Caroline, however, have been badly brought up, and are 'shamefully ignorant'. The book 'attempts to cure those faults by reason, which ought never to have taken root in the infant mind', though 'good habits' are preferable to 'precepts of reason'. Here Wollstonecraft echoes Rousseau, who attacks Locke's idea that one can reason with children. Mary and Caroline have already been deformed by their upbringing – as Wollstonecraft in the *Vindication of the Rights of Woman* argued most women had been, their faults and limitations being socially, not naturally, produced. The project of *Original Stories*, then, is to rescue and rehabilitate the girls, and also the readers, whose parents often don't have the

---

43 Kenyon-Jones, p. 62, footnote 23.
44 Rousseau, pp. 225–7, 282.

ability to do the job themselves.[45] To bring this about, Wollstonecraft creates Mrs Mason, the governess in charge of the girls' re-education. She is in the position of Mr Barlow in relation to Tommy Merton, but has no Sandford to help in her task. Mrs Mason herself becomes the model for her charges to aspire to.

What is interesting here, is the importance of animals in Mrs Mason's educational plan. Chapter One is headed, 'The treatment of animals – The ant – the bee – Goodness – The lark's nest – The asses'. Chapter Two continues 'The treatment of animals. The differences between them and man – Parental affection of a dog – Brutality punished'. Animals function to teach sympathy and morality, which can be transferred to the human world; and also to teach the children their place in the hierarchy of beings, not so much in order to support the idea of hierarchy, as to make them aware of their weakness and dependence, and wish to grow into the superior status of Mrs Mason herself. Mrs Mason's first lesson to the children is not to kill small creatures: she herself has just stepped into the wet grass to avoid stepping on a snail. She asks Caroline 'How dare she kill anything, but to prevent it hurting her?' Like Trimmer, she cites God as Creator to justify this care, and demonstrates her own tolerance by letting a caterpillar and spider creep on her hand. At the same time, like Day, she recognises the exigencies of the food chain, and like Trimmer puts this in the context of a nature created to benefit mankind: birds are permitted to eat insects, which otherwise would proliferate too much and destroy our fruit and vegetables. Mrs Mason's language is often harsh and violent when making these points to her charges ('How dare she ... '); when Mary protests that worms are too insignificant to care for, Mrs Mason says, 'You are often troublesome – I am stronger than you – yet I do not kill you.'[46] This is reminiscent of Rousseau's advice on treating small children: 'Let him only know that he is weak and you are strong, that from your respective situations he necessarily lies at your mercy ... let him from the first feel on his proud neck the hard yoke which nature has imposed on man, the heavy yoke of necessity.'[47] One of Mrs Mason's aims is to humble her charges, by pointing out their place in the hierarchy of beings.

Surprisingly, when writing for children, Wollstonecraft is as keen to teach hierarchy as Trimmer is, though their political perspectives were quite different. Trimmer is essentially a conservative, while Wollstonecraft wrote the anti-hierarchical *Vindication of the Rights of Men* (1790). Mrs Mason teaches that animals are inferior to men, as men are to angels, who do good to men. Here the point is that men should therefore do good to animals; but where the children are concerned, the lesson is always harsher: Mrs Mason stresses that children are inferior to servants, and 'It is only to animals that children *can* do good, men are their superiors.'[48] A rationale is provided here for the proliferation of animals in children's books, as a childish stage in the exercise of benevolence. Later, the girls do graduate to helping a poor

---

45 Mary Wollstonecraft, *Original Stories from Real Life* (London, 1788), p. v.
46 Ibid., pp. 2, 3, 5.
47 Rousseau, p. 96.
48 Ibid., p. 16.

family: but this is part of their growing-up, and becoming like Mrs Mason, who does good to both animals and men. Mrs Mason's hierarchy does not include, however, the subordination of women to men, as Mrs Gatty's Victorian one does (see p. 98 above). Wollstonecraft's idea of an equality between man and woman may be the reason for her wish to stress the weakness and insufficiency of animals and children, to both of which women have been compared, in order to elevate the grown woman by contrast.[49] Mrs Mason is all wise, and morally fully developed.

Her courage and decision are shown when she kills with a quick twist of the neck a suffering lark who has been shot by some 'idle boys' (7). A similar incident occurs later in Anne Brontë's *Agnes Grey*, when Agnes kills some nestlings that the boy she is nominally in charge of plans to torture. There is a significant gender difference here between the ways male and female tutors/governesses demonstrate their heroism with regard to animals, Mr Barlow facing down a large wild creature on the loose, and Mrs Mason killing a small hurt bird. Each is equally courageous and decisive, and Mrs Mason in fact the more violent, but her action is the desperate measure of the powerless, and the stories she tells the girls centre more on suffering than on heroic action. As Mitzi Myers puts it, 'that is what the world looks like through women's eyes, empathetically tuned to disadvantage and injustice.'[50] This female empathy unites women and suffering creatures, and even makes up for one of the disadvantages possessed by animals, their lack of language. They may appear 'dumb', says Mrs Mason, but God understands their language, and Caroline could understand very well 'the mother's agonising cries', which prompted her to replace a stolen bird's nest.[51] Though not possessing reason, animals possess the same language of feeling as human beings, and a particularly female connection is made here through motherhood. I will be returning later to this idea of a special identification between women writers of children's books, and the small creatures they write about.

Other children's writers with affinities to Rousseau are Anna Barbauld and John Aikin, who published *Evenings at Home*, a miscellany of stories, articles and dialogues in 1792–96. Kenyon-Jones finds a Rousseauesque moral in a fable about 'Nature and Education':

> While *Nature* was feeding her pine with plenty of wholesome juices, *Education* passed a strong rope round its top, and pulling it downwards with all her force, fastened it to the trunk of a neighbouring oak. The pine laboured to ascend, but not being able to surmount the obstacle, it pushed out to one side, and presently bent like a bow. Still, such was its

---

49 For the comparison of woman and child, see Rousseau, 217–52; Barker-Benfield, p. 235

50 Mitzi Myers, 'Impeccable Governesses, Rational Dames and Moral Mothers', *Children's Literature,* 14 (1986): 47.

51 Wollstonecraft, p. 12.

vigour, that its top, after descending as low as its branches, made a new shoot upwards: but its beauty and usefulness were quite destroyed.[52]

This certainly fits in with Rousseau's images of the mutilations imposed on Nature by man; but in the fable this incident is only part of a contest between the two forces: despite the efforts of Nature, Education is able, by grafting, to make a crab-apple bear 'tolerable fruit' at last. The two conclude: '"Ah, sister!" (said *Nature*) "I see it is in your power to spoil the best of my works." "Ah, sister!" (said *Education*) "it is a hard matter to contend against you – however, something may be done by taking pains enough."'[53] The further implied moral is that two 'sisters' should not be contending like this, but should be co-operating.

Charles Lamb, however, fastens on the educational rather than the 'natural' side of Barbauld's enterprise, in his famous attack:

'Goody Two-Shoes' is almost out of print. Mrs Barbauld's stuff has banished all the old classics of the nursery: & the Shopman at Newbery's hardly deign'd to reach them off an old exploded corner of a shelf, when Mary ask'd for them. Mrs B and Mrs Trimmer's nonsense lay in piles about. Knowledge, insignificant & vapid as Mrs B's books convey, it seems, must come to the child in the shape of knowledge, & his empty noddle must be turned with conceit of its own powers, when he has learned that a Horse is an Animal, & Billy is better than a Horse, & such like: instead of that beautiful Interest in wild tales, which made the child a man, while all the time he suspected himself to be no bigger than a child. Science has succeeded to Poetry no less in the little walks of Children than with Men. – Is there no possibility of averting this sore evil? Think what you would have been now, if instead of being fed with Tales and old wives fables in childhood, you had been crammed with Geography and Natural History? Damn them. I mean the cursed Barbauld Crew, those Blights and Blasts of all that is Human in man and child.[54]

Lamb's outburst has been re-examined and attacked by several recent critics, who point out how it has helped to structure subsequent debates on children's literature within false dichotomies that oppose instruction 'to amusement, morality to fun, and the "real" world to fantasy, as if these categories were guarded by impermeable boundaries'.[55] Critics have also put Lamb's ideas into context, as part both of a wider Romantic ideology (Reason versus Imagination), and the period's misogyny (only women writers are named).[56] Lamb is clearly wrong in his implicit categorisation of

---

52 Kenyon-Jones, p. 60; Anna Barbauld and John Aikin, *Evenings at Home* (Edinburgh, n.d.), pp. 166–7.

53 Ibid., p. 167.

54 Charles Lamb, *Letters of Charles and Mary Lamb* (Ithaca, NY, 1976), vol. 2, pp. 81–2, 23rd October 1802.

55 Norma Clarke, 'The Cursed Barbauld Crew', in Hilton and Styles (eds), pp. 91–2.

56 Ibid.; Kenyon-Jones, pp. 51–2; Mitzi Myers, 'Of Mice and Mothers', in Louise Weatherbee Phelps and Janet Emig (eds), *Feminine Principles and Women's Experience in American Composition and Rhetoric* (Pittsburgh, PA, 1995), pp. 255–88; Donelle Ruwe, 'Guarding the British Bible from Rousseau', *Children's Literature*, 29 (2001): 1–17.

Goody Two-Shoes with 'wild tales' and 'old wives fables': as we have seen, the book
upholds rationality, and debunks witches and fairies in favour of animals. Barbauld's
fable of 'Nature and Education' also suggests that she is not so one-sidedly in favour
of instruction as Lamb supposes.

Mary Jackson to some extent reiterates Lamb's dichotomy, but cannot help
praising 'the beauties of Barbauld's work, the strength and cleverness of Trimmer's,
the near pure delight of some of the Kilners'. She blames Trimmer's later 'minions'
for appropriating children's literature to 'conservative bourgeois ideals', while
Newbery had a more radical attitude to social hierarchy.[57] On the other hand, Alan
Richardson points out the conservative agenda of Romantics who praised fantasy
and imagination.[58] Barbauld herself could be categorised as a radical, who, unlike
Wordsworth and Coleridge, did not let developments in France sway her beliefs.
Trimmer, on the other hand, is usually seen as a conservative, as we will see in the
next chapter. This does not stop her praising Barbauld's works for children, just as
Wollstonecraft the radical praises Trimmer's in *Original Stories*. Children's literature
seems to cross political divides. Moreover, the works of both Barbauld and Trimmer
are by no means the grimly instructional 'scientific' treatises that Lamb seems to
imagine. These writers wanted to combine instruction and delight, as well as saving
children from the terrors of superstitious beliefs which could lead to injustices like
Margery Two-Shoes' trial for witchcraft. Lamb speaks with the confidence of an
age for which such beliefs are beginning to be unreal threats, and therefore can be
presented as charming and harmless fantasy, suitable for children.

Lamb's example of Billy and the Horse is a parody of a real story in *Evenings At
Home*, and his version may be the origin of an incident in Dickens' *Hard Times*
(1854) that takes place in Mr M'Choakumchild's school. Sissy, a girl who has
worked with horses in the circus, is reprimanded because she is 'unable to define a
horse', while Bitzer, an inhumanly selfish and mechanical child, gives the 'correct'
definition: 'Quadruped. Gramnivorous. Forty teeth, namely twenty-four grinders,
four eye-teeth, and twelve incisive. Sheds coat in the spring; in marshy countries,
sheds hoofs too. Hoofs hard, but requiring to be shod with iron. Age known by marks
in mouth'. Dickens is satirising a purely factual education that takes no account
of either experience or fantasy: half the children give the 'wrong' answer when
asked if they would like horses on their wallpaper, and later Sissy insists 'wrongly'
that individual suffering is more important than statistical averages.[59] If we look at
'A Lesson in the Art of Distinguishing' in *Evenings At Home*, however, it is quite
different from Dickens' scene, and much less banal than Lamb's parody. In the first
place, it follows the account of a legend concerning Flying Fish – the wonderful is

---

57 Jackson, p. 249.

58 Alan Richardson, 'Wordsworth, Fairy Tales, and the Politics of Children's Reading',
in James Holt McGavran (ed.), *Romanticism and Children's Literature in Nineteenth-Century
England* (Athens, GA, 1991), pp. 34–53.

59 Charles Dickens, *Hard Times* (Harmondsworth, 1969), pp. 49–51.

not missing from the book. Secondly, it takes place not in a classroom, but outside, while Father and Charles look at an actual horse. Thirdly, the point of the lesson is to introduce the child, very gently, to close observation and principles of categorisation, that will help it to understand the world – it is an 'Art' that is being taught, not just inert, useless facts: 'I have not given you a definition to teach you what a horse is, but to teach you to *think*.'[60] The dialogue is not without humour:

F[ather]: Are all horses alike, then?
C[harles]: Yes.
F: If they are so much alike, how do you know one horse from another?
C: They are not quite alike.
F: But they are so much alike, that you can easily distinguish a horse from a cow?
C: Yes, indeed.
F: Or from a cabbage?
C: A horse from a cabbage! Yes, surely I can.

More comic and even surreal comparisons follow:

F: I think a salmon could not walk upon the ground, even if it could live out of the water?
C: No, indeed; it has no legs.
F: And a bird could not gallop like a horse?
C: No; it would hop away upon its two slender legs.[61]

Gradually father and son home in on a definition: 'A horse is an animal of the quadruped kind, whole-hoofed, with short erect ears, a flowing mane, and a tail covered in every part with long hairs.' This is like Bitzer's definition, but is arrived at by questioning and observation. Even so, Charles is unimpressed: 'this does not tell us a great deal about him.' Father tries to make 'definition' sound exciting: 'It is a kind of chase, and resembles the manner of hunting in some countries', where the game is gradually enclosed in a smaller and smaller circle. Charles, however, insists on preferring description to definition, and is allowed to recite 'some verses upon the horse' from Pope's *Homer* in illustration. Father concedes that at Charles's age he too preferred descriptions.[62] The dialogue then incorporates its own critique, including both Father's abstract ideas, and Charles's concrete experience and down-to-earth objections. Barbauld's Charles is almost voicing Charles Lamb's position, opposing poetry to science. But, as in 'Nature and Education', Barbauld's project is not to dichotomise, but to reconcile. Her Charles will see the value of definition when he grows up but he need not give up his sensuous experience of horses or poetry. The idea that the experience of childhood is nearer to poetry than science is of course a very Romantic one. In all this, the horse itself functions as the object of both scientific categorisation, and poetic description.

---

60 Barbauld and Aikin, *Evenings At Home*, p. 111.
61 Ibid., p. 106.
62 Ibid., pp. 106–11.

Other tales in Barbauld and Aikin's collection add empathetic understanding of animals to this mixture, as well as metaphorical meanings, social and moral. Barbauld and Aikin ring the changes on the different ways animal and child can be related, compared and differentiated. Some of their animals talk, some are fabular, some are purely realistic objects of study. This polyphony is excused by the fiction of the book's origins. The Introduction sets the scene in the mansion-house of the Fairborne family, whose numerous visitors would 'frequently produce a fable, a story, or dialogue, adapted to the age and understanding of the young people'.[63] These pieces are put into a box, and in the holidays the children are sent each evening to fetch some of them to be read out. The various pieces that make up *Evenings at Home* are not necessarily original, frequently making intertextual reference to preceding animal stories. So the dog who warns his master that the house is about to collapse reappears here from *Goody Two-Shoes,* but in a fable about the usefulness of servants to masters, and man to God. The animal (an owl this time) mistaken for a ghost reappears in a realistic 'Farmyard Journal' that a boy on holiday sends to his friend. The defamiliarising animals'-eye view that Trimmer uses in *Fabulous Histories* (see next chapter), is developed in several fables and tales, and the animal autobiography, inaugurated by Kilner (see Chapter Three), appears as the 'History and Adventures of a Cat'. *Evenings at Home* then represents the wealth of sometimes conflicting ways animals were presented to children at the end of the eighteenth century. We can see a development from the rather static fable, in which each animal represents one emblematic quality, for the purposes of social satire and moral advice, to stories that also give natural historical information, plead for kindness to animals, and attempt to create animals as subjects as well as objects of study and use to man.

A number of fables in the collection concern pairs of animals, with contrasting qualities: 'Wasp and Bee', 'Goldfinch and Linnet', 'Goose and Horse', 'Swallow and Tortoise'. 'Mouse, Lap-Dog and Monkey', and 'The Hog and Other Animals', also work in this simple way. Modest worth is usually contrasted with boastful laziness. The stories do make use of actual characteristics of the animals concerned, but each represents one static, human quality. 'The Discontented Squirrel' puts the squirrel in a natural setting, but its discontented desire to travel is purely human, and its relief at getting home is likely to appeal to child readers. On the other hand, the travelling swallow in 'Swallow and Tortoise' triumphs over the stupid, stay-at-home tortoise. Consistency does not seem to be the point in the selection of fables: the moral, rather than being the aim of the story, gives an excuse to create humorous animal/human characters. The dialogue 'On the Martin' is more complex, and the animals have several different qualities. Papa is showing little William some martins, and proceeds to explain their nature and habits. He includes a couple of 'stories', which give more information, but also present the birds in terms of human values and qualities, and a moral about right behaviour: "'I'll tell you a story about the great care they take of their young ... How cunning that was!" cried William. "Yes", said his father; "and I

---

63 Ibid., p. 5.

can tell you another story of their sagacity, and also of their disposition to help one another.'" The dialogue ends with a reminder not to 'knock down their nests, or take their eggs or young ones'.[64] Sympathy has been created for the birds, by describing their real activities in recognisable human terms.

The autobiographical 'History and Adventures of a Cat' takes us further into an animal's point of view, as Grimalkin tells of her near-escape from drowning as a kitten, and the way even kindly disposed children mistreat her: 'her fondness, indeed, was sometimes troublesome, as she pinched my sides with carrying me, and once or twice hurt me a good deal by letting me fall.' The cat delights in hunting mice and rats, fulfilling her nature, but there is a reversion to stereotype, and to an inappropriate humanisation of her actions, when she kills a pet linnet and some pigeons. Here, she feels she has transgressed against man by killing her fellow pets, and she confirms the 'treacherous' character given to her race by humans: 'Notwithstanding the danger I had run from killing the linnet, I am sorry to confess that I was again guilty of a similar offence.' Shut in the pigeon house, 'I was obliged to wait trembling in the place where I had committed all these murders ... We cats lie under a bad name for treacherous dispositions in this respect, and with shame I must acknowledge it is but too well merited.' This is very different from Mr Barlow explaining to Tommy that it was not his cat's fault that it killed his pet robin, or Mary Pilkington's autobiographical cat, who argues strongly against the reputation for cruelty and treachery that humans have given cats. The 'Farmyard Journal' also describes a dog's action in killing sheep as 'murder', but here it is more of a mock heroic joke: 'the dead bodies were taken to the squire's, with an indictment of wilful murder against the dog, ... [who] is supposed to have fled the country through consciousness of his heinous offence.'[65] Grimalkin's story also descends into humour, as the cat laments the fact that a fat friend of her mistress has suffocated a whole brood of her kittens by sitting on them. The humour distances us from the cat, who by this time lives with 'Mrs Petlove', an over-indulgent mistress with a monkey and a lap-dog, very like Mrs Addis in Trimmer's story (see next chapter), a woman who is too kind to animals.

The astonishing story 'The Transmigrations of Indur', however, celebrates animal being with no such moralising. The story is set in a mythical past, 'when Fairies and Genii possessed the power which they have now lost'. Children are thus discouraged from any belief in the supernatural, while being able to enjoy a story that depends on a fairy granting a wish. The story is set in India, and depends on the idea of the transmigration of souls – far away and long ago enough to be acceptable as part of the magic. The story is, however, overwhelmingly concerned with nature, not magic. Indur is a naturalist, who delights in observing animals, and helping them. One day Indur saves a monkey from a snake, getting bitten by the snake in the process; the monkey turns out to be a fairy, who cannot save his present life, but grants his wish to inhabit in his next lives a series of animal bodies, while retaining his 'rational

---

64 bid., pp. 53–5.
65 Ibid., pp. 45, 48, 96

soul', and his memory. In each succeeding life, we see Indur enjoying the physicality and particularity of his animal host: 'Indur was highly delighted with the ease and rapidity of his motions; and snuffing the keen air of the desert, bounded away'; 'with vast delight he sprung forward on easy wing through the immense fields of air.' Each host dies a violent death, but Indur springs on to the next life. Animal life may be short and violent, but it is also full of enjoyment. Child readers are being incidently educated in the habits and habitats of various animals. Indur's last animal incarnation is as a rather stereotypical dog who dies saving his master, but till then moral messages have been refreshingly absent from this story.[66]

Many, though not all, of Indur's deaths are occasioned by humans and their weapons. There is no comment in the story on this fact, just a description of the process. The story 'The Council of Quadrupeds' shows a group of African animals coming together to plan revenge on the European hunters who are destroying them. The story is partly focalised through the wise Elephant, who tells the other animals how he saw the white men tricking and killing a group of natives; this makes him feel the plan of revenge will not work. Sympathy is entirely on the side of the animals, until they start to kill one another, reverting to their usual roles of hunter and hunted. The story ends as a fable, with the moral drawn by the dignified elephant: 'the folly of attempting to subdue their common foe while they were at variance with each other'. The fabular ending does not, however, cancel out the animal's-eye view of man we have been given. The point of view of this story contrasts with the dialogue 'On Man'. Charles and his father, having defined a horse, attempt to define man. He is distinguished from the animals by his powers of speech, tool-making and improvement. Charles wonders at the existence of unimproved savages, and is told that some nations are more advanced than others, namely in Northern Europe and North America: 'in these countries man may be said to be *most man*.' For the African animals, however, it is superior destructiveness and treachery that characterise the Europeans.[67]

Another way in which *Evenings at Home* gives us an animal's-eye view is through a defamiliarising technique, in which objects we recognise are described from the unfamiliar perspective and scale of an animal protagonist. These stories have the effect of a riddle, as the child readers try to guess what the object is, while the animal is still mystified. The story 'Traveller's Wonders' uses this technique without an animal protagonist, as the Captain Compass describes familiar British objects and scenes as they might look to a foreigner, rather like Craig Raine's poem, 'A Martian Sends a Postcard Home'. Animals' perspectives add changes of scale to the format – a likely source for the device is Swift's *Gulliver's Travels*. 'The Young Mouse' and 'The Travelled Ant' both use this technique. The young mouse exclaims excitedly about a perfect house she has found:

---

66 Ibid., pp. 62–4.
67 Ibid., pp. 337, 122.

Mother! said she, the good people of this family have built me a house to live in; it is in the cupboard: I am sure it is for me, for it is just big enough: covered all over with wires; and I dare say they have made it on purpose to screen me from that terrible cat, which ran after me so often: there is an entrance just big enough for me, but puss cannot follow; and they have been so good as to put in some toasted cheese, which smells so deliciously, that I should have run in directly and taken possession of my new house, but I thought I would tell you first that we might go in together, and both lodge there tonight, for it will hold us both.[68]

The house is obviously a trap: this is the riddle for the child to solve. The mouse's perspective is, however, brilliantly created, and her eagerness and simplicity asks for empathy. As Mitzi Myers points out, this is a child-voice, in its breathless excitement and naivety, its mixture of self-centredness ('just big enough for me') and generosity ('it will hold us both'): 'almost entirely one sentence, it speaks to child readers in their own vernacular.... the tumbling words and enthusiastic projections of Barbauld's tailed imaginist insert the "real" child's voice into narrative pedagogy.'[69] The old mother mouse is luckily wise to the ways of humans, and reveals the truth, drawing an animal-centred, anti-human moral: 'Though man has not so fierce a look as a cat, he is as much our enemy, and has still more cunning.' These mice are much more thoroughly characterised, and yet less purely human, than the mouse in the fable, 'Mouse, Lap-dog and Monkey', who stood only for 'poverty and distress'.[70]

Myers assumes this particular story is by Barbauld, though most of the pieces in the collection were in fact by Aikin. She has good reason for this assumption: in 1773 Barbauld had published a poem entitled 'The Mouse's Petition', subtitled 'Found in the trap where he had been confined all night'. In later editions a footnote adds to this subtitle, '[confined all night] by Dr Priestley, for the sake of making experiments with different kinds of air'. The poem was written for adults, but soon appropriated for children. Barbauld points out that it has been misread as 'the plea of humanity against cruelty', rather than 'mercy against justice', for 'cruelty could never have been apprehended from the Gentleman to whom this is addressed; and the poor animal would have suffered more as a victim of domestic economy, than of philosophical curiosity'.[71] It is not, then, a piece of early anti-vivisection or animal rights polemic. Barbauld approves of science and its methods; she was a close friend of Priestley. She is just asking him to be more humane in his necessary experiments. Nevertheless, in imagining the situation from the mouse's perspective, she uses some powerful emotional and political rhetoric:

---

68 Ibid., p. 12.
69 Myers, 'Portrait of the Female Artist', p. 234.
70 Barbauld and Aikin, *Evenings at Home*, pp. 12, 42.
71 Anna Barbauld, *Poems* (London, 1773), p. 37.

For here forlorn and sad I sit,
Within the wiry grate;
And tremble at th'approaching morn,
Which brings impending fate.

If e'er thy breast with freedom glow'd,
And spurned a tyrant's chain,
Let not thy strong oppressive force
A free-born mouse detain.

The poem works at first to put scientist and mouse on the same level, as 'brothers':

If mind, as ancient sages taught,
A never dying flame,
Still shifts through matter's varying forms,
In every form the same,

Beware, lest in the worm you crush,
A brother's soul you find;
And tremble lest thy luckless hand
Dislodge a kindred mind.

Here Barbauld makes use of Pythagorean ideas of the transmution of souls – ideas that were to reappear in the story of Indur in *Evenings at Home*. Julia Saunders puts these concepts in the context of contemporary debates about the nature of life, in which Priestley was keenly interested.[72] In his *Disquisitions Relating to Matter and Spirit* (1777), he was to put forward a theory of the individual as an indestructible pattern made up of matter. The reference to mind as a 'never dying flame', in 'every form the same', of the poem could be alluding to Priestley's idea. Barbauld presents this idea as only speculation, and also offers an alternative: 'Or, if this transient gleam of day/ Be *all* of life we share'. Here she alludes to continuing theological debates about whether animals have souls, or only share a material life with man, while he is destined for immortality. Even if so, kindness is indicated: 'Let pity plead within thy breast/ That little *all* to spare.'[73]

Trimmer, as we will see, is more orthodox, and quite firm about the spiritual difference between man and animals. Barbauld, as a Unitarian, may have felt freer to speculate. The poem touches lightly on these ideas: it is a serious plea for the mouse's life (which Priestley apparently heeded, freeing the prisoner when he found the poem attached to its cage), but also a mock-heroic *jeu-d'esprit*. There is a jokiness about seeing the mouse in terms of these grand theories. What interests me here is how far these ideas about the nature of life are presented to children, if at all. Material written specifically for children seems to avoid such speculation. In Indur's

---

72 Julia Saunders, '"The Mouse's Petition": Anna Laetitia Barbauld and the Scientific Revolution', *Review of English Studies*, 53 (2002): 513.

73 Barbauld, *Poems*, p. 39.

tale, the idea of the transmigration of souls is explained as a fairy-tale. This absence of scientific controversy contrasts with later children's stories by Margaret Gatty and Charles Kingsley, which overtly take on evolutionary ideas, and are concerned to push specific interpretations, however disguised as fairy-tale.

More evident in eighteenth-century children's animal stories are the traces of political debates. In 'The Mouse's Petition', Barbauld, also half-jokingly, sees the mouse's plight in verse one (see above) in terms of freedom, tyranny and oppression. But such language is used seriously in Samuel Pratt's story 'The Brothers and the Blackbird', when the good brother who wants to free the bird is 'ashamed that I suffered anything to prevent my taking part with the unprotected in the cause of liberty'.[74] Trimmer, in a review of Edward Augustus Kendall's popular children's book, *Keeper's Travels in Search of his Master* (1798), pounced on what she saw as an application of radical political rhetoric to animals: 'We have long been used to hear of the RIGHTS OF MAN, and RIGHTS OF WOMEN; but the levelling system, which includes the RIGHTS OF ANIMALS, is here carried to the most ridiculous extreme.'[75] Kendall's book is in fact a fairly innocuous adventure story with an unexceptionable moral: Trimmer's animosity towards Kendall comes from his radical political associations. Trimmer uses animals to enforce a contrasting idea of social hierarchy; and even Wollstonecraft, despite publishing on the 'Rights' of men and women, reverts to hierarchical ideas in her children's books, as we have seen.

Barbauld too returns to hierarchical ideas in her poem. At first she seems to flatten out the hierarchy by appealing to Priestley as the mouse's 'brother', but she restores hierarchy in the last verse, where, as in Wollstonecraft, angels are to men as men are to animals:

So when destruction lurks unseen,
Which men like mice may share,
May some kind angel clear thy path,
And break the hidden snare.

But the story 'The Travelled Ant', in *Evenings at Home,* once again implicitly questions hierarchy, and the comforting assurances of Natural Theology. In this story, whatever the ant encounters is described from his point of view, and so defamiliarised. The sea becomes 'this great plain ... of that fluid which sometimes falls from the sky'; men are 'those enormous two-legged animals', a carriage is 'a prodigious rolling mountain'.[76] Like the mouse's 'house', these are riddles for children to unmask. But the ant's-eye view also provides a satire on natural theology, and man's assumption of his own centrality in Creation:

I do not know how far I have benefited from my travels, but one important conclusion I

74 Pratt, p. 11.
75 Sarah Trimmer, *The Guardian of Education*, 1 (1802): 400.
76 Barbauld and Aikin, *Evenings at Home*, pp. 272–5.

have drawn from them.

What is that? said his friend,

Why, you know it is the current opinion with us that everything in this world was made for our use. Now, I have seen such vast tracts not at all fit for our residence, and peopled with creatures so much larger and stronger than ourselves, that I cannot help being convinced that the Creator had in view their accommodation as well as ours, in making this world.

I confess this seems probable enough; but you had better keep your opinion to yourself.

Why so?

You know ants are a vain race, and make high pretensions to wisdom as well as antiquity. We shall be affronted with any attempts to lessen our importance in our own eyes.[77]

The ants become a parody of men in their vain assumption that all of Creation is for their use. This use of an animal's-eye view to demolish human pride and reverse hierarchical assumptions is developed further by Margaret Gatty in her story 'Whereunto', where a whole number of different sea-creatures all assume the natural environment is centred on them. Interestingly, the version of Natural Theology taught in *Evenings at Home*, in a dialogue entitled 'What are Animals Made For', is also not wholly centred on man, and includes a fly's-eye view of humans. Sophia asks her papa what flies are for. He replies: 'Suppose a fly capable of thinking, would he not be equally puzzled to find out what men were good for? This great two-legged monster, he might say, instead of helping us to live, devours more food at a meal than would serve a whole legion of flies.'[78] The answer to Sophia's question, is that flies were made to be happy. Papa then backtracks, and says we are superior, in that we may make reasonable use of all animals, and kill those that harm us. The talking animal stories and poems that I investigate in the next chapter take further the animal's eye perspective of the ant or the fly here, while also maintaining a hierarchical relationship between animal and human, and a hierarchical framework within the animal world. As in other eighteenth-century children's books, animals become a means to convey natural historical information, to inculcate kindness, and to combine delight with instruction.

---

77 Ibid., p. 277.
78 Ibid., p. 233.

Chapter Two

Fabulous Histories and Papillonades

The founding text of this study is perhaps Sarah Trimmer's *Fabulous Histories* (1786) (later published as *The Story of the Robins*), which concerns a family of birds who talk among themselves, but also exist as 'real' robins in the garden of a human family whose children gradually come to understand and appreciate the birds. The book was reprinted throughout the nineteenth century, and into the twentieth: Betty Goldstone calculates it had a life-span of one hundred and thirty-three years.[1] The publishers Griffith and Farran advertise *The Story of the Robins* in 1877 as part of their 'Original Juvenile Library', quoting favourable reviews: 'the delicious story of Dicksy, Flapsy, and Pecksy, who can have forgotten it? It is as fresh today as it was half a century ago.' The work appears several times in their list, in different editions at different prices. The shilling edition is listed together with a number of other related favourite animal stories from the past: *The Life and Perambulations of a Mouse* (Dorothy Kilner, 1783), *Memoirs of Bob, the Spotted Terrier* (Anon., 1801), and *Keeper's Travels in Search of his Master* (Edward Augustus Kendall, 1798).[2] The similarity of the names Dicksy, Pecksy, Flapsy and Robin (Trimmer's young robins) to Flopsy, Mopsy, Cottontail and Peter in Beatrix Potter's 1902 *Peter Rabbit* has often been noted, testifying again to the long life and influence of Trimmer's story.

The original title of Trimmer's book, *Fabulous Histories*, signals the basic contradiction that my book is concerned with: how and why does anyone write stories about talking animals for children in an age of Enlightenment and Reason, of Progress and Modernity? The question becomes more urgent, as political and scientific discourses begin to erode the boundaries between humans and animals. One answer is of course that children are different from adults – less rational, more 'animal' themselves. But if the writer's task is seen to be educational, should they not be leading the child reader away from irrational and superstitious beliefs? Many eighteenth-century writers for children clearly saw this as a problem: published in 1783, *Fables in Monosyllables* by Mrs Teachwell (Lady Eleanor Fenn) begins with this dialogue:

---

1   Bette Goldstone, *Lessons to be Learned* (London, 1984), p. 113.

2   Griffith and Farran, catalogue dated 1877, in Francis Power Cobbe, *The Confessions of a Lost Dog* (London, 1867), pp. 13, 26.

Lady. Can Ants speak?

Boy. No, Aunt,

Lady. Can Flies Talk?

Boy. No, Aunt.

Lady. Why then does this Book talk of what they say?

Boy. I do not know, Aunt.

Lady. I will tell you then, my dear, I write in the way I think will please a child – You love to read of a Fox, a Hen, or a Dog; do you not?

Boy. Yes I do, Aunt.

Lady. These are all to please and teach you. There is one of the Boys and the Frogs.[3]

After the story, the Lady returns to her point, in case it was not sufficiently clear to the child:

Lady. How is this? Can Frogs speak?

Boy. They can croak, and make a noise, but they cannot speak; can they, Aunt?

Lady. No, my dear; but this man says for the Frog, what we may think the poor thing would say, if it could speak.

Boy. Why, aunt?

Lady. To teach you, my dear.[4]

In her Preface, Mrs Teachwell had already worried in more grown-up language about her enterprise: 'there must always remain one accusation against Fables, namely, Falsehood; but surely it is easily explained to the children, that it is but their own usual favourite sport of "*make believe*" as they call feigning visits, trading, &c. &c. with no design to deceive'. In the same year, Dorothy Kilner wrote her delightful 'Introduction' to the *Perambulations of a Mouse*, in which the mouse hero engages the human writer to tell his story. She concludes like this:

> But, before I proceed to relate my new little companion's history, I must beg leave to assure my readers, that, in earnest, I never heard a mouse speak in all my life; and only wrote the following narrative as being far more entertaining, and not less instructive, than my own life would have been.[5]

Sarah Trimmer approaches the issue a little differently, claiming that the idea of animals' speech comes from her child audience themselves. She begins the Introduction to *Fabulous Histories* by reminding her readers of her previous book, in which Henry and his sister Catherine were introduced to the wonders of nature by their indulgent mamma: 'the consequence of this was, that they contracted a great fondness for animals; and used often to express a wish that their birds, cats, dogs,

---

3 Fenn, pp. 15–16.

4 Ibid., p. 19.

5 Dorothy Kilner, *The Life and Perambulations of a Mouse* (London, 1783), p. 8.

&c. could *talk*, that they might hold conversations with them'.[6] So their mamma, 'to amuse them', wrote this book, but before the children were allowed to read it,

> ... they were taught to consider them, not as containing the real conversations of birds (for that is impossible we should ever understand), but as a series of FABLES, intended to convey moral instruction applicable to themselves, at the same time that they excite compassion and tenderness for those interesting and delightful creatures, on which such wanton cruelties are frequently inflicted, and recommend *universal benevolence*.[7]

This double purpose – to instil both social morality, and compassion for animals, so that the animals are both metaphorical and representative – is true of all three writers I've been quoting, Fenn, Kilner and Trimmer. In Fenn's fable about the frogs, they plead with the boys not to mistreat them, and Kilner's mouse provides many lessons against cruelty to mice. It is this compassionate purpose, together with the desire to convey accurate natural historical information to their audiences, that distinguishes these eighteenth-century works from the tradition of Aesopian Fables, in which animal stories convey morals about conduct in the human world. However anthropomorphised, these eighteenth-century children's talking animals are not just metaphorical or allegorical, but convey lessons about animals in the real world, what they are like, and how we should behave towards them.

To allow one's animal characters to talk, then, is for these writers the most effective way to amuse and interest a juvenile audience, and to arouse their sympathy and benevolent instincts. But these purposes conflict with the aim of accuracy and natural historical truth: animals in the real world cannot talk. This is why we have these protestations of the fabular and 'make-believe' nature of the material, which, on another level, is meant to be taken seriously. Mary Jackson rather scorns these writers for their prevarications:

> They accepted Aesop and dug their own pit: If animals talk and display human motives, what cannot happen? Having opened the door to Aesop, they tried to monitor its use with elaborate proscriptions based on the equivocations used in [Fenn's] *Fables*. At fancy's feeblest stirring, they trotted this out, mainly in their prefaces.[8]

But this is to ignore the delicate fancy and playful 'make-believe' with which they present the paradox to their juvenile audience. Jackson's book partakes of the bi-polar model that critics (all the way from Charles Lamb) have imposed on the history of early children's books – reason versus imagination, instruction versus delight, Locke versus Rousseau, conservatives versus revolutionaries – which is now being questioned. It is clear that the dilemma Trimmer, Fenn and Kilner find themselves in comes from their determination to be *both* amusing and instructional, following the lead of Locke and of Newbery. Playful metafictional and intertextual devices

---

6 Sarah Trimmer, *Fabulous Histories Designed for the Instruction of Children, respecting their Treatment of Animals* (London, 1786), p. viii.

7 Ibid., pp. vii–viii.

8 Jackson, pp. 136–8.

animate their 'elaborate proscriptions'. A kind of joke with the readers is going on, which is carried forward in later texts. In Mary Wollstonecraft's *Original Stories from Real Life*, Mrs Mason gives her charges Mrs Trimmer's *Fabulous Histories*. They are delighted: 'I never read such a pretty book, may I read it over again to Mrs B's little Fanny? Certainly, said Mrs Mason, if you can make her understand that birds never talk.'[9] The disclaimers in these texts also free them from any criticism on religious grounds: since God only granted speech to humans, could it be thought blasphemous to make animals talk? But this difficulty is never directly alluded to by these writers. Perhaps they felt themselves empowered by a text like Proverbs 31:8, 'Lift up your voice for the dumb', which was used as an epigraph by the Reverend Humphrey Primatt in his 1776 *Dissertation on the Duty of Mercy and Sin of Cruelty to Brute Animals*, and reappears later in the literature of animal protection (see p. 65 below).

Sarah Trimmer is often characterised as a rather formidable and joyless writer for children. She features as part of Lamb's 'cursed Barbauld crew' (see p. 27 above). This reputation may be largely created by her other activities – she produced a magazine called *The Guardian of Education*, from 1802 to 1806, in which she provided the first serious criticism of children's books, tending towards the conservative and instructional in her judgements. She was also an active publicist for the Sunday School movement, as a way of educating the lower classes, and wrote many books for charity schools. But it is her 'later works' rather than *Fabulous Histories* that Pickering considers liable to Lamb's critique; while Jackson blames Trimmer's 'minions' for their overly conservative agenda, and cannot help confessing her own delight in 'the strength and cleverness' of works like *Fabulous Histories*.[10] Jackson still imitates Lamb in setting up a dichotomy within eighteenth-century children's literature, partly based on political affiliation – Newbery's enthusiasm for social climbing, as against Trimmer's conservative affirmation of hierarchy. Jackson also contrasts Trimmer's work with an eruption of fairytale literature, which is presented as a riposte to the over-instructional works of Trimmer and her followers. A numerous genre of animal poems for children which Jackson aptly names 'papillonades' are seen by her as part of the same liberating movement as the fairytales.

These poems are all sequels to or imitations of William Roscoe's (1807) *The Butterfly's Ball and the Grasshopper's Feast*, the most successful of which was Catherine Dorset's *The Peacock at Home*, itself generating more sequels and imitations: *The Lioness's Rout, The Peacock and Parrot, On Their Tour, to Discover, the Author of, 'The Peacock at Home', The Fishes Grand Gala*, and many more. A consideration of these fantastical talking animal poems occupies the second part of this chapter. I argue that, however fanciful, the papillonades are not so different from *Fabulous Histories* as has been allowed. They also attempt to convey accurate natural history, and generate animal's-eye views of the world and of human society.

---

9   Wollstonecraft, *Original Stories*, pp. 11, 19.
10 Pickering, p. 151; Jackson, p. 249.

The underwater world of *The Fishes Grand Gala, The Water-King's Levee*, and *The Lobster's Voyage to the Brazils* clearly had an influence on the strange combination of carnivalesque playfulness, moral instruction and natural history that is Charles Kingsley's *The Water Babies*. Catherine Dorset, the anonymous author of *The Peacock at Home*, was the sister of Charlotte Smith, the poet. Smith also wrote for children, including a volume to which Dorset contributed that contains perfectly serious animal poems, and a Natural History. The affiliations of Trimmer and Dorset are not so separate after all. At the end of the chapter, I will also be looking at the poems in *Signor Topsy-Turvy's Wonderful Magic Lantern* (1810), a playful series by Ann and Jane Taylor. As suggested by the title, these poems invert hierarchies, and give voice and agency to animal victims of human actions. They are allied to the papillonades through their carnivalesque qualities, but also to the moral purposes of Trimmer.

Harriet Ritvo has pointed out the ubiquity of hierarchical arrangements and implications in children's natural histories of the eighteenth and nineteenth centuries.[11] She sees these as allegories and justifications of the hierarchical arrangements of human society. But, as we have seen in Chapter One, hierarchy can be differently invoked by children's writers of different political persuasion. Thomas Day uses animal stories to flatten hierarchies, and reduce class pride. Mary Wollstonecraft reinforces the lowly hierarchical position of children, only just above animals, but perhaps in order to elevate grown-up women. Anna Barbauld and John Aikin use animal's-eye views to undermine man's position at the top of the earthly hierarchy. While I have stressed that despite political differences, Trimmer and these other writers for children all appreciated each other's works, it is important to notice that the notion of hierarchy that underpins *Fabulous Histories* is relatively stable and fixed. Parents are above children in terms of authority, and humans above animals, in terms both of dominion and compassion: poor people should be fed before hungry animals. The book was subtitled, 'Designed for the Instruction of Children Respecting Their Treatment of Animals', and the narrator and her surrogate in the text, Mrs Benson, are explicit and repetitive in driving home these hierarchical lessons. As we have seen, Trimmer was vocal in attacking any notion of the 'Rights' of animals which would overturn the status quo. On the other hand, as in Wollstonecraft, the hierarchical relation of men and women is not so clearly enforced in *Fabulous Histories*. The father robin has some degree of authority over the mother robin, but mostly they act in concert. He explicitly tells his nestlings that though their mother is 'no songstress herself … yet she is very clever'. On the first page of the story, the human father, Mr Benson, authoritatively sets up his orchard as a safe haven for the robins, having 'strictly charged his domestics not to destroy the labours of those little songsters'.[12] But he then disappears from the story, leaving Mrs Benson to dispense knowledge, wisdom and morality to the children. Mitzi Myers has written about this new, powerful role

---

11 Ritvo, *Learning from Animals*.
12 Sarah Trimmer, *The Story of the Robins* (London, 1873), pp. 13, 1.

of maternal instructress, which was created by female children's writers such as Trimmer, Barbauld and Wollstonecraft.[13]

In Chapter Thirteen of *Fabulous Histories*, Trimmer articulates a deeper rationale for allowing her animals to talk than the one she had used in her Introduction. The device is not just an amusing game for children, but is part of her moral and compassionate purpose. Mrs Benson, in a conversation with Mrs Wilson the farmer's wife, declares that 'I am of the opinion … that it would be a good way to accustom one's self, before one kills anything, to change situations with it in imagination, and to suppose how we should feel were we bees, or ants, or birds, or kittens.' This exchange of situations is ubiquitous in children's literature as a teaching tool, as can be seen in examples from *Goody Two-Shoes*, *Sandford and Merton* and *Original Stories* in the previous chapter, and, more recently, in Roald Dahl's story *The Magic Finger*. In *The Story of the Robins*, Frederick, the younger of the two Benson children, is warned away from catching a butterfly like this: 'Should you like … when you were going out to play, to have anybody lay hold of you violently, scratch you all over, then offer you something to eat which is very disagreeable, and perhaps poisonous, and shut you up in a little dark room?'[14] The anthropomorphism here is a way to develop a child's moral imagination with regard to animals.

In the conversation in Chapter Thirteen, Mrs Wilson takes the point further: 'I have often wished that poor dumb creatures had somebody to speak for them', and Harriet, the older Benson child follows with the resolution, 'I am sure I shall never kill anything without first magnifying it in my mind, and thinking what it would say for itself if able to speak', an obvious reference to Trimmer's practice in this book.[15] To imagine speech for an animal is to put oneself in its place. It is also not purely fanciful: the basis in fact is 'what it would say for itself'. The most striking examples of this technique in the book, are when the father and mother robin tell each other (and therefore the reader), in first-person narratives, what happened to their previous mates and broods, all the victims of schoolboys' birds'-nesting activities. Their speech gives an unavoidable affirmative answer to the question posed in *Goody Two-Shoes*: 'Do you think the poor birds, whose nests and young ones that wicked boy, Dick Wilson, ran away with yesterday, do not feel as much pain as your father and mother would feel, was any one to pull down their house and run away with you?'[16] Harriet's resolve to 'first magnify' the creature (a spider in this case) she might otherwise kill, relates to conversations with her mother about the microscope, which, as in *Easy Introduction*, is an instrument of compassion (see p. 18 above). Mrs Benson affirms the connection of natural history and kindness to animals: 'you must study natural history, from whence you will learn how wonderful their construction

---

13 Myers, Mitzi, 'Impeccable Governesses, Rational Dames and Moral Mothers', *Children's Literature*, 14 (1986): 31–59.

14 Trimmer, *Story of the Robins*, pp. 150, 9.

15 Ibid., p. 151.

16 *Goody Two-Shoes*, p. 37.

is, how carefully and tenderly the inferior creatures tend their young, how ingenious their various employments are, how far they are from harbouring malice against the human species.'[17]

Mrs Wilson's wish that 'dumb' animals should have 'someone to speak for them', evokes the powerful idea of animal 'advocacy'. Farmer Wilson in fact uses courtroom terminology to characterise his compassionate attitude to animals: 'As there are no courts in which beasts can seek redress, I set up one for them in my own breast, where humanity pleads their cause.' Mrs Benson replies, 'I wish they had such an advocate in every breast.' I will be pursuing this courtroom analogy, together with ideas of testimony and witness, in relation to animal autobiography in the next chapter: first-person narrations by animals are a logical extension of the attitudes expressed by the Bensons and Wilsons here. Another similarity between Trimmer's story and the populous genre of animal autobiography, is the convention by which the animals speak in human language among themselves, but cannot be understood by the humans in the story. Only the reader and the narrator, as privileged humans, can understand the animals. This convention preserves the idea that animals cannot in fact speak. Mrs Benson and Harriet have a conversation about the 'Learned Pig', who has recently been exhibited in London. The Pig appears to spell out words, but Mrs Benson is not impressed: 'great cruelty must have been used in teaching him things foreign to his nature.' She does not believe 'animals capable of attaining human sciences'.[18] This attitude is very different from the cheerful acceptance of performing animals in *Goody Two-Shoes*.

While Mrs Benson is sure that animals cannot speak human language, or attain to reason, she is willing to believe they have their own language, to some degree. This conviction comes from careful study of nature: 'I have been an attentive observer'. She has credentials as a natural historian – something reaffirmed in her talk about the microscope. In this capacity she has noticed that 'though they have not the gift of speech, like us, all kinds of birds have particular notes, which answer in some measure the purpose of words among them, by means of which they can call to their young ones, express their love for them, their fears for their safety, their anger towards those who would hurt them, &c; from which we may infer it is cruel to rob birds of their young.'[19] This explanation of the meaningful nature of birdsong, its limitations and its possibilities, helps to insure that the speech of the robin characters in the story is not taken literally, as well as providing yet another reason to treat birds well. The study of birdsong reveals that it is *feeling* that the animals share with us, and through sympathetic feeling we can interpret their language. Interestingly, animal language is seen by Mrs Benson in terms of *expression,* rather than *communication,* an emphasis that persists up to Darwin and his book *Expression of the Emotions in Man and Animals.*

---

17 Trimmer, *Story of the Robins*, p. 152.

18 Ibid., pp. 170, 67.

19 Ibid., pp. 58–9.

In particular, it is parental emotion that is stressed over and over again in this and other eighteenth-century stories for children. This is partly for practical reasons: the stories are designed to prevent the cruelty of birds'-nesting, by appealing to a sympathy with the parent birds. The nestlings, presumably, are too young to articulate their feelings, though it is strange that there are rarely appeals to how the children might feel at being torn from their parents. It is striking how the robins' story in *Fabulous Histories* is told from the parent robins' perspective. At the end of the book, we are told, 'as the old robins, who were the hero and heroine of my tale, are made happy, it is time for me to put an end to it.' It is not that Trimmer is unaware of her juvenile audience: she carefully leads them between her two narratives, what the Bensons are doing, and what the robins are doing concurrently: 'Let us now return to the redbreasts'; 'It is now time to inquire after Harriet and her brother'; 'You may remember, my young readers … '. When an adult conversation about the nature of animals begins, the narrator cuts it short: 'This led to a conversation on the instinct of animals, which young readers would not understand; it would therefore be useless to insert it.'[20]

The story then operates as one of those comparative rarities among children's books that let children into the feelings of their parents – more recent examples would be F. Anstey's *Vice Versa* (1882), or Mary Rodger's *Freaky Friday* (1973), both stories in which children change places with parents for a while, though the reversal here is between children and adult birds, not between children and parents, and is metaphorical rather than literal. Of course Trimmer's book is from an entirely different context, but I make these comparisons to jolt us out of conventional and condescending readings of the text, or the assumption that Trimmer's approach is somehow inappropriate for a children's book. By telling the parents' story through the birds, Trimmer maintains the authority of the human mother in the text, and as animals are nearer to children in terms of the hierarchy Trimmer is using, this device allows for more sympathy and identification between children and parent birds. The human children are also allowed to keep more of their dignity, while the robin children are more directly scolded for bad behaviour, and reminded continually of their parents' care and sacrifice. The burdens of parenthood are made clear to children, without their having to feel too personally guilty. Mrs Benson teases Frederick gently about his greediness, while Dicky is punished for not sharing his worm with his siblings

The story begins with the parent robins building their nest, and goes on to emphasise the parent robins' tenderness and rapture at producing a brood of nestlings. The first words, which are spoken by the father robin, stress both the pleasures and costs of parenthood: '"We may promise ourselves much delight in rearing our little family,' said he, 'but it will give us a great deal of trouble."' By using animal protagonists, Trimmer brings out the material conditions of parental labour, and childhood dependence: the nest must be built, the worms must be caught, making 'a hard day's work' for the father. Mother robin also must work to fetch

---

20 Ibid., pp. 207, 72, 100, 124, 65.

food. Infringements of parental instructions have direct physical consequences: Robin injures his wing by disregarding his father's advice on how to fly; and an expiring redstart whom the robins observe exclaims: 'Oh, my dear father! Why did I not listen to your kind admonitions, which I now find, too late, were the dictates of tenderness!'[21]

These physical consequences could be easier for children to understand than the real dangers that human parents might fear for them in the outside world: the birds' adventures are allegories for these more nebulous perils. Mrs Benson occasionally makes explicit the comparison between the robin children and her own, using a further parallel between children's relationship to animals, and parents' relationship to children: 'you depend as much on your papa and me for everything you want as these little birds do on you; nay, more so, for they could find food in other places but children can do nothing towards their own support; they should therefore be dutiful and respectful to those whose tenderness and care they constantly experience.' The definition of childhood as a period of helpless dependence is very historically and socially specific: previous periods and other classes might see children as workers too, able to contribute to their family income. The book is helping to create a new definition of childhood as a protected space, as the robins are protected in the nest and in the orchard. But it also makes explicit the labour and care involved in maintaining this space. The robins speak like careful middle-class parents: 'this great increase of family renders it prudent to make use of every means for supplying our necessities.'[22]

However, as well as being like the Benson parents in working hard for their children, the robin parents, being lower down the hierarchy, are also dependent on the human children: they are described as the children's 'little pensioners', their 'winged suppliants'. In relation to them, the children are 'young benefactors'. On seeing the birds, Harriet is 'quite impatient to exercise her benevolence'. The robins then correspond to the poor but deserving human family that Mrs Benson helps, but it is made clear that human needs always take precedence over animal needs: '"It is not right to cut pieces from a loaf on purpose for birds, because there are many children who want bread, to whom we should give the preference."'[23] Benevolence can be practised on animals, but is more important in regard to humans. Trimmer is very concerned to maintain a hierarchical relation between humans and animals. This means that her book is to some extent pulled in two different directions. On the one hand, there is the sympathetic anthropomorphising of the robin family, and their function as a metaphor for the human family. On the other hand, Mrs Benson is keen not to let sympathy for the robins and other animals get out of hand and upset her hierarchical system.

Donald Worster has identified a related tension in the ecological implications of eighteenth-century natural history, between the idea that man has dominion over the

---

21 Ibid., pp. 2, 3, 178.
22 Ibid., pp. 17, 3.
23 Ibid., pp. 16, 6, 7, 5.

animals, who have been created to serve him, and the idea that the natural world is an interlocking system of which man is only a part.[24] Trimmer's natural theological framework has an analogous problem: God created all creatures to be happy, and yet we are allowed to kill and eat some of them. Mrs Benson has to both excite and rein in her children's compassion for animals. When the robin nestlings are big enough to leave the nest, 'a wonderful change took place' in the father robin's heart. All his 'ardent affection for his young' vanishes, and Mrs Benson explains that 'it was the nature of animals in general to dismiss their young as soon as they were able to provide for themselves.'[25] The children are therefore to feel no more distress on the parents' behalf. Mrs Benson also points out the difference between humans and animals at this point: God has ordained that 'parental affection, when once awakened, always remains in the human breast.' All the understanding aroused earlier in the story for the parent birds can now be transferred by the child readers to their own human parents.

Compassion for animals is also limited in other ways. Several of the nestlings the children adopt from a thoughtless nest-stealer die, in graphically described ways, so that the issue of animal death can be faced. When animals die, their mother explains, we should not grieve as for humans, because animals are not 'accountable beings' – that is, they have no souls, and will not have to answer to God for their actions. Once they are dead, their troubles cease. Animals provide children with the pleasure of benevolence without the pain of grief. The animals we eat have no foreknowledge of their fates. Part of Frederick and Harriet's education is to be taken by their mother to see Farmer Wilson's farm. This expedition teaches them the correct way to regard farm animals, that is, to make them as happy as possible in their short lives. Harriet is also taken to visit Mrs Addis, who lavishes excessive attention on her exotic pets, a monkey, parrot and parroquet. These pets create havoc, and the point is made that Mrs Addis neglects her own children, and the local poor, because of her infatuation with animals. We learn later that she dies alone, neglected by her children, one of whom develops an exaggerated fear of animals, while the other treats them cruelly. The human/animal hierarchy has become unbalanced. The disasters are traced back to Mrs Addis's own childhood, when she was allowed to indulge her 'immoderate fondness' for animals to the neglect of 'studying natural history, and other useful things'.[26] Education is essential to maintain the proper relation between humans and animals, justifying the purpose of the book. A more detached, scientific interest in animals is also recommended, rather than an overly sentimental one. Pets are not encouraged by Mrs Benson, who prefers useful farm animals, or hard-working, family-minded wild birds.

The contrast between the farm, where animals are treated properly, and their improper treatment by Mrs Addis, educates the children away from any overly-sentimental feeling for animals. In the end, man is the master: Mrs Benson explains

---

24 Donald Worster, *Nature's Economy* (Cambridge, 1994).

25 Trimmer, *Story of the Robins*, pp. 198, 201.

26 Ibid., p. 210.

that the world has been 'principally designed for the use and comfort of mankind, who, by divine appointment, have dominion over the inferior creatures'. Numerous beasts are 'indebted to men for many of the necessities of life', and so 'men have a right to their labour in return.' Others have been 'expressly designed by the Supreme Governor as food for mankind'. Trimmer here disposes of any political ideas of animals' 'rights'. This confidence in human centrality is, however, challenged by the central position of the robins in the story. There are some interesting attempts to see the human world from their perspective, rather like the ant's-eye view in Barbauld and Aikin's later story (see p. 35 above). This animal's-eye perception is achieved partly by changes in scale, which must owe something to Swift's *Gulliver.* In her discussion of the microscope, Mrs Benson contends:

> Neither do I know how we can precisely call anything great or little, since it is only so by comparing it with others. An ant or a fly, may appear, to one of its own species, whose eyes are formed to see those parts which we cannot discover without glasses, as considerable as men and women do to each other; and to creatures of the dimensions of a mite, one of the size of an ant doubtless looks formidable and gigantic. I therefore think it but justice to them to view insects with microscopic eyes before we do anything to them that is likely to give them pain.[27]

The robins partake of this relativity. To them, the human gardener is a 'monster':

> … a great round red face appeared before the nest, with a pair of enormous staring eyes, a very large beak, and below that a wide mouth with two rows of bones, that looked as if they could grind us all to pieces in an instant. About the top of this round face, and round the sides, hung something black, but not like feathers.[28]

The children are also described in this way, when they climb up to see the nest:

> Instead of being all over red, it had on each side two spots of a more beautiful hue than Dicky's breast; the rest of it was of a deep red, like the cherry you brought us the other day, and between these two streaks were rows of white bones, but by no means dreadful to behold, like those of the great monster.[29]

There are also some other attempts to see human behaviour from a robin's-eye view. The father robin cannot understand gunfire, but has observed its effects: 'some men carry instruments from which they discharge what proves fatal to many a bird.' Even more frightening is father robin's account of seeing some partridges killed and cooked: 'she put them before a place which glowed with a brightness something resembling the setting sun.' In his terms, the birds have been 'murdered'.[30] This

---

27 Ibid., pp. 203–4, 151–2.
28 Ibid., p. 35.
29 Ibid., pp. 30–1.
30 Ibid., pp. 180, 192.

description comes near the end of the book, and rather detracts from Mrs Benson's assurances about the rightness of eating animals.

In fact, while Mrs Benson has been taking her children around on visits to teach them the right way to regard animals, the father robin has been taking his brood around to observe the lives that different birds lead. Just as Mrs Benson urges a careful study of natural history, so the robins carefully observe the ways humans treat birds: 'watch here with me a little while', urges the father. They see boys stealing nests, a bird-catcher caging birds, partridges and pheasants being reared to be shot and eaten, and an aviary, where again bird and human perceptions differ. The imprisoned lark 'would, to a human eye, have appeared in raptures of joy; but the redbreasts perceived that he was inflamed with rage'.[31] In the aviary, they also find some canaries, who are very grateful for their accommodation. As foreign birds, they would be mobbed outside, and could not survive the climate – a point Mrs Benson has made to her children earlier, excepting canaries to her disapproval of caging birds. Moira Ferguson has seized on this and other instances in the book, to find hidden xenophobia behind the happy façade of *Fabulous Histories*.[32]

But the attitudes to foreigners deployed by both Mrs Benson and the robins are not so negative, nor are they concealed. Though we see native birds mobbing a cuckoo, with cries of 'Get back to your own country', mother robin explains 'I am far from bearing enmity to foreign birds in general ... How different is the character of the swallow! He comes here to enjoy the mildness of the climate, and confers a benefit on the land by destroying many noxious insects. I rejoice to see that race sporting in the air, and have had high pleasure in conversing with them; for, as they are great travellers, they have much to relate.' Mrs Benson, rescuing a canary from the persecution of other birds, remarks, 'I could not help fancying the little creature to be like a foreigner just landed from some distant country, followed by a rude rabble of boys, who were ridiculing him because his dress and language were strange to them.' The children are being educated to respect difference here. The father robin gives his brood a similar lesson, when Dicky takes against a strange-looking foreign stork: '"Take care, Dicky ... how you form an ill opinion of any one on slight grounds. You cannot possibly tell what the character of this stork is merely from his appearance; you are a stranger to his language, and cannot see the disposition of his heart."' In fact, the stork 'is remarkable for his filial affection', and was carrying his aged father on his back when he was cruelly captured by a man.[33] Mrs Benson's attitude to the foreign pets that Mrs Addis keeps – that they would be better off in their native habitats – could not be disputed today. It is cruel and impractical to keep such animals as pets.

I think, then, we need to beware of reading too many metaphorical meanings into the text. On one level it is merely dispensing practical advice on how to treat

31 Ibid., pp. 186, 173.

32 Moira Ferguson, 'Sarah Trimmer's Warring Worlds', *Children's Literature Association Quarterly*, 21/3 (1996): 105–10.

33 Trimmer, *Story of the Robins*, pp. 131, 31, 196–7.

animals. There are also plenty of quite overt metaphorical meanings attached to animal behaviour. It is this mixture of natural historical verisimilitude and overt moral allegory that characterises the book. At some points, the two are in tension: when a mocking-bird is introduced, to show the little robins how rude mimicry is, Trimmer adds an anxious footnote: 'The Mocking-bird is properly a native of America, but is introduced here for the sake of the moral.' Many of the birds the redbreasts observe function rather like the beasts in fables, who stand for only one quality: the mocking-bird for mimicry, the stork for filial piety, the ornamental pheasants for pride in appearance, and so on. The robins themselves, however, are given a more complex characterisation, though here anthropomorphism can clash with natural historical truth, as when naughty Robin has to abase himself before his father before he receives forgiveness for his disobedience: 'he cast himself in the most supplicating posture at the feet of his father.' It is this rich and sometimes contradictory mixture of the animal and the human, the moral and the scientific, the fantastic and the instructional, that characterises *Fabulous Histories* and the tradition it helps to inaugurate.[34]

A similar mixture, though in different proportions, can be found in the papillonades and the topsy-turvy poems. These children's poems, as I will explain, draw overtly on specific carnivalesque traditions: the eighteenth century masquerade, and the 'world-turned-upside-down' chapbook. But Trimmer, though not overtly carnivalesque, cannot help hints of subversion entering her story, once she has allowed human speech to animal characters. Paradoxically, the poems that label themselves as carnivalesque are more affirmative of hierarchy than Trimmer's book. The talking animals in the poems inhabit a comic and fantastic space outside the normal hierarchical rules that pertain in the rest of the world. At the same time, these poems also make serious links to natural historical fact and the everyday treatment of animals.

Catherine Ann Dorset, the chief inaugurator of the papillonades, began her career as a children's writer by contributing to her sister, Charlotte Smith's book, Conversations, Introducing Poetry; chiefly on subjects of Natural History, for the use of children and young persons (1804). Smith, a well-known poet, used a familiar formula for this book, in which Mrs Talbot instructs George and Emily in natural history and poetic form, while also inculcating kindness towards animals. The animals in the interspersed poems do not talk – instead they are apostrophised (e.g. 'To a greenchafer, on a white rose') as objects of contemplation. Even so, it must be explained to the children, in the manner of Trimmer, that the animals addressed cannot understand human language: 'prose, or poetry, we know to be equally unintelligible to an insect, as to a bird, a tree, or a flower, or any other animate, or inanimate being, that does not possess speech or reason.'[35] This form of address does not rule out sympathy, for instance for the persecuted hedgehog: 'Wherefore should man or thoughtless boy / Thy quiet harmless life destroy?' The poems are heavily annotated

---

34 Ibid., pp. 136, 96.
35 Charlotte Smith, *Conversations* (London, 1804), p. 5.

with the Latin names of plants and animals. This practice of scientific footnoting is something Smith also uses in her poems for adults: it is not merely there to add instructional content for children, but it is a way for a woman writer, debarred from the usual scientific forums, to demonstrate her scientific competence. The natural historical references of the footnotes are combined with fable-like morals for human readers. 'The early butterfly' ends:

> Thus unexperienced rashness will presume
> On the fair promise of life's opening day,
> Nor dreams how soon the adverse storms may come,
> 'That hush'd in grim repose, expect their evening prey.'[36]

Smith is however aware of the danger of triteness here: Mrs Talbot comments to the children, 'It is difficult, George, to say anything that is not mere commonplace on so obvious and hackneyed a subject.' But useful facts can still be conveyed: the butterfly is 'Rhamni, which makes its appearance early in March'.[37] A poem addressed to a Jamaican firefly, now a specimen in a collection, introduces a more particular and contemporary moral: the firefly can no longer either terrify the escaped slave, or comfort the slave at work. The dead specimen evokes the living landscape, and a lesson in natural history leads to sympathy for the oppressed slave. The sequence of footnotes is interesting, mingling different types of information:

1. The wretched Negro, fearing punishment, or driven to despair by continual labour, often secretes himself in these obscure recesses, and preys in his turn on his oppressor at the hazard of his life.
2. Bats bigger than crows are found in the gullies and caverns among the woods of Jamaica. And monkeys hide there, sallying forth in numbers to prey on the canes and fruits.
3. After the toils of the day, the poor African often walks many miles, and for a few hours loses the sense of his misery among his friends and companions.
4. Cocoa. Coco-nut tree, *Cocos*.
5. Banana. *Muse Paradisiacus*, Plantain or Banana ... [38] (my numbering)

Catherine Dorset must not have felt out of place in the serious moral and instructional context of her sister's *Conversations,* as she reprinted her poems from that collection in *The Peacock at Home, and Other Poems* (1809). The poems, on such subjects as 'The Mimosa', 'The Captive Fly', or 'The Glow-Worm' are indistinguishable in tone and form from Smith's. Dorset comments in her Preface that 'being principally on subjects of Natural History, they may be considered as no improper accompaniment

---

36 Charlotte Smith, *Poems*, ed. Stuart Curran (Oxford, 1993). The poem quotes Gray, 'The Bard', line 76.

37 Smith, *Conversations*, Vol. 1, p. 52.

38 Smith, *Poems*.

to the "Peacock at Home"', making it clear that she considers 'The Peacock at Home' to be also a 'Natural History' poem.[39]

In 1807 William Roscoe's phenomenally successful comic poem for children, *The Butterfly's Ball* was published. Almost at once, a multitude of imitations and sequels appeared, including Dorset's *The Peacock at Home*, which became even more famous than Roscoe's original, and itself spawned several sequels, such as *The Lion's Masquerade* (by Dorset), *The Lioness's Ball, a companion to The Lion's Masquerade*, and *The Peacock and Parrot, On Their Tour, to Discover, the Author of, 'The Peacock at Home'*. Many of these were collected together and published by John Harris in *Harris's Cabinet of Amusement and Instruction* (1807–09). The title of the collection refers back to Newbery's winning formula, based on Locke: the combination of the playful and the didactic in literature for children. These popular poems exploit the comic potential of animals performing human activities: holding parties, dancing, talking, wearing clothes. There are interesting variations in their degrees of anthropomorphism, and all retain some reference to the naturalistic. In most of them the ubiquitous framework of hierarchy is apparent, but often reversed: the humour comes from a carnivalesque inversion of proper order, as animals imitate humans. But the hierarchies are often quite complex, as hierarchical structures within the animal world are also invoked, sometimes as comic parallels with human class structures. The topsy-turvey world of the 'papillonades' (as Mary Jackson has dubbed them) bears an obvious relation not only to the general idea of carnival, but to the specific eighteenth-century masquerade, an allusion which is made very explicit in some of them.

Roscoe's original poem is simpler than many of its imitations, and with an overt address to children which is sometimes lost in the later poems. Rather like the nursery-rhyme 'Girls and Boys Come Out to Play', it invites its child listeners to the insects' party:

> Come take up your hats, and away let us haste
> To the *Butterfly's* Ball and the *Grasshopper's* Feast.
> The Trumpeter, *Gadfly*, has summon'd the Crew,
> And the Revels are now only waiting for you.

These words are then revealed to be spoken by 'little Robert', who leads his 'merry Companions' to what is surely an ancestor of the Teddy Bears' Picnic in the woods. At the end of the poem, Robert leads his companions back home at bedtime: 'Then Home let us go, while yet we can see.' We have here both a child addressee, with whom the reader can easily identify, and a child speaker, who invites the reader into the poem. The insects in the poem do not talk, but perform human actions that are also appropriate to their real habits: for instance, the spider performs on the tightrope. Falling off, he is able to save himself, hanging by a thread. The insects use a mushroom as table, a leaf as a cloth, as children might in a game of miniaturisation.

---

39 Catherine Dorset, *The Peacock At Home, and Other Poems* (London, 1809), p. iii.

Figure 2.1 Illustration by William Mulready in William Roscoe, *The Butterfly's Ball* **(1807).**

Figure 2.2 Illustration by William Mulready in William Roscoe, *The Butterfly's Ball* **(1807).**

While the insects are not overly anthropomorphised in the poem, the illustrations in the first edition present them quite differently, in what must be a reference to the eighteenth-century masquerade. The insects appear as creatures riding on people, or people using animals as costume – for instance, a lady with a snail on her head like a hat; but the snail is also depicted as a man with a shell on his back, or is it a snail with the upper body of a man? (See Figures 2.1 and 2.2). Different ways in which humans might disguise themselves as animals are explored. Terry Castle, in her detailed study of the eighteenth-century masquerade, refers to the popularity of animal costumes: 'eighteenth-century masqueraders metamorphosed into dancing bears, birds, donkeys and apes.'[40] The masquerade theme is more overt in *The Lioness's Rout*. A party game at the Rout requires the animals to dress up as their opposites: 'The Giraffe was an elegant Girl in her bloom, / And the Bear was a Fairy, and tripped round the room.'[41] Here we have an inverse reversal, animals dressing as humans, just as humans dress as animals. Castle points out the emphasis on dressing as one's opposite at a masquerade: 'Costume ideally represented an inversion of one's nature … one was obliged to impersonate a being opposite, in some essential feature, to oneself.' '"Everyone here wears a Habit which speaks him the Reverse of what he is"', wrote one commentator.[42] Dorset's *Lion's Masquerade*, her own sequel to *The Peacock at Home*, is even more explicit in its reference. The various costumes are elaborately jokey, making intertextual references to allegorical and fictional associations of the animals concerned, and satirising human types. So, the Horse comes as a 'Hounyhm of Gulliver', the Fox as a country attorney, the Wolf in sheep's clothing, the Bear as Caliban, the Greyhound as Vanity, the Mastiff as a brave English sailor, the chattering Monkey as a 'Frenchified beau', the Bull as Taurus, the Ass as King Midas, the Elephant as King of Siam, and the Lioness as Britannia.[43]

In Castle's account, the public masquerade was already in decline by the 1780s and 1790s. The eighteenth-century masquerade, unlike the folk carnival, did not take place out of doors in unconfined space, but in an assembly room or ballroom. Yet it was 'open', in that tickets could be purchased for entry, and people of all kinds and ranks would mingle. Its decline was signalled by the predominance of more exclusive, private variants. The Peacock and the Lion send out invitations to selected, aristocratic guests, the Peacock of course being 'At Home'. By the nineteenth century, the masquerade had been reduced to a quaint object of nostalgia, and, significantly, took on 'juvenile associations'. 'Costume parties' were now mostly for children: these poems mirror this movement to the childish. The masquerade in its heyday allowed adults to become children and animals, with its 'affirmation of childhood over adulthood', and 'descent from adulthood and from full humanity', fulfilling

---

40 Terry Castle, *Masquerade and Civilisation* (London, 1986), p. 67.
41 *The Lioness's Rout* (London, n.d.), p. 19.
42 Castle, pp. 5–6.
43 Catherine Dorset, *The Lion's Masquerade* (London, 1807), pp. 8–12.

childish wishes.[44] But the masquerades in the 'papillonades' instead allow children to participate in comic versions of adult revelry.

It is notable that Dorset's *Peacock at Home* has a more adult tone and a more aristocratic setting than Roscoe's simple nursery-rhyme poem. Instead of the voice of little Robert, we have the voices of the adult animals: Dorset is the first to introduce *talking* animals into the genre. Her poems contain satire on adult social behaviour, and were read as such by adults. The edition of the *Peacock at Home* with Dorset's other, shorter poems hopes to fulfil the desire of adult readers 'to see it transplanted from the nursery, to a more honourable station'.[45] At times her address does seem unsuitable for children. In *The Lion's Masquerade*, for instance, the Lion reproaches mankind for the bad example men give to the animals, remarking on human festivities:

> How oft have their gala's a tragical end,
> One loses a mistress, another a friend –
> The wife of a third has elop'd from a ball,
> A fourth the next day in a duel must fall.[46]

These extraneous events perhaps reflect the masquerade's function as a 'plot-catalyst' in eighteenth-century fiction. They presuppose a knowing, adult audience. Is Dorset using the cover of a children's poem to address a social commentary to adults? Here she seems to echo earlier critics of the immorality of masquerade, who saw it as 'a foolish, irrational and corrupt activity perpetrated by irresponsible people of fashion'.[47] On the other hand, it is only human galas that are condemned: the children's animals provide a safe, playful, moral form of masquerade. Other poems, like the *The Fishes Grand Gala*, reinstate the child audience as miniature adults, addressing 'little beaus' and 'little fair'. The fashionable world is being imitated by children and by animals, in a game of dressing up.

So how subversive are these poems? Great effects have been claimed for the carnivalesque as a loosener of hierarchical power structures and an expression of suppressed desires: 'the potent transformations of the masquerade implicitly challenged those hierarchical valuations built into the system of cultural oppositions … the archaic chain of being, with its value-laden system of interlocking vertical contrasts, was gloriously dismantled.'[48] Several poems comment on the topsy-turvy nature of their proceedings. The Lioness remarks on the impropriety of 'Reptiles and Birds to be giving a rout/ As if old Dame Nature was turned inside out'.[49] The Fishes 'resolv'd they would do as they did ABOVE STAIRS'.[50] Both social and natural

---

44 Castle, pp. 36, 74, 101.
45 Dorset, *The Peacock at Home and Other Poems*, p. i.
46 Dorset, *Lion's Masquerade*, p. 15.
47 Castle, pp. viii, 2.
48 Ibid., pp. 78–9.
49 *The Lioness's Rout*, p. 3.
50 Mrs Cockle, *The Fishes Grand Gala* (London, 1808), p. 4.

hierarchies are being inverted. But on the other hand, the primary effect is comic: the comedy stems from the incongruity and impossibility of the situations, and could be seen as reinforcing normality.

It is interesting that several of the poems also assume a hierarchy within the animal world. So the Peacock determines to hold his 'At Home' in order to assert his rank over other birds, and over the Crickets and Butterflies of Roscoe's poem:

> Shall we, like domestic, inelegant Fowls,
> As unpolish'd as *Geese*, and as stupid as *Owls*
> Sit tamely at home, hum drum with our Spouses,
> While *Crickets* and *Butterflies* open their houses?
> Shall such mean little insects pretend to the fashion … ?[51]

The Peacock himself is described as 'Imperial, the pride of his race', quite different from one of the guests, 'a London-bred *Sparrow* – a pert forward Cit!'[52] The presence of the Sparrow suggests the sort of mixing of classes that Castle describes in the public Masquerade. But in another poem, *The Fishes Grand Gala*, class and taxonomical barriers are kept up, when a seal is refused admission as an 'amphibious creature'.[53] It is difficult to judge whether the poems are reinforcing such hierarchies, or making fun of them. In *The Peacock and Parrot*, 'our birds of *haut-ton*' visit their silly country cousins, the turtle doves, and both ranks are made fun of.[54] *The Jackdaw at Home* shows the disreputable Jackdaw giving a disorderly feast, to which he invites his Irish friend, the Heathcock, 'Foremost in impudence, freedom and fun,' parodying the Peacock's party, as that party parodies human assemblies.[55] The level of intertextual parody and self-referentiality within these texts is high: the epigraph to *Madame Grimalkin's Party* reads:

> Birds, beasts and fishes, are so learned grown,
> They speak the English language as their own;
> At least so modern poetasters tell ye,
> Some of whom write to fill an empty belly.[56]

To be taken more seriously are the nationalistic and patriotic sentiments expressed in many of the poems. England was by now at war with France, and the French are often vilified through unfavourable animal comparisons, as when the monkey dresses up as a 'Frenchified beau'. So in *The Fishes Grand Gala*, the Swordfish dresses like 'a bold British sailor', while the shark dresses like a Frenchman, and Neptune speaks up against the French.[57] *The Lioness's Rout* ends with a patriotic

---

51 Catherine Dorset, *The Peacock at Home* (London, 1807), p. 1.

52 Ibid., pp. 1, 12.

53 Cockle, p. 13.

54 Catherine Dorset, *The Peacock and Parrot* (London, 1816), p. 24.

55 *The Jackdaw at Home* (London, 1808), p. 7.

56 *Madame Grimalkin's Party* (London, 1808), title page.

57 Cockle, pp. 2, 5.

toast to the Lion and Lioness, 'Rex and Regina', whose subjects will never 'bow to an insolent foe'.[58] *The Lion's Masquerade* similarly ends with all the guests roaring 'Rule Britannia!' in praise of the Lioness, and at the end of *The Elephant's Ball* the Lion sings 'Britannia Rules', and the Tiger, 'English Roast Beef'.[59] Other prejudices are evident: *Madame Grimalkin's Party* makes fun of Italian opera, when Puss sings 'In a language few can understand / Who're born in Britain's happy land'. Fashion, however, decrees approval, so, 'Though her language no-one knew / They all admired her charming mew.'[60] The canary, in *The Peacock at Home* is, however, described as a 'much admir'd foreign musician', in keeping with the friendly attitude to canaries as foreigners in *Fabulous Histories*.[61] The anti-French xenophobia and corresponding British patriotism in these poems is very overt: there is no need to dig into the subtext to find it.

A surprising piece of overt propaganda in one of these poems is the pro-Catholic message in *The Water-King's Levee; or, the Gala of the Lake: A Sequel to The Peacock at Home, for Children of all Ages and Sizes*. We are told that fish are all Catholics, and 'The Pike calmly own'd – that he cordially hated / To see others thus *persecuted* and *baited*!' The fishes ask for toleration, and a footnote adds 'not *under*, but *over* the water', with a punning reference to the Jacobite toast. The poem ends with a wish that St Anthony may 'baffle No Popery's mischievous howl'.[62] The political content here must be addressed to the children of larger size addressed in the title, while the younger readers enjoy the comedy of talking fishes.

Though the animals in these poems perform human activities – talking, masquerading, playing cards, sending invitations, taking up patriotic and religious causes – they also retain their reference to the natural. The habits and habitats of the birds the Peacock invites to his 'at home' are correctly described –

> The *Woodcock* preferr'd his lone haunt on the moor
> And the Traveller, *Swallow*, was still on his tour,
> While the *Cuckoo*, who should have been one of the guests,
> Was rambling on visits to other Birds' nests.[63]

The birds' orchestra is not a group of animals dressed up and playing human instruments, but a tree full of songbirds. The food eaten at the feast also hovers between the natural and the anthropomorphic: 'Wasps *a la sauce piquante*' and 'Flies *en croute compote*', 'Worms and Frogs *en friture*' and barbecued Mouse, as well as 'Nuts, grains, fruit and fish'. The birds' human actions are suited to their natural characteristics: the Spoonbill ladles the soup, the Trumpeter announces the feast, the

---

58 *Lioness's Rout*, p. 32.

59 *The Elephant's Ball* (London, 1807), p. 15.

60 *Madame Grimalkin*, p. 10.

61 Dorset, *Peacock at Home*, p. 11.

62 *The Water-King's Levee* (London, 1808), pp. 20–22.

63 Dorset, *Peacock at Home*, p.5.

Bantam is criticised for wearing ridiculous pantaloons.[64] The delicate manoeuvrings between the natural and human are very reminiscent of Beatrix Potter, and especially in the matter of dress. Carole Scott points out the ways that Potter uses clothing to blur the dividing line between the natural and the social. While in *Peter Rabbit*, 'clothes, and the social self they represent, are imprisoning; they mar and hide the real, natural self', in *Mrs Tiggy-winkle* the animals' natural covering is presented as clothing.[65] For instance, drying on the washing line are the hens' long yellow stockings. Something similar happens in *The Peacock at Home* when the Taylor-Bird makes 'new clothes / for all the young Birdlings who wish'd to be Beaux'.[66] The Robin gets a doublet of red, the Goldfinch a velvet cap, the Kingfisher a blue bodice.

The Lioness's Rout includes more natural historical information in the poem: camels, who live in the desert, are 'famous for bearing of thirst', and 'lay in such store' of water, that 'for days, even weeks, they can do without more.' Here, the singular Camel, the guest at the party, becomes briefly the plural species, camels, who really have such instincts. While in *The Elephant's Ball* the Lion and Unicorn dance patriotically together, in *The Lioness's Rout*, when the Lion suddenly realises he has forgotten to invite the Unicorn, the Lioness reassures him with fact: 'There exists no such creature.' A passage on the usefulness of the Roebuck (perhaps the Reindeer is meant) in providing food and clothing for the human inhabitants of Lapland, leads to a Natural Theological message: 'And there we may see how Kind Nature produces / From the Pole to the Equator, all things for our uses.'[67] Natural history is allied to religion: after a passage on the characteristics of the Hippopotamus, the reader is urged to look him up in Job, where he is described as Behemoth.

The Water-King's Levee and *The Lobster's Voyage to the Brazils* also include accurate and attractive natural descriptions. For instance, in the latter we meet the 'Muscle' 'at his two folding doors/ Which the purple of Morn, in her beautiful hue / Had just painted with crimson, with gold, and with blue'.[68] Several of these poems also make great use of prosaic footnotes to convey natural historical information, in the manner of Charlotte Smith. *The Lobster's Voyage* has a note or more for every page. Though Dorset claims that footnotes were only added to *The Peacock at Home* when it was published with her other poems, there are already two notes in the first edition, on the Indicator and the Trumpeter. Dorset also ascribes the absence of footnotes in the first edition to an educational purpose: 'for as the poem was written expressly for the amusement of very young readers, it was rather my wish to excite than to satisfy curiosity, by inducing them to apply to other books for that information, which a short note can very imperfectly supply.' On the advice of 'others', she has added

---

64 Ibid., p. 14.

65 Carole Scott, 'Between Me and the World', *The Lion and the Unicorn*, 16 (1992): 192–98.

66 Dorset, *Peacock at Home*, p. 5.

67 *Lioness's Rout*, pp. 5–7, 12, 21–2.

68 *The Lobster's Voyage to the Brazils*, p. 3.

notes to this edition, which she hopes will be of interest to adult readers as well. For extra credibility, she cites her sources: Wood's *Zoography*, Bewick's *British Birds*, and Bingley's *Animals Biography*.[69] In *The Fishes Grand Gala*, the notes often refer back to the illustrations, implying they are accurate representations of the creatures, even though some of the pictures show animals dressed up in human clothes. In this poem and in *The Lobster's Voyage*, the notes refer the reader to other sources of information: 'see Shaw's Naturalist Miscellany Plate 124', 'Dictionary of Natural History published by Harris, St Paul's churchyard', 'specimen in the British museum', 'Chaetodon Enceledus Linnaei Syst Nat p 462'.[70] Once again, instruction is being combined with delight, perhaps because this would make the poems more saleable to parents, and might also send them back to Harris's shop to buy a Natural History.

While these poems combine comic inversion with natural historical instruction, they hardly touch on the other ingredient of *Fabulous Histories*, and other eighteenth-century animal stories, the anti-cruelty message. Perhaps this kind of material would be too inappropriate to their pervading light-heartedness: *The Peacock at Home* is punningly humorous about birds who are hunted and eaten by humans:

> The *Partridge* was ask'd; but a Neighbour hard by
> Had engaged a snug party to meet in a Pie;
> And the *Wheat-ear* declined, recollecting her Cousins,
> Last year, to a feast were invited by dozens, –
> But, alas! They returned not; and she had no taste
> To appear in a costume of vine-leaves or paste.[71]

The only hint of the humane strand of the animal story is the Pike's words in *The Water-King*: 'he cordially hated / To see others thus *persecuted* and *baited*!', and it is the human, pro-Catholic message that predominates here, rather than a serious plea against angling.[72] But a different set of poems show it is possible to combine anti-cruelty and comic inversion, while omitting any natural historical information. These can be found in Ann and Jane Taylor's *Signor Topsy-Turvy's Wonderful Magic Lantern* (1810). This collection of poems takes its origin from a more popular carnivalesque tradition than the masquerade. The 'Advertisement' to the book confesses that some of its ideas have been 'stolen' from 'a little volume entitled, "The World turned upside down"', which 'those grandmammas and aunts who are versed in the nursery learning of fifty years ago, may perhaps recollect', and which the present authors have been asked to revise for a modern audience.[73] Matthew

---

69   Dorset, *The Peacock at Home and Other Poems*, p ii.

70   Cockle, pp. 12–16; *Lobster's Voyage*, p. 17.

71   Dorset, *Peacock at Home*, p. 5.

72   *Water-King's Levee*, p. 21.

73   Ann and Jane Taylor, *Signor Topsy-Turvy's Wonderful Magic Lantern* (London, 1810), p. 2.

Grenby explains that there were many 'World Turned Upside Down' chapbooks in the eighteenth century which 'took an absurd concept – a dog playing the flute, a man attempting to swallow himself, a goat becoming a Jewish old clothes seller – and presented the reader with a woodcut image, a verse to explain the scene, and perhaps another to offer a moral or an apposite joke.'[74]

While turning the world 'Topsy-Turvy' is the stuff of carnival, it is also the strategy used by serious and moral children's writers to evoke sympathy for the animal creation. As Mrs Benson says, in Trimmer's *Fabulous Histories*: 'it would be a good way to accustom one's self, before one kills anything, to change situations with it in imagination, and to suppose how we should feel were we bees, or ants, or birds, or kittens.'[75] In the Taylors' poems, animals often turn the tables on cruel humans, just as children in some tales are punished for mistreating animals by having the same done to them, in imagination or reality. Like the 'papillonades', the Topsy-Turvy poems are balanced between the purely nonsensical, which can serve to reinforce normality, and the subversive. They belong to a genre which Margaret Blount calls 'The Tables Turned at the Zoo', after a Du Maurier cartoon showing animals feeding and viewing humans in cages.[76] Much later, P. L. Travers developed the idea in *Mary Poppins*, when the children pay a visit to the Zoo after dark, and find animals in charge and humans caged. The same type of idea is exploited by Roald Dahl, in *The Magic Finger*, when hunters and ducks change places, and *Dirty Beasts* when an intelligent pig eats the farmer.

The equivalent Topsy-Turvy poems have titles such as 'Birds Turned Fowlers', 'Game Turned Sportsmen', 'The Hogs' Court of Inquiry', and 'Fish Turned Fishers' (also the topic of a Mary Poppins story). The morals of these stories often contradict each other, ranging from the folly of those who 'attempt to rule over their betters' in 'The Ass Turned Miller', to 'some men behave little better than brutes' in 'Servants Turned Masters'. All the stories are placed within the framework of Signor Topsy-Turvy's magic lantern show, in which the slides are shown upside down: they are to some extent discredited from the start. The book did not in fact sell well, and Matthew Grenby hypothesises that the potentially seditious content – taken seriously, some of the poems could be read as fomenting rebellion – was not well received, in spite of the comic framing. Different poems in the collection use concepts with different political and moral connotations: rebellion, revenge, justice, mercy. In 'The Cook Cooked', the language of seditious assembly and treachery is used. A hare, hanging in the kitchen and seeming dead, 'really brew'd sedition'. She unites with other food animals, also obviously dead: the turkey has been in the larder 'half a week'.[77] They make a compact, described as if it were an illegal trade union, or revolutionary council:

---

74 Mathew Grenby, Introduction to Taylor, *Signor Topsy-Turvy's*, Hockliffe Project website.

75 Trimmer, *Story of the Robins*, p. 150.

76 Margaret Blount, *Animal Land* (London, 1974), p. 12.

77 Taylor, *Signor Topsy-Turvy's*, pp. 28, 44, 8,

So hand and foot, and fin and paw,
  In mutual faith were shaken;
And all the patriots made a law
To murder every cook they saw
  The moment he was taken.[78]

A human victim is found, and roasted on 'the traitor of a jack', and the poem concludes without further moral.[79]

In 'Game Turned Sportsmen', a similar compact to kill and eat the gamekeeper is made between a stag, fox and hare. But in this poem, the incompetent animals forget to load their gun, and conclude 'I very much doubt if we lawfully may / Revenge ourselves thus upon man.' In 'The Fish Turned Fishers', however, we have another 'rebellion', 'the tenants of wood and of water among, / Against the dominion of man'. Here man is seen as an invader: 'a great living thing with a gun, / Our rightful dominion invades.' The animals speak feelingly about their sufferings, their wounds and their bereavements, and decide to take arms for freedom. Their plan succeeds, and 'Poor gentlemen anglers were hook'd by the nose, / And the whole race of fox-hunters died.' In 'Servants Turned Masters', we are told of a magic place where man is not 'lord of the flocks and the herds', but cattle are in charge (perhaps inspired by the Houyhnms), men pull ploughs, and 'fat farmers' are traded. The poem ends in Swiftian mode, turning its critique onto men, who sometimes behave 'little better than brutes'. 'The Hog's Court of Inquiry' debates similar issues, in what seems to be an allusion to early evolutionary thinking: 'A report having lately prevail'd in the corps, / That both [hogs and men] were related some ages before.'[80] Evolutionary ideas had already been mooted in England by Erasmus Darwin in *Zoonomia* (1794) and *The Temple of Nature* (1803). The idea of animals debating evolution is later taken up by Margaret Gatty (see Chapter Four). While Gatty is concerned to parody and discredit evolutionary ideas, here the concept is used as a device to show up man's moral failings. Evolution is presented as a comic idea, not to be taken seriously, but equally not to be discredited. The hogs point out the laziness and greed of men:

Mere gluttons! – contented to grovel in mire,
To feast and to revel, to sleep and expire;
Say, citizen pigs, can it ever be true,
Such wretches as these were related to you?[81]

The word 'citizens', however, discredits the hogs as revolutionaries, who then cruelly resolve, like the cooked animals, to eat 'two or three fricasseed butchers at least' at a yearly celebration. The moral finally turns back on the hogs, since their criticisms of men could be equally applied to pigs: 'to themselves, even pigs may be blind!'[82]

---

78 Ibid., p. 10.
79 Ibid.
80 Ibid., pp. 65, 13, 16, 42–4, 57.
81 Ibid., p. 58.
82 Ibid., p. 59.

If the evolutionary idea were to be pursued, the poem seems to be saying that yes, pigs and men *are* related: the hogs are arrogant to think otherwise. But the moral, seemingly directed at the hogs, is a metaphor for human conduct, warning us to be aware of our own faults.

The same could be said about the other poems, which warn humans, in the guise of animals, not to rebel, or use animal rebellions to point out human faults. But those human faults include bad treatment of animals, and this aspect is emphasised in some of the poems to put across a message against cruelty to animals. This strategy is very evident in 'The Horse Turned Driver', when 'a poor-looking hack' turns the tables on a cruel groom, forcing him to wear 'stirrup and bit' controlling him with 'bridle and spur'. This device is not so very different from Black Beauty's later invitation to his readers to imagine themselves being broken in. The horse treats the groom badly: 'If he dare complain, / She but tightens the rein, / And whips him for going no faster.' The moral explicitly advocates kindness to horses: 'She had trudg'd to this day, / If he'd been a merciful master.'[83] Similarly the poem 'Birds Turned Fowlers' takes up the campaign against bird-nesting that was so prominent in eighteenth-century children's literature. Here we have a debate and compact among animals that is not discredited by revolutionary language. The birds assemble and agree to make a net to catch 'a great bird-nesting boy in.' The idea is to provide a deterrent: 'if once he were caught, / It would stop the vile practice for ever.' They catch the robber, but he gets away. The poem concludes, 'Tho' none of them yet, ever made such a net, / *It would serve him just right if they were.*'[84]

Like the papillonades, then, these poems mix comic inversions, political references, and messages about real animals in the world outside the book. We could see their mixture of meanings as merely contradictory, but it could also be read as a reflection of what can and cannot be said about animal/human relations in a children's book. That animals should protest about being eaten or exploited by humans is presented as absurd, and metaphorically related to seditious revolutionary activity. But humane treatment of animals, wild and domestic, is something to be advocated through sympathy with animal suffering. The attitudes to animals are not that different from Trimmer's, though displayed through a different genre. In these poems and in the papillonades, there is no need for the kind of apology and explanation for allowing animals to talk that Trimmer and Fenn go in for. The comic and fantastic mode is excuse enough not to take animal language seriously: the poems are funny precisely because the readers know animals do not behave like this. But the poems also show how the carnivalesque talking animal story can work as a means to convey natural historical information and to inculcate kindness to animals, as well as raising evolutionary issues – propensities which will be further developed by Gatty and Kingsley later in the century. Before I pursue these ideas, however, I want to follow the development throughout the 'long' nineteenth century of a highly influential genre: the animal autobiography.

---

83 Ibid., pp. 32–3.
84 Ibid., pp. 68–71.

Chapter Three

Animal Autobiography

In the long nineteenth century, animal autobiography is one of the most persistent and popular genres of animal story, from Dorothy Kilner's *Life and Perambulations of a Mouse* (1783) right through to *Pussy Meow: The Autobiography of a Cat*, by S. Louise Patteson (1901).[1] In these stories an animal, usually domestic or in close relation to humans, gives a first-person account of their life and experiences. The most famous of these stories, and the only one still popular today, is Anna Sewell's *Black Beauty*, published in 1877, but *Black Beauty* is part of a long tradition, and one aim of this chapter is to restore this neglected context. *Black Beauty* is not the earliest animal life-story to call itself an 'autobiography', and it shares many actual scenes with Arabella Argus's 1815 *The Adventures of a Donkey*. The project of the animal autobiography is nearly always to argue for the better treatment of animals by humans: they actualise Trimmer's resolve to speak up for a 'dumb' animal, and to think 'what it would say for itself if able to speak'. The full-scale autobiography is after all only a longer development of the life-stories father and mother robin tell each other in Trimmer's book. While the genre invites human readers to 'change situations' with the animal protagonist, and imagine its feelings, this is done in a realistic mode, not in the fantastic, comic mode of the *Topsy-Turvy* poems. The only fantastic element in the animal autobiography is the ability of the animal narrator to speak to the reader. Animals speak, but they do not turn round and force humans into animal situations, though they may take their revenge in more realistic ways, by throwing off a cruel rider for instance.

The majority of these books are addressed to children, as part of their education in sympathy. The child audience excuses the device of a talking animal, and licences moral instruction. Jemmy the Donkey in Arabella Argus's book is firm about addressing 'juvenile readers', as part of his plan to improve the treatment of donkeys. Another donkey questions this plan: "'If I am not misinformed, Mr Jemmy, your proposed publication is designed for the amusement of young people; then how do you hope to benefit your species by an address to children?'" Jemmy replies, "'children of amiable manners have much influence in society, particularly amongst their inferiors. A well-educated child may, in the most graceful manner, reprove the inhumanity of the less informed.'"[2] 'Well-educated' children, like Mrs Trimmer's

---

1   Though this book is about British texts, I have included *Pussy Meow*, and Marshall Saunders' *Beautiful Joe*, as they are so strongly influenced by *Black Beauty*, purposely written as feline and canine equivalents of that text.

2   Arabella Argus, *The Adventures of a Donkey* (London, 1815), p. 173.

Harriet and Frederick are being appealed to. In *Beautiful Joe* (1894) which won an American competition for a canine equivalent of *Black Beauty*, Joe reports his mistress's belief that 'if all the boys and girls in the world would rise up and say that there should be no more cruelty to animals, they could put a stop to it.'[3] In these two instances, then, the animal voice is transparently a mask for the human author addressing her preferred readership. Not just the message of kindness, but the ethical purpose of the story in getting this message across is made clear. Child characters help to enforce the message: the contrast between bad and good little boys, in their treatment of animals, is deployed in extended episodes in Dorothy Kilner's *Life and Perambulations of a Mouse* (1783), Mrs Pilkington's *Marvellous Adventures, or the Vicissitudes of a Cat* (1802), Elizabeth Sandham's *The Adventures of Poor Puss* (1809), and in Argus's *Adventures of a Donkey*. Dorothy Kilner addresses her story explicitly to 'little readers', begging them to follow the Mouse's good advice and give up their 'follies and vices'.[4] Many of the mouse's stories involve children who are either afraid of animals, or mistreat them, and who all come to bad ends. The mouse observes children's behaviour, and overhears stories about them told by reliable adults.

In addition to these didactic functions, the genre can also be used to satirize human behaviour more generally, especially as the domestic animal's movements between various owners, up and down the social scale, can give a comprehensive picture of society and its failings. This is the main feature of the earliest dog book, *Pompey the Little* (1751), a biography rather than an autobiography. Ouida's much later novel *Puck* (1870), uses the autobiographical form for a similar purpose: 'for a vantage point from which to survey all the tricks and trades, the devilries, and the frivolities, the sins and the shams, the shifts and the scandals of this world of yours, commend me to a cosy nook under a woman's laces!'[5] The dog provides a 'vantage point' from which to tell a human story. Neither of these books is especially directed at children, but there is a series of children's books that use inanimate objects as a similar fictional device, and which are closely allied to the children's animal autobiography. Dorothy Kilner, author of *The Life and Perambulations of a Mouse*, published *The Adventures of a Whipping Top* in 1784, and her sister, Mary Ann, published *Memoirs of a Peg-Top* and *The Adventures of a Pincushion* in 1783. Picaresque adventure for its own sake can also be part of these books' appeal, as suggested for instance by the title of Mrs Pilkington's *Marvellous Adventures, or the Vicissitudes of a Cat*. Some animal autobiographies, mostly of wild creatures, also sought to impart natural historical information. An example here is *Rambles of a Rat* (1857): 'I would suggest to my readers how wide and delightful a field of knowledge Natural History must open to all, when there is so much to interest and

3   Marshall Saunders, *Beautiful Joe, The Autobiography of a Dog* (London, 1901), p. 14.

4   Dorothy Kilner, *Life and Perambulations of a Mouse,* vol. 1, p. 3, vol. 2, p. 57.

5   Ouida, *Puck* (London, n.d.), p. 2.

admire even in those animals which we usually regard with contempt and disgust.'[6] Both Pilkington and Tucker address themselves to children, and also argue for better treatment of their cat and rat protagonists, who are shown to be both lovable and useful to man.

In this chapter, I want to investigate the consequences of writing 'autobiography' from an animal's point of view. How is animal subjectivity created, and how is this subjectivity linked to the books' ethical purposes? I am going to concentrate on several interlinked problems and issues. How is the issue of animal language dealt with? How is the actual scene of writing or narration imagined? Who is the narratee or implied audience for these stories? Do animal narrators have a different kind of consciousness to the human, and/or are they built up through analogies with human types? Here I will be investigating analogies with children, women, slaves and servants. The parallel made in some of these books between domestic animals and slaves leads me to explore similarities between the genre of animal autobiography and the slave narrative, a comparison that raises issues of testimony and witness, while the servant analogy suggests the idea of the autobiography as testimonial. I will also ask how tensions between individuality and representativeness are negotiated, and, in particular, what is the animal's relation to its *name*? In the majority of these books there are crucial 'recognition' scenes, where the protagonists are recognised by former owners and given back their 'original' names. This scene forms part of the happy ending: here, differences between the patterns of human and animal life-stories emerge.

The basic problem of animal autobiography is encapsulated by the illustration from *Beautiful Joe: The Autobiography of a Dog*, by Marshall Saunders in Figure 3.1. The tell-tale human hand holding the ball here, making the dog sit up and beg, reveals only too clearly the human manipulation going on, while the caption seems to stress the animal's independence. The following illustration is a wider shot of the same scene, fully revealing the human owner holding the ball, while the caption explains the 'contract' behind this sort of autobiography: 'Lift up your voice for the dumb.'[7] The author is, following Trimmer's precepts, speaking up for the speechless, giving a voice to the voiceless. The unvarying convention in all of these stories is that the animals can speak to us and to each other, and can also understand human speech, but humans, apart from the readers, and occasionally children, cannot understand them. The *Memoirs of Dick, the Little Poney* present this convention as a learning process: 'these words, which I could now understand (for human language had now become intelligible to my ears)', but most other texts provide no explanation.[8] Token examples of the animals not fully understanding what the humans are saying are put in, and, on the other hand, there are instances when they report to us human doings

---

6   Charlotte Tucker, *Rambles of a Rat* (London, 1857), p. vi.

7   Proverbs 31:8. This Biblical quote is also used as an epigraph by Humphrey Primatt in his 1776 *Dissertation on the Duty of Mercy and Sin of Cruelty to Brute Animals*.

8   *Memoirs of Dick, the Little Poney* (London, 1799), p. 104.

Figure 3.1 'Billy would take his ball and go off by himself.' Illustration in Marshall Saunders, *Beautiful Joe* **(1901).**

and sayings they could not have known about, in order that the story may progress. Lucy Thornton's *The Story of a Poodle, by Himself and His Mistress* (1889) solves this problem by allowing the mistress to narrate four out of the nine chapters. Jemmy the Donkey, in Arabella Argus's book, draws attention to his limitations as narrator, when he regrets that 'the habits of a Donkey precluded him from knowing what occurs within doors'.[9] The problem is solved here by the groom, Robert, coming out and relating the indoor happenings to a fellow servant. Dick the Little Poney admits that 'what passed in the parlour, I can only guess', which he proceeds to do, telling us what is 'probable'.[10] Mouse, cat and dog narrators find it easier to observe human indoor behaviour.

The Adventures of a Donkey and *Black Beauty* share many features, and several actual scenes, but an important difference is the way Argus playfully and metafictionally directs our attention to the incongruities of the convention she is using. For instance, Jemmy asserts 'I will never lend a foot, the scribbling member in all asinine literatures, to publish what could not edify the public.'[11] Similarly, the later *Autobiography of a Cat, and the Cream of Cats Too* (1864) claims to be written

---

9   Argus, *Adventures of a Donkey*, p. 24.
10 *Dick, the Little Poney*, p. 53.
11 Argus, *Adventures of a Donkey*, p. 115.

'while this paw can hold a pen'. The autobiographer refers to her family history, consisting of 'ten *closely written* rats' skins'.[12] Before publication, Jemmy must get his idea passed by a committee of donkeys. This reminds us that for animals to talk, or to write, can be presented as a *joke*, especially one to be shared with 'juvenile readers', who may once have thought animals *could* talk, but now know they cannot. Jemmy writing with his foot passes as a joke; *Beautiful Joe*, a more serious text, stumbles over this problem: 'I am an old dog now, and am writing, or rather getting a friend to write, the story of my life.'[13] Dorothy Kilner solves the problem more neatly, through the device of a charming framing narrative. The author and a group of friends are trapped by bad weather in a country house. They determine to pass the time by telling their autobiographies. Time is allowed for people to prepare their stories. Our narrator is in despair: her life story '"will be insipid and unentertaining to others ..." – "Then write mine, which may be more diverting," said a little squeaking voice.' The author locates the mouse looking out of its hole. The mouse agrees to dictate, '"if you will not hurt me." – "Not for the world," returned I; "come, therefore, and sit upon my table, that I may hear more distinctly what you have to relate."'[14]

Figure 3.2 'Luath tells his story.' Illustration by Harrison Weir in Gordon Stables, *Sable and White* **(1894).**

---

12 *Autobiography of a Cat* (London, 1864), pp. iv, 5.

13 Saunders, p. 13.

14 Dorothy Kilner, *Life and Perambulations of a Mouse*, vol. 1, pp. 8–9.

Elizabeth Sandham's *The Adventures of Poor Puss* (1809) imagines the narratees and the scene of narration rather differently: two 'gossiping' cats on a wall are telling each other their life-stories. An omniscient narrator is also present to set the scene. *Sable and White: the Autobiography of a Show Dog* (1894) by Gordon-Stables, provides a further elaboration on this type of narration (see Figure 3.2). A dog is narrating to other dog listeners. This scenario, however, can only be realised through the mediation of human imagination. The book opens with an idyllic garden setting. The master sees the 'trio of dogs' sitting on the lawn:

> He looks up now and his wife's eyes follow his.
>   'Wouldn't you really think, dear?' she says, 'they were talking of old times?'
>   'Yes, but note, it is the Newfoundland who is listening, and also, with half closed eyes, Mr Consequential, the pug, and Luath, honest Luath, is telling the story of his life.'[15]

There is a break in the text, and then the 'autobiography' begins: 'You must remember, Luath was saying, I wasn't always a show dog.'[16] The humans here are being fanciful, and yet there is something in the animals' behaviour that suggests intelligence and the wish to communicate. In *Tuppy, or the Autobiography of a Donkey* (1859), a groom remarks, 'Why, Neddy, you have got such intelligent eyes, you look a'most as if you could speak. I wonder what you have got to say to me.'[17] Attributing speech to animals is only an extension of a belief in their intelligence. The role of human imagination in animal speech is also alluded to in *Poor Puss*, when a later owner suggests, 'No doubt ... this cat could tell us some entertaining adventures, if she could speak.'[18] The remark labels the story as a kind of thought-experiment, like *Fabulous Histories*, in which Trimmer tries to imagine what the robins would say if they could.

The narration by animals to each other can give a conspiratorial sense of solidarity against humans. For instance, Luath asks his friends, 'I wonder ... whether human bipeds – human beings, I mean, – ever do think and feel as deeply and acutely as we kings of the canine race do?'[19] But this canine self-importance is also comic, set up by the author and his stand-in, the good master. A metafictional element is also in evidence: before describing some of the horrible mutilations show dogs are subject to, Luath remarks to his dog listeners:

> I fear, my dear Chummie, that if I describe graphically what follows, you may be very much shocked. And yet I consider it my duty to tell the truth. You see it may do good, because I note that our friend, the jackdaw, is listening intently. And as he has all the

---

15 Gordon Stables, *Sable and White* (London, 1894), p. 14.
16 Ibid.
17 E. Burrows, *Tuppy* (London, 1859), p. 8.
18 Elizabeth Sandham, *Poor Puss* (London, 1809), pp. 60–61.
19 Stables, p. 29

appearance of a literary character, what I now tell you may one day find its way into the public prints, and so help to mitigate the evils it depicts.[20]

In *Black Beauty*, by contrast, the scene of writing or telling is elided almost completely. 'Translated from the equine by Anna Sewell', on the title page of the original edition, gives us our only clue, implying that the text exists in some other form. 'Translating' is a very apt metaphor for the way that Sewell imagines a human voice for animal experiences. It does not, however, account for the horses' ability to understand human language. And, in addition to this understanding, a quite different kind of communication goes on from human to animal, via tone and touch. For instance, John Manly, the groom 'had his own ways of making me understand by the tone of his voice or the touch of the rein'.[21] These instances are very reminiscent of anecdotes about Anna Sewell's actual dealings with horses: 'She seemed simply to hold the reins in her hand, trusting to her voice to give all needed directions to her horse.'[22] The book's need to promote this kind of sympathetic communication with animals is at odds with the convention that the animals can understand everything the humans say anyway. That animals have other, more effective ways to communicate with humans than using human language is also admitted by other writers: Bob the Spotted Terrier incongruously says, 'Dogs indeed cannot speak ... but they can feel obligation, and express it, without the intervention of language.'[23] Alfred Elwes, who also claims to be 'translating' *The Adventures of a Dog* (1857), writes in his Preface about the bodily dimension of dog-language: 'its meaning is associated by gestures of the body ... a good portion finds its way to his tail. The motion of that member is full of meaning.'[24] Tuppy the donkey's owner claims, 'Tuppy understands me ... look how sensibly he looks up into my face ... he can do almost everything but speak.' The donkey comments, 'and though perhaps I did not understand everything she said in just the sense which you would apply to it, kind reader, yet I took in quite sufficient.'[25] An interest in the ways animals really communicate with humans co-exists with the convention that they can speak our language. This may be inconsistent, but the inconsistency also points up the fictionality of animal speech in these stories, with a similar effect to Trimmer's apologetic Preface. It could be seen as a way of using anthropomorphism without being misled by it.

'Who is the narratee in *Black Beauty*?' wonders Timothy Morris.[26] It is never made clear to whom Black Beauty is talking, and it is this unspecificity of the narratee that allows the reader to slide in and out of horse-consciousness, blurring the human/animal divide perhaps more effectively than the more self-conscious address to children in *Adventures of A Donkey* or *Beautiful Joe*. Here is Black Beauty

20 Ibid., p. 153.
21 Anna Sewell, *Black Beauty* (London, 1994), p. 27.
22 Susan Chitty, *The Woman Who Wrote Black Beauty* (London, 1971), p. 108.
23 *The Dog of Knowledge* (London, 1801), p. 66.
24 Alfred Elwes, *The Adventures of a Dog* (London, 1857), p. iii.
25 Burrows, *Tuppy*, p. 43.
26 Morris, Timothy, *You're Only Young Twice* (Urbana, IL, 2000), p. 24.

describing his experience of the process of 'breaking in': 'Everyone may not know what breaking in is, therefore I will describe it.'[27] 'Everyone' includes both humans and animals, breakers and the broken. First-person accounts of the sensations of being broken in also occur in *Dick* and *Tuppy*: 'I was girded till I could scarcely breathe. I had only a piece of iron to chew'; 'I felt some tight thing passing over my forehead, and a hard cutting substance pressing against my teeth.'[28] But Beauty then begins by describing the process as happening to a horse, in the third person: 'He must never start at what he sees, nor speak to other horses, nor bite, nor kick, nor have any will of his own.'[29] Then he moves on to use pronouns that increasingly confound the ambiguously human or animal narratees with the narrator:

> Those who have never had a bit in their mouths, cannot think how bad it feels; a great piece of cold hard steel as thick as a man's finger to be pushed into one's mouth, between one's teeth and over one's tongue, with the ends coming out at the corner of your mouth and held fast there by straps over your head, under your throat, round your nose, and under your chin; so that no way in the world can you get rid of the nasty hard thing.[30]

The human reader is being pushed to identify with horse experience. Sewell is developing the strategy of reversal that is explored in earlier texts. For instance, in *Adventures of A Donkey*, Jemmy tells us of a Turkish story he hears in which cruel human owners are forced to take the places of their donkeys for a day. This embedded story is similar to the strategies of the Topsy Turvy poems. All donkeys, Jemmy assures us, love this story. As we have seen, Mrs Benson in *Story of the Robins* asks us 'to suppose how we should feel were we bees, or ants, or birds, or kittens, and so on'.[31]

The project of creating identification between the human reader and the animal protagonist means that the differences between animal and human consciousness are not much explored. There is one incident when Black Beauty, by instinct, knows more than his owners. They attempt to make him cross a bridge which has been damaged by floods. He refuses, and is proved right. He attempts to explain his state of mind to us, emphasising here how he does not fully understand the humans either: 'I felt sure there was something wrong. I dare not go forward, and I made a dead stop … I could not understand much of what they said, but I found they thought, if I had gone on as the master wanted me, most likely the bridge would have given way under us.' The master then delivers an explanation of animal instinct: 'God had given man reason, by which they could find out things for themselves, but He had given animals knowledge which did not depend on reason, and which was much more prompt and perfect in its way.'[32]

---

27 Sewell, p. 10.
28 *Dick*, p. 44; Burrows, *Tuppy*, p. 27.
29 Sewell, p. 11.
30 Ibid.
31 Trimmer, *Story of the Robins*, p. 150.
32 Sewell, pp. 61–2.

There is a similar explanation in *Sable and White*, again in praise of this different faculty: 'Our knowledge again differs in kind from that of men. They may be all at home in politics or algebra, but in a stubble field among the partridges, which is the nobler animal, that blind, pottering old biped, or the noble Irish setter, that ... knows without seeing them even, where the birds are to be found?'[33] 'Instinct', particularly the hunting instinct, can be a problem in books which are dedicated to teaching kindness to animals, through the voice of a rational animal narrator. What of the violence and cruelty of animals to each other? This is a subject that Trimmer and Barbauld were able to deal with openly in the context of a natural theological ecology. But it is harder to introduce the topic when there is a strong identification with an exemplary animal narrator. It is the carnivores, dogs and cats, that raise the most problems. What happens in the dog and cat stories is a mixture of protestations by the narrator that he or she is not really cruel, and assertions that killing smaller animals is natural to the animal concerned and part of their duty to humans. Hunting figures sometimes as a natural activity in which the animal joins, and sometimes as cruel behaviour by humans towards animals.

Mary Pilkington's cat insists on her good feelings: 'my species, I know, are accused of torturing their victims; but I cannot think it possible that any of them can delight in giving pain; I know, however, that it is not in my disposition.' She does, however, derive a 'sensation of delight' from first killing a rat, and 'being able to exercise those talents for which our species were originally designed', though 'I certainly was not, by nature, of a sanguinary temper.'[34] Bob the Spotted Terrier, learning to be a sporting dog, finds it hard to be violent: 'it was long before I could reconcile myself to blood, or feel that delight which I communicated to others, in terrifying and tearing other creatures, which had the same original claim to the blessings of life as myself.'[35] Dick the Little Poney is also disgusted with hunting, and pities the animal victims, 'two poor hares', 'a poor little creature with a long tail'.[36] But Luath, as we have seen, celebrates the skill of dogs 'in a stubble field among the partridges'.

In Luath's story there are some attempts to create a non-human consciousness for the dog narrator: 'I think an old boot is the finest thing in the world. First you pick up the boot and give it a shake or two as if you mean to kill it.' Luath supposes that if his old master had known how cruel his new master was, 'I am sure he would have come back and bitten him.'[37] In *Bob, the Spotted Terrier*, 'scent' works well as a metaphor to describe the narrative trajectory, as the dog narrator struggles to stick to the point: 'But I am again straggling, and here must make a pause, in order to recover the proper scent.'[38] Natalia, in *Autobiography of a Cat*, uses animal's-eye

---

33 Stables, p. 70.
34 Mary Pilkington, *Marvellous Adventures* (London, 1802), pp. 50–51.
35 *Dog of Knowledge*, p. 125.
36 *Dick*, pp. 128, 135.
37 Stables, pp. 15, 17.
38 *Dog of Knowledge*, p. 130.

similes: the harness she was forced to wear looked like 'a number of very black rats' tails fastened together'.[39] But these catty or doggy ways of thinking are not sustained, and there is no attempt to create a different, canine consciousness, through the use of a special language, as there is in Kipling's later *Thy Servant, A Dog* (1930). As Luath converses with his young mistress Etheldene, it is the dog who speaks 'proper' English, as opposed to both the lispings of the little girl, and the 'rustic English' of the cows, which he has to translate for us. The cows, however, are given a strictly limited bovine consciousness: 'nothing is ever, ever, going to happen, and the meadow will never, never, go bare. Summer will never, never end, and the sun will always, always shine.'[40] A hierarchy within the animal world is being created, involving degrees of rationality, sensitivity and imagination. Implicitly, it is all right to eat the unimaginative cows, who live in an eternal present.

A hierarchy of different styles of speech for different animals is also explored in *Further Adventures of Jemmy the Donkey, interspersed with biographical sketches of the horse* (1821). The horse claims closer kin to humans than the donkey: 'I write particularly to rational animals, creatures endowed with reason; capable of arranging and *revising* their sentiments, and consequently less liable to fall into those self-delusions, which deform the donkey character.' Cavalry horses, however, have a more elevated style. The horse narrator remarks on 'the loftiness of their expressions; their style is flowing and more figurative than ours.'[41] In the first book about him, Jemmy the Donkey has occasional difficulties in understanding the human world: 'I saw Jenkins and his companions drinking, and afterwards playing with spotted pieces of paper which I have since learned were "cards".'[42] In such passages, we have an animal's eye view of human activities, rather like the ant's-eye view in *Evenings At Home*. Other animals, like the rats in Charlotte Tucker's book, are mystified at first by books and writing:

> '... he brings back something which puzzles my brain – something white, with black marks upon it. He and little Billy sit poring over it by the hour. They don't eat it, they don't smell it, they don't wear it: I can't make out that it is of any use to them at all; and yet they seem as much pleased, as they study it together, as if it were a piece of Dutch cheese!'[43]

But on the whole the animals in these books are very literate and even literary. Luath becomes a dog who not only understands, but composes poetry.

Luath's poem is an elegy in praise of his friend, the mastiff Professor Huxley. The name here is used to satirise scientific attitudes to animal consciousness: 'Professor Huxley, the champion mastiff, was of the opinion that nearly all actions of human beings are mechanical, and that the moving power was external, and very often

---

39 *Autobiography of a Cat*, p. 10.
40 Stables, pp. 60–62.
41 Arabella Argus, *Further Adventures of Jemmy Donkey* (London, 1821), pp. 40–41.
42 Argus, *Adventures*, p. 51.
43 Tucker, p. 69.

atmospheric.'[44] These books do not pick up the Darwinian affirmation of our kindred with the beasts, but instead attack what they see as a scientific categorisation of beast with machine. This is especially so in *Black Beauty*, where the equation of animal and steam-engine is critiqued several times. For instance, 'they always seemed to think that a horse was something like a steam engine, only smaller. At any rate, they think that if only they pay for it, a horse is bound to go just as far, and with just as heavy a load as they please.'[45] The attribution of speech and subjecthood to an animal in these texts is an obvious counter to these mechanical or 'mechanomorphic' constructions of animals.

In assuming for the most part that animal consciousness is similar to human consciousness, or at least that human consciousness can serve as a metaphor for animal consciousness, these books deploy various analogies between animals and types or classes of humans: children, women, slaves, servants. The child analogy is the most obvious: as we have seen, most of the books address themselves to children, and provide examples of good and bad behaviour to animals by child characters. With this audience in mind, they also use animal behaviour and attitudes to give moral lessons on child behaviour. So Jemmy the Donkey, when young, foolishly longs for a beautiful white saddle and bridle he has seen on another donkey, providing the juvenile readers with a lesson against vanity. Dick the Little Poney learns 'the folly of unlimited indugence', through over-eating in a corn field.[46] Kilner's mouse hero, Nimble, also acts as a negative model for children: he attributes many of his early troubles to not having listened to his mother's advice. Mrs Burrows' Newfoundland dog, Neptune, makes fun of what must have become a convention in these stories, by promising to spare the readers 'parental admonitions' from his mother, but nevertheless, a few pages later, he laments, 'how often had my mother warned me to beware of the jealousy and the vanity that were the besetting sins of my nature.'[47] Mary Pilkington's dog narrator in *The Sorrows of Caesar* (1813) makes explicit the connection between good behaviour in children and animals, and the lessons to be learnt from his story:

> As children, as well as animals, are liable to the vicissitudes of fortune, and change of situation, how necessary it is, that even the most affluent should endeavour to acquire those habits which are likely to insure general esteem! Sweetness of temper, and conciliating manners, are, I have no doubt, the certain method of procuring friends ...[48]

Tuppy the donkey, addressing his 'little friends', also draws a moral from his experiences: 'make the most of your present blessings. If you have gentle loving

---

44 Stables, p. 29.
45 Sewell, p. 144.
46 *Dick*, p. 26.
47 E. Burrows, *Neptune* (London, 1869) pp. 5, 9.
48 Mary Pilkington, *The Sorrows of Caesar* (London, 1813), p. 172.

mothers and kind teachers, be thankful … Do not champ upon the bit because you find the restraint irksome.'[49]

There is also an address to parents in some of these books, which holds up the treatment of the animal narrator as an example of how to treat children. Neptune recommends his 'training' as a model: 'well would it be for parents, and well would it be for children themselves, if the rules by which my education was conducted could be introduced into the nursery as well as into the kennel.'[50] In *Black Beauty* there is a hint of this sort of moralising when we are told by Merrylegs the pony that human young also require 'breaking in'.[51] This metaphor is reminiscent of Margaret Gatty's 'breaking in' story, 'Kicking' (see p. 98 below). One of Tuppy's owners, however, recommends kind treatment for both animals and children: 'It is much easier to whip a child into a bad humour than a good one; of that I am sure, and I think animals are much the same.'[52] *Sable and White* uses the animal/child parallel rather differently, but also in a way that is probably addressed to adults. The dog's early companion, Etheldene, is a little girl who is just able to talk. She and the dog converse with each other, and with other animals. As in all these stories, the animals cannot be understood by most humans, except the readers. The child, 'nearer' to the animal, can understand them here:

> 'I is so happy,' she said, after gazing away up into the sky for a moment, 'but I fink – '
> 'What do you think, little mistress?' I said, licking her ear.
> 'Oh!' she said, 'I fink it won't last always, always, for ever But I cannot speak all my finks. What oo think?'
> 'I don't know,' I said, 'I hope it will last.'
> 'Let us go and ask the moo cow what she finks.'[53]

The affinity between animal and child is not, however, emphasised in *Black Beauty.* There is instead an increased seriousness in the address to adults in what was still seen as a children's genre. *Black Beauty* had a specific effect in the world: it helped in the abolition of the bearing-rein , a fashionable device that forced horses to hold their heads up unnaturally high. Reviewers praised it as both 'a capital book for the young – boys and girls', and 'an excellent book to put into the hands of stable boys'. George T. Angell, founder of the Massachusetts Society for the Prevention of Cruelty to Animals, went around giving free copies to cabmen.[54] The reference in the title to 'his grooms and companions' puts the human emphasis on those who work with Black Beauty. Though children occasionally appear, and are criticised for thoughtless treatment of horses, there is not an obvious address to them. Instead, the animal/child analogy is deployed to shock the reader into imagining human children

---

49 Burrows, *Tuppy*, pp. 28–9.
50 Burrows, *Neptune*, p. 15.
51 Sewell, p. 42.
52 Burrows, *Tuppy*, p. 25.
53 Stables, p. 60.
54 Chitty, pp. 188, 223–5.

being treated as animals are treated. For instance, the old horse Sir Oliver asks, 'Why don't they cut their own children's ears into points to make them look sharp? Why don't they cut the end off their noses to make them look plucky?'[55] Sewell could be elaborating here on a point made in the earlier *Memoirs of Dick, the Little Poney*, and by Rousseau: 'Ye tasteless sons of men, is Nature such a bungling performer, that her works must submit to your improvements in almost every instance? Why do you not practice the same experiments on yourselves?'[56] This use of the animal/child analogy prioritizes the animal and its feelings, forcing the human to stand in for the animal, as opposed to the moral lessons of Kilner, Argus and Pilkington, which use the animal as a stand-in for the human. Anna Kingsford, a prominent anti-vivisection campaigner, deploys a similar analogy: she reports a dream in which a tortured rabbit becomes a child: 'your victim is of your own kind, a child that is human.'[57]

This kind of comparison is obviously addressed to adults, attempting to extend their sympathy for children into a sympathy for animals. Vivisection as a topic or event rarely figures in the stories addressed to children. In *Sable and White*, the dog heroes are briefly entrapped in a vivisector's den, and describe, in vivid terms, the scenes of torture they witness there:

> Here we could see in the ghostly moonlight, not only rabbits and birds alive and half-dissected, fastened down to the tables and stools just as the operator had left them, but many dogs as well. One was face downwards on a species of saddle like a grating, and even as we looked at him he lifted up his head, and once more the thrilling and terrible medley of mingled barking, howling, and moaning resounded through the rooms ... another wretched dog had both its jaws tied to bars that kept the mouth open wide, and from the throat protruded strange-looking pipes and instruments.[58]

Vivisection was an especial danger for dogs and cats. *Pussy Meow* (1901), written as a feline equivalent of *Black Beauty* and *Beautiful Joe*, also includes an anti-vivisection message, though it does not risk upsetting its child readers by any actual description. The cats are indignant at the idea, but do not act as witnesses:

> I had heard Guy tell mistress that very day not to let us stay out much evenings, because he had been told that it was the fashion in schools and colleges to dissect cats, so they could see how they were put together ... When I told this to Jack [another cat], it made him very indignant. 'The idea of such an outrage perpetrated on us poor unsuspecting cats,' said he.[59]

The analogy between animal and woman has been persuasively argued by Coral Lansbury, in relation to *Black Beauty* in particular, and the anti-vivisection

---

55 Sewell, p. 49.

56 *Dick*, p. 31

57 Coral Lansbury, *The Old Brown Dog* (Madison, WI, 1985), p. 92.

58 Stables, p. 266.

59 S. Louise Patteson, *Beautiful Joe* (London, 1901), p. 14.

movement in general. This movement was notable for its large number of women supporters, and Lansbury focuses on an incident when female and working-class support for anti-vivisection came together. She argues a parallel between the way women are described in Victorian pornographic texts, and the way animals were treated in vivisection. She does not claim that the women who supported the anti-vivisection movement were consciously aware of this parallel, but that it must have subconsciously affected their attitudes. She uses *Black Beauty* to illustrate what she means, focusing on Ginger's account of her treatment, which can sound to a modern reader like a rape scene:

> But when it came to breaking in, that was a bad time for me; several men came to catch me, and when at last they closed me in at one corner of the field, one caught me by the fore-lock, another caught me by the nose, and held it so tight I could hardly draw my breath; then another took my under jaw in his hard hand and wrenched my mouth open, and so by force they got on the halter and the bar into my mouth; then one dragged me along by the halter, another flogging behind, and this was the first experience I had of men's kindness, it was all force.[60]

Ginger's conclusion, 'that men were my natural enemies and that I must defend myself' can then be taken two ways, from the animal or the female point of view. The word 'ruined', conventionally applied to fallen women, is repeatedly used of both Ginger and Beauty in Chapter Twenty-Seven, 'Ruined and Going Down-hill'. Ginger remarks: 'here we are – ruined in the prime of our youth and strength – you by a drunkard, and I by a fool.'[61]

While the sexual subtext here does support Lansbury's point, I have not discovered this particular analogy between animals and women in any of the other animal autobiographies I have found, pre or post the anti-vivisection movement. There are some disquieting undertones in E. Burrows' *Neptune* (1869), which work in quite an opposite direction: Neptune insists how right it is of his mistress to whip him when he is at fault, and worships her, while despising the kind servant maid. Otherwise, sexuality, overt or covert, is largely absent from these stories. Sandham's Tabby, Frances Power Cobbe's 'Lost Dog' Hajin, Natalia the Cream of Cats, and Pussy Meow all have litters, but the process by which they are conceived is passed over. Commentators have also pointed out that Black Beauty himself must be gelded, but this is never made clear, and the process is not described. In the earlier *Memoirs of Dick*, however, the narrator is a little more explicit, though still modest:

> … they next proceeded to an operation, the exquisite torture and fatal consequences of which I still feel in reflection, though delicacy forbids me to explain it. Nature produced me a male, but my tyrants were not satisfied with her decrees, and they deprived me of all the privileges of my sex.[62]

---

60 Sewell, p. 30.
61 Ibid., pp. 39, 137, 138.
62 *Dick*, p. 17.

Some other sections of this book are very close to *Black Beauty*: Sewell's total silence on this matter must be the deliberate result of a stricter Victorian moral code.

Though sexuality is hidden in these texts, gender differences are overtly important. In a general sense, dogs are male, cats female, though Cobbe's 'Lost Dog' is an exception here. Authors are overwhelmingly female, perhaps reflecting women's role in socialising children into kindness towards animals; perhaps also suggesting a hidden affinity with oppressed creatures. Feminists such as Frances Power Cobbe and Bessie Raynor Parkes wrote the life-stories of their pets, and the anonymous *Autobiography of a Cat* (1864) was published by Emily Faithfull's feminist press. The tormenting of Sandham's Tabby could be a description of the way Charlotte Bronte's Jane Eyre is tormented by her male cousin: 'I am expected to make a return by suffering quietly the pinches and pulls of the dear little George, as he is called.' Cat and poor female relation are both entrapped in the houses of their 'benefactors', and expected to put up with any treatment from favoured boys. Tabby also complains of her stay with a rich mistress who pampers her: this is 'the most disagreeable' of all her 'situations', because she lacks 'liberty'. There is an implied analogy here with the rich, idle mistress herself, as well as with her servants. Maternal feeling is another area of analogy between women and animals, though one that raises some difficulties. As we saw in *Fabulous Histories*, the parental (not just maternal) feelings of the robins are both sympathised with, and then dismissed when their brood grows up. Domestic animals often have no paternal relation, and are soon removed from their mothers. Maternal wisdom and advice is stressed, to be remembered later (often too late); and the anguished maternal feelings of cats whose litters are drowned are dwelt on, while at the same time the short duration of maternal feeling in animals is explained. Tabby, her mother's one remaining kitten, remarks: 'I have never found any treatment like her's; though, when she left me to the wide world, we neither of us seemed to care any longer for each other.' But when Tabby's kittens are removed, she is inconsolable until she meets with another mother cat, and they both share the feeding and caring for this new litter. Tabby becomes extremely humanised here, confessing 'I know too well the tenderness of a mother', as the 'tears rolled down my cheeks'.[63]

Sable and White has a noticeably more masculine tone, as Luath and his friend take to the roads as happy vagabonds, contrasting with the terrified female lost dog Hajin in Cobbe's book. But Sandham's Tabby enjoys the time she travels with a party of honest beggars ('disabled seamen'): 'from a lady's cat, shut up in a warm carpeted room, and fed with the greatest delicacies, I became a beggar's follower … yet became so pleased with their way of life.'[64] The thought that she may be eating food that really belongs to the beggars' children is all that sends her away – a very maternal point of view. Charlotte Tucker's rats (all male) also have exciting adventures on the high seas and in St Petersburg, and are shipwrecked at one point.

---

63 Elizabeth Sandham, *The Adventures of Poor Puss* (London, 1809), pp. 6, 44–5, 7, 66–7.

64 Ibid., pp. 57–8.

These adventures are lead by the desperado, Whiskerandos, whose role is balanced by the tame rat, Oddity, who plays a more feminine role. Jemmy the Donkey's story includes a strange meditation by the protagonist on the uncomfortable role of a 'male pet':

> It may be a silly remark I am going to make, but to me there is not in existence so laughable a character as a male pet.
> Judging by what is to expected to constitute the masculine character in our class, I can make no allowance for the irritable petulances, the tearful complaints, and the jealous whims these creatures exhibit towards the softer sex; and until these weaknesses are totally disowned by the masculine gender, I beg leave to say, the word Hero must remain an indefinite expression.[65]

The convoluted ironies here are difficult to follow, but there is no mistaking the scorn for the 'feminine' attributes of the 'pet' role. Jemmy at this point has been bought as a pet for an aristocratic child. His masculine anxiety strengthens the analogy between pets and women.

Though male and female pets may have different roles, the roles of master and mistress are quite similar – both have authority over the animals in the hierarchical scheme of things. The authority and wisdom of the mistress may have recommended her as a character to female writers. Both the American animals here, Beautiful Joe and Pussy Meow, have well-informed and expert mistresses, whose doings and sayings provide a large part of the plot. Black Beauty ends up with some kind female owners, and women as well as men speak up for the better treatment of animals. Neptune's mistress, rather differently, inspires his masculine respect by violent punishments. He does, however, play a traditional masculine role in saving her from drowning. In other books women characters of all ages are also there to be rescued by brave, masculine pets.

The analogies between animals and slaves have been extensively investigated in the critical literature about *Black Beauty*. They were also clearly recognised at the time of writing: the book was advertised in America as 'The Uncle Tom's Cabin of the Horse'. The emphasis on Beauty's blackness cannot be coincidental. Sewell is using the emotive power of anti-slavery discourse, and applying it to another cause. The earlier *Bob, the Spotted Terrier* had made the connection between animals and slaves more overtly, using an animal autobiography to critique slavery. Bob sees slaves in Jamaica:

> I felicitated myself on being born a dog, and not a Negro … To be sure, they had not the complexion of Europeans, and perhaps possessed none of the same delicate sensibilities, yet they walked on two legs like the rest of the species, and seemed to me to differ in nothing but the colour of their skin and the contour of their face. However, there certainly must be a fallacy in appearances; and those can only be a particular, though singular kind of animals, that are born to subjection, the same as dogs or horses. Man surely could

---

65 Argus, *Adventures,* p. 57.

never tyrannize over his fellow-man without compunction, nor dare to injure him with impunity.[66]

Bob's naïve animal's-eye view of humanity, and his equation of slaves and animals, is to be read ironically, as a fierce criticism of the treatment of human beings as 'dogs or horses'. Bob's master confirms this, by reciting a couplet: 'Say, does th'eternal principle within / Change with the casual colour of the skin?'[67] The slaves are treated like animals, but they are not animals: the difference is essential here.

This difference causes some difficulties when Sewell reverses the metaphor, to show us animals being treated like slaves. Robert Dingley has argued that *Black Beauty* compares badly with anti-slavery literature. While a book like *Uncle Tom's Cabin* can have liberty as its project, *Black Beauty* depends on an acceptance that it is right for horses to be the slaves of man. As Bob says, animals are 'born to subjection'. Black Beauty does long for liberty, as the one thing he cannot have, but all the happiest ending can offer him is a good master or mistress, and he accepts this dispensation:

> What more could I want? Why, liberty! … I must stand up in a stable night and day except when I am wanted, and then I must be just as steady and quiet as any old horse who has worked twenty years. Straps here and straps there, a bit in my mouth, and blinkers over my eyes. Now, I am not complaining for I know it must be so.[68]

It is the mare Ginger who most uncompromisingly expresses rebellion against this version of slavery, in a chapter entitled 'A Strike for Liberty'. Here, she rebels against the bearing-rein : 'plunging, rearing, and kicking in a most desperate manner'. But Ginger is ground down and defeated. At their last meeting, Beauty says, 'You used to stand up for yourself if you were ill-used', and she replies, 'I did once, but it's no use; men are strongest, and if they are cruel and have no feeling, there is nothing that we can do, but just bear it, bear it on and on to the end.'[69] Shortly after, Beauty sees Ginger's dead body on a cart.

Ginger's role here as the defeated rebellious horse, has been read to mean that the text as a whole endorses Beauty's more accepting attitude. But the text has many voices, and one is Ginger's protest: her death can be taken as a moral lesson, or as a tragic defeat. The acceptance of enforced servitude and the impossibility of 'liberty' resonates with the way all these animal autobiographies endorse hierarchy, but they often also express a reluctant acceptance. Tuppy the donkey, like Ginger, reveals the arbitrariness of human power, and the way servitude is enforced on animals:

> We forget that we are servants, and that our master has a right to expect our obedience in return for the food he gives us, and the care which he bestows upon us. We are apt to grow proud, and to think that our service is entirely optional … and then it is not until we feel

---

66 *Dog of Knowledge*, p. 70.
67 Ibid.
68 Sewell, p. 26.
69 Ibid., pp. 112, 212–13.

his strong hand upon us, conquering our wills and doing with us according to his pleasure, that we begin to understand that we are only servants of a higher power than our own, and that we should have been wiser to have submitted patiently and done our duty cheerfully, than to have struggled against an authority which, after all, we are powerless to resist.[70]

The hard moral here is not just confined to animals: 'we must all take the bits in our mouths' says Tuppy's mistress. After he is punished for rebelling, she tells him, 'We have all got our cross to bear, Tuppy.'[71] An animal's acceptance of human mastery is implicitly likened to human acceptance of God and his decrees, 'a higher power'. This implication does not make the situation any easier to bear: necessary submission to a higher power provokes bitterness and rebellion:

> And if you should be tempted to turn aside and follow your own devices, and the rein tightens, and the bit cuts your mouth, and you are sharply turned back again, take my advice, be thankful for the pain, and instead of struggling and hurting yourself more, just retrace your steps, and be grateful the cuts were not deeper, nor the sores more incurable.[72]

Anna Sewell and other writers of animal autobiography, may have viewed their own lives in terms of an enforced servitude to God's will and to human hierarchies, balancing an acceptance of their place and destiny with a longing for something more. It is not just animals who are denied 'liberty' and forced to know their places.

While there may be different attitudes to liberty and servitude in animal autobiography and abolitionist writings, there is a clear *formal* parallel between the animal autobiography and the slave narrative, as published by the abolitionists to advance their cause. This generic parallel raises interesting questions about the usefulness of concepts of testimony and witness in understanding animal autobiography. In using the autobiographical form, slave narratives were not just providing eyewitness evidence of the abuses of slavery, they were also attesting to the fully human subjectivity of their slave narrators, who had been classed as objects to be used, bought and sold. Similarly, animal autobiographers by writing in the first person bear witness to their human-like subjectivity, and often protest against humans who treat them like machines, rather than sentient beings. Another effect of both these kinds of autobiography is the creation of empathy between narrator and reader, across a gulf of dissimilarity. Harriet Jacobs, in *Incidents in the Life of a Slave Girl* (1861), insists on the great differences between the lives of her white women readers, and her own life; at the same time, she invites them to imagine themselves in her situation, by insisting on the underlying similarity of her desires to theirs. This kind of invitation to empathy is a strong part of the didactic purpose of animal autobiography. The autobiographical testimony of slave witnesses played an important part in the abolitionist movement. Similarly, animal autobiography is

---

70   Burrows, *Tuppy*, p. 70.
71   Ibid., pp. 27, 43.
72   Ibid., p. 29.

part of a wider movement for animal protection. Frances Power Cobbe is an example of a woman who was active in the anti-vivisection campaign, and wrote an animal autobiography, *Confessions of a Lost Dog* (1867), though vivisection is not dealt with in this book – its reforming purpose is to promote homes for lost dogs. Anna Sewell was not herself active in animal protection movements, though she made her own personal interventions. *Black Beauty* was, however, endorsed by the RSPCA in 1894, and had a specific reforming purpose in the abolition of the bearing-rein. In the cases of both slave narrative and animal autobiography, a testimonial genre worked together with a social and political movement to try and bring about changes in the law and in attitudes. This use of testimony and witness is rather different from their retrospective and historiographical uses in the work of, for instance, Shoshanna Felman and Dori Laub, where witnesses both memorialise the past and seek to heal their own trauma. Slave and animal testimonies have more immediate purposes.

But of course there are also important differences between them. Though detractors sometimes insisted slave narratives were the work not of the slaves themselves, but of their abolitionist patronesses, this is not now generally believed. Animal autobiographies, however, are obviously ventriloquised or at least 'translated' by human authors. Dwight A. McBride, in his book on slave narrative, points out that in order for their testimony to be heard, slave witnesses had to adopt the discourses of the abolitionists.[73] The animals here have to adopt rational, human discourse. It is the relation of the human writer to the animal's voice that is central to the status and effect of these books as 'testimony'. Can there be testimony by proxy, or by 'translation' of a silent or incomprehensible witness's meaning? Jan-Melissa Schramm has described the important effect of the decision to allow advocates to speak for the accused in trials for felonies, in 1836, with the Prisoner's Counsel Act.[74] 'Animal advocacy' is a phrase often used to describe the activities of animal protectionists in the nineteenth century, and the courtroom metaphor first appears in Trimmer's *Fabulous Histories*, as we have seen: 'As there are no courts in which beasts can seek redress, I set up one for them in my own breast, where humanity pleads their cause', says farmer Wilson, and Mrs Benson replies, 'I wish they had such an advocate in every breast.'[75] Are these writers then advocates, speaking for their clients? But in the courtroom, it is the accused who has an advocate. The animal autobiographer is instead the victim and accuser.

The animal, through their 'advocate' is testifying to us, the readers, who perform the function of jury or of accused, depending on our treatment of animals. At the same time, to the human characters, the animals are dumb, and this speechlessness is linked to truth-telling – they cannot deceive, as humans can through their possession of language. Alfred Elwes claims in his preface to *The Adventures of a Dog*, that he is translating the story from 'the great canine tongue'. He remarks,

---

73 Dwight A. McBride, *Impossible Witnesses* (New York, 2001).

74 Jan-Melissa Schramm, *Testimony and Advocacy in Victorian Law, Literature and Theology* (Cambridge, 2000).

75 Trimmer, *Story of the Robins*, p. 170.

... there is a simplicity about it that often shames the dialects of man; which have been so altered and refined that we discover people often saying one thing when they mean exactly the reverse ... a dog never sullies his mouth with an untruth. His emotions of pleasure are genuine; never forced. His grief is not the semblance of woe, but comes from the heart.[76]

Bob the Spotted Terrier holds a similar view: 'Dogs are by nature honest; they fawn not where they wish to bite; they lick not the hand which they do not love.'[77] The point is reinforced by a central courtroom scene in Burrows' *Tuppy*. The epigraph to this book claims that, 'the idea of this little story, the main incident of which is strictly true, was suggested by reading a curious trial published in the Times about three years ago.' Chapter Five is headed, 'A Recognition – I make my 1ˢᵗ Appearance in a Police Court, and prove myself a Valuable Witness'.

What happens in this chapter is a consequence of Tuppy, the donkey autobiographer, having been stolen by a gypsy hawker, who puts him to hard, menial work. His former mistress, however, recognises him in a London street, and claims him back. The court case is to decide who really owns him, and the judge asks that Tuppy himself be brought into the courtroom and 'judge for himself'. Tuppy ignores the blandishments of his false master, and goes straight to his real mistress when she calls. The court erupts first in laughter and then in tears at this evidence of 'real, genuine affection'. The judge comments: 'I am quite satisfied ... no witnesses that could be produced could speak half so strongly to the truth of your case as does the affectionate remembrance of the poor dumb beast. That the donkey is the one that was stolen from you three years ago, there can be no doubt'. Later, an onlooker comments, 'The man told a wonderful plausible tale. But this dumb beast here told a better ... there was many a one who thought it no shame to be seen with tears in their eyes. That donkey is a first-rate witness.'[78] Animal witnesses in these books have the double authority of the affective genuineness of the speechless, and the rational speech of the autobiographer to the reader.

Tuppy's appearance as witness in the courtroom flouts the nineteenth-century exclusionary rules of evidence, which ruled out the testimonies of incompetent witnesses such as children who did not understand the religious meaning of taking the oath. Animals would seem to be similarly excluded, though Tuppy's story claims to be based on a real case. Schramm sees fiction taking up the role of voicing the testimonies of those witnesses, especially the poor and oppressed, whose words have been excluded from official courtrooms. She is, however, interested in showing the applicability of this idea to third-person fiction, taking it for granted that autobiography and fictional autobiography are necessarily 'testimonial'. I would argue that the word applies in a special sense to these animal autobiographies that have the explicit aim of 'advocacy' through animal witness.

Within the animal autobiographies, it is interesting that there are a number of other first-person narrations or speeches, adding extra testimony to that of

---

76 Alfred Elwes, *The Adventures of a Dog* (London, 1857), pp. iii–iv.

77 *Dog of Knowledge*, p. 66.

78 Ibid., pp. 81, 87.

the main narrator/protagonist. Often, several other animals tell their stories to the autobiographer, building up a composite indictment of human mistreatment of animals. The most notable example of this is Argus's *Further Adventures of Jemmy Donkey, interspersed with biographical sketches of the horse* (1821). The biographical sketches are in fact in first person, and are very like Black Beauty. In *Black Beauty* too, other horses, including Ginger the mare, tell their experiences to the autobiographer. There is also another class of witnesses in these books, whose existence could easily be overlooked, but who are, I think, very important. These are human characters, who function as 'by-standers', witnesses of cruelty to animals. They either intervene, or report the perpetrators to the authorities. Hilda Kean comments on the emphasis on personal engagement and observation of cruelty in the campaigns for animal protection. These human witnesses act as role-models for the readers – this is what you must do if you witness something like this. Quite precise advice is often given: a man who remonstrates with Jemmy the donkey's owner only causes poor Jemmy to be beaten further in private; another man, more effectively, notes down the name of the carter, written on his cart, and reports him. This very same scene is repeated in *Black Beauty*.

These human witnesses can also be seen as surrogates for the human writers, hidden behind the animal autobiographer. In *Black Beauty* a lady intervenes to explain rationally and politely to a carter that his overladen horse can only get up the hill if he removes the constricting bearing-rein. This lady has often been identified with Anna Sewell speaking as herself. A whole other set of meanings for witness and testimony come in here – Anna Sewell was a Quaker originally, and the importance of testifying to one's beliefs and religious experience is central to Quaker practice. What this suggests, however, is that as well as testifying on the part of silent animal witnesses, these writers are indirectly testifying to what they themselves have witnessed.

On finding a kind master, Dick the Little Poney exclaims, 'I now felt myself a servant, and not a slave.'[79] The servant analogy is often used in these texts, and is in tension with an opposite class analogy that insists the animal autobiographer is well-born or upwardly mobile: Dick claims, after a period with the gypsies, 'if I rose, it was by merit alone.' There are some interesting exceptions here: Beautiful Joe insists he is only a mongrel: 'I know that I am not a thoroughbred. I am only a cur.'[80] He also does not use the language of service. Perhaps this indicates an American egalitarianism, though a parallel with slavery undercuts this (see p. 87 below). Luath by contrast is proud of his pedigree, and only mongrels behave badly in his story. But the servant analogy is not emphasised. Instead, the dogs become vagabonds, living and performing with a travelling circus, a different kind of de-classing. In contrast, the ancestry of Dorothy Kilner's mouse is not particularly emphasised, but an analogy with servants runs throughout the book, though the mouse itself does

---

79 *Dick*, p. 95.
80 Saunders, p. 13.

not act directly as a servant to humans. The mouse's stories parallel children who are unkind to servants, with children who are unkind to mice. One cruel little boy is made to imagine himself in the place of a tortured mouse; another, who plans to ruin the servants' work so that they have to do it over again, is made himself to do their tasks. Neptune, the Newfoundland dog, is himself rude and unkind to servants, and is punished for it.

The tension between class aspirations and servitude is clear in Mary Pilkington's *Marvellous Adventures* (1802). The cat heroine, settled with a poor family, at first feels 'convinced that *happiness* did not depend upon *situation*, but on a perfect heart and a contented mind', but is soon pleased when she is taken elsewhere, because 'I never could be happy except in society where I thought my mind could be improved.'[81] She finds her true home with aristocrats, but partly because her new owners are always able to receive a good 'character' from her previous owners, in the manner of a servant. She also very much enjoys fulfilling her duty of catching rats and mice. Poor Tabby is treated well by the servants, 'however, I knew what was for my own advantage too well to continue among them': this is from a cat whose happiest time was wandering with beggars, and who also talks about her different 'situations' in different households.[82] The rats in Charlotte Tucker's book are also proud of their ancestry, but they are implicitly paralleled with the ragged and starving little boys who seek shelter with them. The one rat who does become a pet, insists on his loyalty to his master, and the boys find service in the same house. Jemmy the Donkey does not associate with lower-class donkeys he meets, but he draws parallels between his situation and that of human servants. Similarly, Black Beauty is told by his mother not to associate with the 'rough' colts in the meadow: 'they are cart-horse colts, and, of course, they have not learned manners. You have been well bred and well born.'[83] But his story is regularly punctuated by the passing on of 'character' references, and the importance of keeping a good 'name'. Here, there is a very obvious parallel with Black Beauty's grooms, who also depend on having a good 'name' and finding a good 'place'. Dick, the Little Poney makes this parallel explicit, when he admonishes himself against 'dissatisfaction with our allotments': 'I have heard a groom murmuring because he was not a squire … and a footman, that he was obliged to wait on his master at table, when he was hungry himself.' Dick too relies on character references: on throwing a malicious mistress, he is worried that 'my character would again suffer'. At the end of his story all goes well, because someone's 'recommendation ensured my favourable reception. A good introduction is all that merit wants.'[84]

In a recent article on autobiography, Carolyn Steedman suggests that the origins of the genre lie not in the canonical autobiographies of great men, but in the 'characters' and life-stories that were required of the poor by their employers and

---

81 Pilkington, *Marvellous Adventures*, pp. 112, 115.
82 Sandham, p. 61
83 Sewell, p. 4.
84 *Dick*, pp. 142, 121, 171–2.

benefactors. As she says, 'the emerging administrative state demanded that it was in fact the poor who tell their story, in vast proportion to their vast numbers.' She gives as an example, the mid-eighteenth-century London Society for the Encouragement of Honest and Industrious Servants, which 'determined that none should join or have entitlement to a handout unless they gave their account *in writing*: 'Every person applying must deliver in a Petition, a narrative of Information, containing an Account of his or her Service'.[85] Autobiography is something you have to produce to ensure fair treatment. It would not then be surprising that defenders of animals would resort to it. The autobiography is less testimony than testimonial. This idea is borne out by Cobbe's *Confessions of a Lost Dog* (1867), where the dog is narrating her life story to the ladies and gentlemen who run and support the Lost Dogs' Home, explaining how she has come there: 'it is sad to be a dependent on public charity after having had so happy a life as mine.'[86] An additional purpose of the book was perhaps to raise support and funds for the Lost Dogs' Home: the autobiography demonstrates that the recipients of charity are deserving of it.

As testimonials, all the stories work to show the protagonists as faithful and helpful to man. Those dealing with semi-wild creatures have to work the hardest at this: not only does one of Charlotte Tucker's rats become a pet, guarding his master's food against other rats, but the wild rat Whiskerandos explains, 'We are useful to man … by acting the part of a scavenger, and clearing away that which, if left, would poison the air, the race of Mus does good service to man.' The story rehabilitates and recommends 'those animals which we usually regard with contempt and disgust'.[87] As we have seen, Mrs Pilkington's Grimalkin also has to contend with prejudice, and explains that cats do not really delight in giving pain. At one point her 'place' is saved when her noble owner explains to his daughter, 'the character he had received of my fidelity and attachment'.[88] The stories act as self-written, self-recommending 'narrative(s) of Information, containing an Account of his or her Service', and contain within them the 'characters' provided by respectable human others. Here the courtroom comparison is relevant again: Schramm points out the importance of character witnesses in the nineteenth-century courtroom, who could testify to the credit-worthiness of another witness's testimony. Gentility and rank were also important contributors to credit-worthiness of a witness – perhaps this is why nearly all these animal autobiographers insist they are of high birth, despite the analogies made between them and servants.

Black Beauty's 'good name' involves a human being attesting to his good qualities, and does not involve what he is actually called. But even his individual name, 'Black

---

85 Carolyn Steedman, 'Enforced narratives, stories of another self', in Tess Cosslett, Celia Lury and Penny Summerfield (eds), *Feminism and Autobiography* (London, 2000), pp. 28, 30.

86 Frances Power Cobbe, *Confessions of a Lost Dog* (London, 1867), p. 58.

87 Tucker, pp. 157–8, vi.

88 Pilkington, *Marvellous Adventures*, pp. 50, 69.

Beauty', is not securely his, and is given and changed by human owners. In his essay on 'The Autobiographical Pact', Philippe Lejeune emphasises the importance of the 'proper name' of the author/narrator: 'the name received and assumed first – the father's name – and especially the Christian name that distinguishes you from it, are no doubt essential basic principles in the story of *me.*'[89] Feminist critics have already questioned this idea, from the point of view of female autobiographers, whose names are relational to those of the men in their lives. Can the name and the self coincide so neatly for them? Is the name a badge of individuality or of servitude?

All the animals in these stories are speaking as representatives of their species. For instance, the cat in *Marvellous Adventures* hopes that 'though mankind have supposed that my species are incapable of attachment, and that our dispositions are marked with fierceness, treachery and deceit, yet I flatter myself with the hope, that my adventures will convince them that every prejudiced report is not to be believed.'[90] Bob the Spotted Terrier, comparing men unfavourably with dogs, confirms his species' stereotype: 'among my species, the sin of ingratitude is yet unknown.'[91] Tuppy admits his species-specific failings: 'Our race have the character of being obstinate, and though I like to dignify it by the name of perseverance, yet I suppose I am no better than the rest of my species.'[92] Nevertheless, all the animals are accorded the individuality of a name, that both is and is not theirs. The cat is referred to as Grimalkin, a generic cat name, in the chapter headers, but its human owners call it Puss or Tab. Jemmy the Donkey's name is more individual, but we never learn where it comes from. Dick the Little Poney says, 'why I was called Dick, I know not', but Natalia the cat is so named because she was born on the birthday of one of her master's sons.[93] Black Beauty's name also originates from particular owners – not his first owners, but his ideal owners, Squire Gordon and his wife.

> 'Yes,' she said, 'he is really quite a beauty, and he has such a sweet good-tempered face and such a fine intelligent eye – what do you say to calling him Black Beauty?'
> 'Black Beauty – why, yes, I think that is a very good name. If you like it shall be his name,' and so it was.[94]

In the Edenic setting of Birtwick Park, these words have the resonance of a divine fiat. Subsequent owners call him Black Auster, Blackie, and Jack, but at the end of the book, Joe Green, a groom from Birtwick Park, reappears, working for Beauty's final owners, and recognises him by name. Black Beauty has circled back to his true identity, confirmed by the title of the book, his name.

---

89 Philippe Lejeune, *On Autobiography*, ed. Paul John Eakin, trans. Katherine Leary (Minneapolis, MN, 1989), p. 21.

90 Ibid., p. 3.

91 *Dog of Knowledge*, p. 68

92 Burrows, *Tuppy*, p. 10.

93 *Dick*, p. 37; *Autobiography of a Cat*, p. 5.

94 Sewell, p. 23.

Luath in *Sable and White*, also has a degree of named individuality. As in *Black Beauty*, the good master with whom he starts and to whom he returns at the end, knows his name. The dog himself knows where his name comes from: 'Luath, you know, my little chum, was the name given by the great Scottish poet Burns to his favourite collie.'[95] This is reinforced by the epigraph to the book, a quote from Burns: 'I've often wondered, honest Luath / What sort of life poor dogs like you have.' The Burns quote, however, points to this new Luath's status as generic, called after another dog, and representative of 'poor dogs like you'. Beautiful Joe, like Black Beauty, has his name as the title of his book. The name, however, has been given to him by human owners, with an irony that Joe himself cannot appreciate.

> I am not called Beautiful Joe because I am a beauty. Mr Morris, the clergyman, in whose family I have lived for the last twelve years, says that he thinks I must be called Beautiful Joe for the same reason that his grandfather, down South, called a very ugly colored slave-lad Cupid, and his mother Venus.
> I do not know what he means by that, but when he says it, people always look at me and smile'.[96]

The feline equivalent of Joe, Pussy Meow, praises her mistress's habit of giving names to cats, but it is a two-edged process, involving both individuality and servitude:

> And right here let me tell you, a cat with a respectable name feels a sense of dignity and self-respect that is impossible to one only known by the general name of 'kitty'. Moreover, it gives him a chance to exercise promptness and obedience, qualities which are sure to endear an animal to his master; because, when he hears his name called, he can get right up and run, knowing that it means him and not some other cat.[97]

In Lucy Thornton's *The Story of a Poodle* (1889), the dog has two names, given by different owners. Their provisionality is indicated by quotation marks: there is a picture of 'Juan', previously known as 'Gaston'. As with other protagonists, his original name and owner are restored at the end. Only the mice and rats have the independence to award their own names: Longtail, Softdown, Brighteyes and Nimble for the mice, Ratto, Oddity, and Whiskerandos for the rats. But Gaston the Poodle's father, 'Pluto', has his own name for his mate, 'Darling Spot': 'He never cared to call her "Proserpine"'. The poodle comments on the oddity of the 'funny, ugly' official names, but his mother laughs and insists they are 'very interesting ones'. The dog's uncles and aunt also have classical names, Cerberus, Charon, Styx, Ceres. A joke is going on at the expense of the naïve child/animal; at the same time, these high-flown names indicate a pedigree, 'a high-born race'. The poodle-autobiographer's own name has to be explained by his mistress, in a chapter in which she describes Pau in the Pyrenees, where she is living: 'the castle was founded in 1363 by Gaston Phoebus, Comte de Foix. And so you see, wishing to give our little friend, the poodle,

---

95 Stables, p. 50.
96 Saunders, p. 1.
97 Patteson, p. 234.

a name of interest in connection with Pau, he has been called "Gaston".[98] The issue of the name in these books signals an uneasy relationship between animal-as-possession and animal-as-individual, and also between the generic and the specific. Vicki Hearne distinguishes between a 'real' name for an animal, and 'a label for a piece of property, which is what most racehorses' names are'.[99] But the real name for her is also the emblem of a relationship with humanity, in which the animal can be 'called' by its owner.

Lejeune's main point about the importance of the proper name in autobiography, is that the identity between the name on the title page and the protagonist of the narrative creates what he calls 'the autobiographical pact'. This implied contract promises the reader that what is told will be an extension of the reality outside the book, just as the name on the title page is assumed to refer to a real person in the world. In Lejeune's terms, then these are not autobiographies – the animal's name is sometimes the title of the work, but not given as the author. *Black Beauty*, however, first appeared without an author's name, Anna Sewell being, as I said, merely the 'translator'. *Black Beauty* is more like the autobiographies based on oral narratives that Lejeune writes about in 'The Autobiography of Those Who Do Not Write'. Here, 'the writer, who often takes the initiative to create a story which otherwise would remain concealed in silence, appears like a mediator between two worlds, almost like an explorer.' On the other hand, there is no taped or oral narrative behind the story. All these 'autobiographies' are also similar to what Lejeune terms 'imitations', like eighteenth-century novels that pretend to be memoirs or diaries of real people.[100] But there is another aspect to them that does seem to partake of the contract Lejeune writes of, especially in the case of the later books that use photographs. These pictures imply that the protagonists are real dogs in the world – we are being told the stories of real pets who exist outside the books. Cobbe's *Confessions of a Lost Dog* was advertised 'with a photograph of the Dog from Life'. The Author's Preface to *Beautiful Joe* insists on its facticity:

> Beautiful Joe is a real dog, and 'Beautiful Joe' is his real name. He belonged during the first part of his life to a cruel master, who mutilated him in the manner described in the story. He was rescued from him, and is now living in a happy home with pleasant surroundings, and enjoys a wide local celebrity ... and nearly all of the incidents of the story are founded on fact.[101]

Similarly, the epigraph to *Neptune* insists that 'all the incidents told in this little story of the life of Neptune are strictly true'. In the copy in the John Ryelands Library, which is inscribed 'a presentation copy from the Author' on the flyleaf, the epigraph goes on in handwriting after 'strictly true', 'with a few mistakes in those remembered from hearsay only, excepted. The stealing of the bone for instance is

---

98　Lucy D. Thornton, *The Story of a Poodle* (London, 1889), pp. 1, 2, 13.
99　Vicki Hearne, *Adam's Task* (London, 1987), p. 169.
100　Lejeune, pp. 197, 15.
101　Saunders, p. 8.

pure fiction. Neptune never stole, but was the very soul of honour.' When the bone-stealing episode in the text occurs, the same hand has written a disclaimer in the margin to the effect that the bone in question was not really stolen. The truth of the story is a matter of urgent concern. What we are getting in these books might be better defined as biography in the first person.

Black Beauty itself has no photographs, though Anna Sewell's biographer claims to have identified the 'original' of Black Beauty. This text, however, establishes its continuity with the world outside the book by acting as a handbook for grooms and stable-boys on the good treatment of horses. *Beautiful Joe* is also full of practical information on the treatment of various pets. Charlotte Tucker's *The Rambles of a Rat* (1857) claims natural historical truth: 'the courage, presence of mind, fidelity, and kindness which I have attributed to my heroes, have been shown by real rats. Such adventures as I have described have actually happened to them.'[102] Even earlier texts that play metafictionally with matters of truth still refer their readers to real originals. The Advertisement that introduces the *Memoirs of Bob, the Spotted Terrier* makes fun of a bookseller who claims almost first-hand knowledge of the author's previous work, *Dick, the Little Poney*: 'It is a very good little book, and a very true story. The gentleman's servant who groomed Dick, was here the other day, and declared, that he knew his history to be a fact, and that he was still alive and well.' The author expects to hear on his return to the shop that 'some gentleman's huntsman has scraped an acquaintance with Bob, and is ready to vouch for the authenticity of his memoirs also.' While scorning the shopman's trick and the naivety of the customer, the author claims credit for the 'life and nature' of his story, that makes 'every reader think he has met with something similar'. Unlike other children's books, this one contains 'fact' and 'knowledge', and is based on real animals: 'the *original* DICK and BOB have been long favourites of his [the author's] own family.'[103] *Marvellous Adventures* also creates a continuity with the outside world: in a footnote, we are told that the expiring cat's devotion to its dead mistress has a parallel in a true story:

> The latter part of Grimalkin's history is founded upon a fact, that some years ago occurred at Bath:– A cat, who had been long attached to a very amiable young lady, actually refused to quit her tomb; and though she was frequently taken from thence by her connexions, yet the attached creature regularly returned; upon that spot only would she take any sustenance; and upon that spot, in a few months, she died.[104]

This story of a pet's devotion to a dead owner is of course also the stuff of legend and stereotype. It is one way for an animal story to end, emphasising the pet as secondary to the human, and yet as possessing human virtue in excess. How to end an animal autobiography is a problem. The most recurrent pattern I have found is the recognition scene, which leads to a peaceful rural retirement with sympathetic owners. Even the piebald rat, Oddity, now a pet, is recognised by the boys who used

---

102 Tucker, p. v.

103 *Dog of Knowledge*, pp. v–viii.

104 Pilkington, *Marvellous Adventures*, p. 160.

to live with it: 'There – look! If that an't my own pretty spotted rat!'[105] Often, as in *Black Beauty*, the animal is again called by its right name. The scene involves a return to an earlier, paradisal state, originally experienced in infancy, before dog-stealers, horse-thieves, cruel owners, injuries, economic hardship have intervened to create a story. The recognition confirms the animal as an individual. It is analogous in some ways with the marriage ending that closes a romance narrative, or the parent-child reconciliation that ends some children's stories, except that it occurs near the end of the animal's life, as its last scene.

Teresa Mangum has written of the emergence of the 'aged autobiographical dog' in the late nineteenth century, citing passages from *Sable and White*, and *Beautiful Joe*. She sees this fictional voice as a way for the Victorians to examine their feelings about old age, and as part of a struggle to comprehend 'marginal subjectivities' such as animals, and old people.[106] But, as we have seen, the voices of many kinds of domestic animals, dogs included, were present in children's fiction from the late eighteenth century, and there are several reasons why an aged narrator should be telling these stories. In the first place, the autobiographer is looking back over his or her whole life, from the vantage point of old age. Secondly, the comparatively short life-spans of animals mean that the ageing process is more visible in their lives, and the human writer, memorialising a real animal, will probably have experienced its old age and death. Thirdly, one of the issues taken up by humanitarians was the protection of aged animals, especially horses. Several of these books attempt to change attitudes and practice, presenting a peaceful retirement as a humane alternative to the knacker's yard. The horse in *Further Adventures of Jemmy Donkey*, laments his fate:

> ... the horse, on whose agility man will stake his property, is, in old age, discarded; transferred from master to master, and successively degraded in every swift change, as age increases; at length he is consigned to the custody and possession of wandering traders, and finally becomes the food of dogs.[107]

Jemmy himself is writing from a peaceful retirement: in fact, boredom induces him to embark on the horse's story. Tuppy, a later donkey-autobiographer, also writes from retirement: 'now, as in my old age I quietly graze through the summer days in my pleasant green field, or keep myself warm in my comfortable winter shed, I often think over my past career.'[108] Dick the Little Poney is given 'a Paddock and a Shed for Life', as 'a Reward for his Services' (170). The family who own him are determined 'never to distress an old and faithful servant': there is a clear parallel with human employees.[109] The book ends by quoting the whole of a poem by Mr Pratt,

105 Tucker, p. 153.

106 Teresa Mangum, 'Dog years, Human fears', in Nigel Rothfels (ed.), *Representing Animals*, (Bloomington, IN, 2002), pp. 35–47.

107 Argus, *Further Adventures*, pp. 17–18.

108 Burrows, *Tuppy*, p. 1.

109 *Dick*, p. 170.

of the tear-jerking *Pity's Gift* (1798): 'the pathetic address of a superannuated horse to his master, who had sentenced him to be shot, in order to abridge the sufferings of a lingering death'. There is a concerted attempt in these books to make readers sympathise with the sufferings and the relief of the 'superannuated' animal.

Both *The Adventures of Poor Puss*, and *Marvellous Adventures* follow their cat protagonists through to their deaths, by means of an outside narrator. Grimalkin's faithfulness is stressed, in her death by her mistress's tomb, as part of the book's overall project to rehabilitate cats from negative stereotypes. Tabby's death emphasises the humanity of her young owner. Before she dies, her age is also humorously celebrated as accumulated experience and skill: her younger companion offends her by implying she is unable to catch mice any more. Tabby leaves the mouse to her, 'and inwardly laughed at the chase the mouse was likely to lead her'. When they meet again, '"You were a little disappointed," said the old cat smiling.'[110] The old age of the Cream of Cats is also celebrated as achievement:

I am lame, old, grey, have been wounded three or four times, severely burnt once, had the mange once, my paw broken once, my eyes bad twice. I have been starved, beaten, whitewashed, stoned, set upon by dogs and my own species, yet here I am presentable at last, and a standing illustration (though standing only upon three legs) of the truth of the proverb, as many lives as a cat.[111]

This cat, like the horses and donkeys, is enjoying a safe retirement, having been returned to her first owners: 'I live with them still, and write these lines in the garden arbour.'[112]

In the scheme of things these books subscribe to, there is no life for these animals outside human ownership. When a human autobiographer gains social recognition and acceptance, and/or romantic fulfilment, a further phase of active life and independent accomplishment can follow. But for the domestic animal, the only sequel is retirement and death. Ernest Thompson Seton explains the problem involved in writing the life of a wild animal:

For the wild animal there is no such thing as a gentle decline in peaceful old age. Its life is spent at the front, in line of battle, and as soon as its powers begin to wane in the least, its enemies become too strong for it; it falls.

There is only one way to make an animal's history untragic, and that is to stop it before the last chapter.[113]

Seton's conception of wildness is strongly Darwinian, and dictates the form of his animal 'biographies'. The animal autobiographies, however, are structured on a hierarchical model of domestic service, that allows for 'peaceful old age' as a gift that human owners can give to their animal servants. The circular plot that returns

---

110 Sandham, pp. 68–70.
111 *Autobiography of a Cat*, p. 32.
112 Ibid.
113 Ernest Thompson Seton, *Lives of the Hunted* (London, 1924), p. 11.

animals to their first owners and original names also has the virtues of the 'narrative of restoration' that Peter Hunt suggests is preferred in children's fiction to the 'narrative of development': though the ending is old age, it has many similarities to the protected and pastoral way the ideal childhood was being constructed.

Chapter Four

Parables and Fairy-tales

Margaret Gatty's *Parables from Nature* (1855–71) and Charles Kingsley's *The Water Babies* (1863) derive from both the serious, moral, semi-realistic animal story as developed by Trimmer, and the fantastic, grotesque, carnivalesque comic animal poems of the papillonades and *Signor Topsy-Turvy*. The explorations of animal subjectivity and the political purposes of the animal autobiographies are not, however, part of their projects. Their focus instead is on natural history, science and theology. Gatty and Kingsley are writing in an increasingly complex Victorian context of evolutionary controversy. Both were accomplished naturalists, on the borderline between amateur and professional, two categories that were not yet fully distinguished in the mid-Victorian period. Gatty published an authoritative book on seaweeds, and Kingsley wrote popular natural history, while also becoming respected in the adult scientific community. Trimmer's emphasis on an education in natural history, and the use of the microscope, appears in their children's stories as a more thoroughgoing expertise. Both writers choose children's animal stories as a place in which to react specifically to theories of evolution. Gatty uses her parables to oppose scientific materialism, aiming to counter the desponding reactions of Tennyson's poetry to evolutionary theory. Kingsley uses his fairy story to propose a reconciliation between evolutionary theory and religion. He had been famously alluded to as a clerical supporter of Darwin's position in the second edition of *The Origin of Species*:

> A celebrated author and divine has written to me that he has gradually learnt to see that it is just as noble a conception of the Deity to believe that He created a few original forms capable of self-development into other needful forms, as to believe that He required a fresh act of creation to supply the voids caused by the action of his laws.[1]

It is worth asking why both these writers choose children's stories, and talking animals, to put forward or refute complex scientific theories that would be of interest mostly to an adult audience. When contemporary controversies about mechanism and materialism briefly surface in Trimmer's *Fabulous Histories*, Mrs Benson quickly shuts the topic down, as unsuitable for young readers:

> 'I have been,' said a lady who was present, 'for a long time accustomed to consider animals as mere machines, actuated by the unerring hand of Providence to do those things

---

1 Charles Darwin, *The Origin of Species*, 2nd edn [1859] (Oxford, 1996), p. 388.

which are necessary for the preservation of themselves and their offspring; but the sight of the Learned Pig, which has lately been shown in London, has deranged these ideas, and I know not what to think.'

This led to a conversation on the instinct of animals, which young readers would not understand, it would therefore be useless to insert it.[2]

While Harriet afterwards asks to be informed about the Learned Pig, and Mrs Benson obliges, the issue of mechanism is not returned to. But Gatty's and Kingsley's stories are full of allusions that only adults would understand: for instance, Kingsley's references to the 'hippocampus' controversy (see p. 120 below), or Gatty's epigraphs from Tennyson. Gatty even addresses adults specifically at times. Both writers seem to have been influenced by Romantic idealisations of childhood as a time of uncontaminated vision nearer to our divine origins: the child can often see more clearly than the adult scientist. This Romantic nostalgia for childhood appeals more to the adult than the actual child in the present: the child is valued for something the adult has lost and can only regain through the child. The Romantic influence is most evident in the preamble to a parable of Gatty's called 'Inferior Animals' in which a group of talking rooks parody evolutionary theory. Interestingly, childhood vision is linked here to the belief that animals can talk. The narrator laments the 'necessary unlearning' of our childhood instinct for intercommunication with the animals, quoting from Novalis: 'only children, or child-like men ... have any chance of breaking through the charm which holds nature thus as it were frozen around us, like a petrified magic city.'[3] She then appeals to the (grown-up) reader to join her in becoming a child, and approach the rooks. Magically, narrator and readers can now understand the rooks' language.

Kingsley also celebrates the child's powers of belief, which he presents as an open-mindedness which adult scientists have lost. While Professor Ptthmllnsprts refuses to believe in the existence of water-babies, because he has not seen them, Kingsley, the child Ellie, and the reader know better. Interestingly, it is the girl child who believes spontaneously: the boy reader has earlier had to be lectured by the narrator about the need not to believe the limiting pronouncements of scientists about reality. Kingsley quotes Wordsworth's 'Immortality Ode' to the child reader – 'trailing clouds of glory do we come' – to remind him of his divine origins. The assumption is that he may have been already contaminated by 'Cousin Cramchild' and 'Aunt Agitate', the purely factual educationalists. Ellie's belief in water-babies is Keatsian: 'it is so beautiful, that it must be true.' The Professor, however, 'had not the least notion of allowing that things were true, merely because people thought them beautiful ... [he] held that no man was forced to believe anything to be true, but what he could see, taste, or handle.' When he actually catches Tom the water-baby in his fishing net, he is thrown into complete denial, and the narrator comments: 'I believe that the naturalists get dozens of them when they are out dredging; but they

---

2   Trimmer, *Story of the Robins*, p. 65.
3   Margaret Gatty, *Parables from Nature* (London, 1907), pp. 194–6.

say nothing about them, and throw them overboard again, for fear of spoiling their theories.'[4] Here an address to children confirms the adult narrator's value for and affinity with childlike vision. This Romantic belief in the special, counter-factual powers of the child is rather different from Trimmer or Fenn allowing that children like talking animals, and so, for educational purposes, and with apologies, using the device.

Their value for childlike vision does not prevent either of these later writers from, at the same time, promoting a sometimes fierce moral code for children. Gatty uses allegories of 'training', and Kingsley educates Tom through the ministrations of Mrs Bedonebyasyoudid, a personification of natural cause and effect. Evolution provides Tom and the readers with a strenuous programme of moral improvement: degeneration is the alternative. Among the lessons taught, however, kindness to animals, the staple of eighteenth-century animal tales, hardly figures. Tom is cruel at first to the sea-creatures, and is punished later, but there is no serious moral to be drawn about the wrongness of tormenting sea-creatures. The incidents serve instead to show how Tom's aggressive attitude prevents him from conversing with the animals and learning wonderful natural historical facts about them, and later his punishment illustrates the workings of justice. We are in no case asked to sympathise with or pity the sufferings of the creatures. Gatty is not interested in the theme of kindness to animals at all. The talking animals in both works are mostly small wild animals, often sea-creatures, at a great remove from human consciousness. In Gatty's stories not only animals but also plants, and sometimes inanimate objects speak, for the sake of the moral and the natural historical facts, not in order to explore animal subjectivity. The attribution of speech to animals, for both writers, is something of a joke, full of ironic and parodic double meanings that sometimes get out of control.

Margaret Gatty (1809–73) was both a naturalist and a writer for children. Her special object of study was the seashore. In 1862, she published the authoritative two-volume *British Seaweeds*. She also published the *Parables from Nature* (1857–71), a series of moral tales featuring talking animals and plants, and, with her daughter Juliana (later Mrs Ewing, another popular children's author), she edited *Aunt Judy's Magazine* for children. The *Parables* were very popular in the nineteenth century, and Kipling acknowledged their influence on his animal stories.[5] Gatty's interest in seaweeds was of her time. As Anne Shteir remarks, 'during this period several women were well known as seaweed collectors', though Gatty is unusual in this group in writing her own book on the subject, rather than merely providing specimens to male botanical authors.[6] She was the wife of a clergyman, and had ten children in all. In 1848, when she was thirty-nine, she paid a visit to Hastings, where she had

---

4   Charles Kingsley, *The Water Babies* [1863] (London, 1995), pp. 153, 161.

5   Rudyard Kipling, *Something of Myself* (London, 1964), p. 32; J. M. S.Tompkins, *The Art of Rudyard Kipling* (London, 1959), pp. 59–60.

6   Ann B. Shteir, *Cultivating Women, Cultivating Science* (Baltimore, MD and London, 1996), p. 183.

an 'illness', from which she recovered with the help of a sympathetic doctor who 'lent her books that induced her to take up the study of seaweeds'.[7] Shteir reads the 'illness' as 'the effects of too many pregnancies'.[8] Whatever its cause, the mental and physical stimulus of seaweed collection revived her as effectively as any present-day course of therapy or anti-depressants.

Botany was a particularly feminine scientific pursuit for a Victorian lady, but Gatty used it to escape at least some of her constraints. As she wrote:

> The sea-weed collector who has to pick her way to save her boots will never be a loving disciple as long as she lives! Any one, therefore, really intending to *work* in the matter, must lay aside for a time all thought of conventional appearances ... Next to boots comes the question of petticoats ... to make the best of a bad matter, let woollen be in the ascendent as much as possible; and let the petticoats never come below the ankle.[9]

Her activities were something of a family joke: her daughter Juliana wrote a comic poem on the difficulties of getting her away from the seashore. Nature study here figures as an escape from family duties; but in her writing for children, Gatty was seen as combining her roles as scientist and mother: 'she studied closely, and the artist and the mother in her learned to render beautifully and simply the truths she had perceived.'[10]

Gatty read Darwin's *Origin of Species* in 1859, and was fiercely opposed to his views.[11] Like many Victorians, however, she did not fully understand his theory of evolution, which she conflates with earlier theories such as those of Robert Chambers and Jean-Baptiste Lamarck.[12] She also classes Darwin with Voltaire, as another atheistic unbeliever to be combatted.[13] Well before reading Darwin, she was already an opponent of scientific materialism. In the *Parables*, Gatty makes use of her scientific knowledge, her feminine persona, and the metaphoric possibilities of the parable as genre to dismantle the arguments of scientific materialists. She takes up the perspectives of children and animals to mock the pretensions of prideful grown-up evolutionists. At the same time, she attempts to preach the virtues of hierarchy in the animal and human kingdoms, resulting in a rich and contradictory mixture of messages.

The introduction to the 1907 Everyman edition of *Parables* recommends the book for its

---

7　Gatty, *Parables*, p. ix.

8　Shteir, pp. 184–5.

9　Ibid., p. 171, quoting Gatty, *Seaweeds*.

10　Gatty, p. ix.

11　Gillian Beer, *Darwin's Plots* (London, 1985), pp. 140–41; Christabel Maxwell, *Mrs Gatty and Mrs Ewing* (London, 1949), pp. 114, 125; Alan Rauch, 'Parables and Parodies', *Children's Literature*, 25 (1997): 140–47.

12　Alvar Ellegard, *Darwin and the General Reader* (Chicago, IL, 1990).

13　Maxwell, pp. 114, 125

... love for all the small helpless pretty things of nature, an imagination deeply coloured, if rather strictly defined, by Christian doctrine, an unfailing candour, and lastly a spirit of affection that fills the whole book, binding it together and making it possible for the reader to sympathise warmly in the small conversations of bees, crickets, kittens, raindrops and vegetables.[14]

Gatty appears to match the Victorian feminine stereotype perfectly: unquestioning simple faith, sympathy for all small living things, child-like innocence and love. We can find this type described in Tennyson's poem *In Memoriam*: in verse XCVI, the male speaker turns to address a female interlocuter, who has been reproaching him for his religious doubts:

> You say, but with no touch of scorn
> > Sweet-hearted, you, whose light blue eyes
> > Are tender over drowning flies,
> You tell me, doubt is devil-born.

'You' is usually identified as Emily Sellwood, later Tennyson's wife, but is also emblematic of the positioning of Victorian femininity in the discourse of faith and doubt.[15] The more emotional, empathetic woman keeps unproblematically to her simple faith, untouched by the intellectual doubts of the man. For her, Nature is not an evolutionary battlefield, 'red in tooth and claw', but full of small creatures to be pitied and saved. This contrast mirrors the economic division of home and work, in the 'separate spheres' ideal: the man participating in the rough competitive world of work, the woman as guardian of the hearth and the moral and emotional aspects of life. The woman fulfils the role of conscience-keeper for the man. The 'you' of *In Memoriam* also fits into that other important role given to women in the late eighteenth and nineteenth centuries: as Barbara Gates says, 'women were called upon to aid children in developing respect and sympathy for nonhuman species.'[16] In the previous three chapters, we have seen many examples of women fulfilling this didactic and humane role.

In the *Parables*, however, Gatty, like her predecessors, far exceeds this feminine stereotype, though she may be using it as part of an acceptable feminine self-presentation. Her work is informed by scientific knowledge and understanding, and her attitude to the natural world is tough-minded and brisk. Instead of merely 'sympathising' with the problems of small creatures, she cleverly deploys their voices to aid a polemic against religious doubt. In so far as she is orthodox, what comes over is not a passive acceptance, but a rigid insistence on hierarchy, authority and

---

14 Gatty, *Parables*, pp. ix–x.

15 Christopher Ricks (ed.), *The Poems of Tennyson* (London, 1969), p. 440 fn. Emily Sellwood fits the role of conscience-keeper, described below, postponing her marriage to Tennyson because of her doubts about his faith, until finally convinced by the completed *In Memoriam*.

16 Barbara T. Gates, 'Revisioning Darwin with Sympathy', in Barbara T. Gates and Ann B. Shteir (eds), *Natural Eloquence* (1997), p. 164.

obedience, which we can read as an attempt to come to terms with the limitations imposed on her as a woman, and/or the short-hand solution of a harassed mother of ten spirited children. Her insistence on hierarchy allies her with writers like Trimmer and Wollstonecraft, and, more than they do, she also insists on women's subordination to men. And, unlike earlier writers, she is not really interested either in arousing sympathy for animals, or in exploring animal consciousness.

Gatty, like Trimmer and Fenn, is very self-conscious about attributing 'voices' to nature. She refers to an adult, scientific truth which opposes her fictionalising, mythologising tendencies. In a parable about 'Night and Day', she playfully allows that

> ... now the wise men will not allow that Night and Day drive round the world in cars with horses to them. Well, perhaps they don't. Perhaps it is really true that the earth is a dark ball, hanging in the open space which we call the firmament of heaven, moving slowly round the shining sun, but spinning like a top all the time itself, so that first one side and then the other faces the brightness; and thus there is a constant change from lightness to darkness and darkness to light going on all over the world.[17]

The length and carefulness with which this theory is described works against the dismissiveness of 'perhaps': she is in fact giving us a physics lesson. Nevertheless, Gatty asserts, Night and Day still praise the Lord, and we may hear their voices in a new scientific and technological context: 'as musical sounds ... sweep along the wires of the electric telegraph on breezy days'.[18] This emphasis on retaining a spiritual element is rather different from the clear-cut division between natural fact and children's fantasy in the works of earlier writers.

One of the purposes of the *Parables* is to counter scientific naturalism and its attendant disbelief, and evolutionary thought in particular. This purpose leads Gatty to address adults as well as children. For instance, 'Kicking', about a rebellious colt, is clearly at times directed at children: the colts are told that the breaking-in is 'to prepare them for being taught a thousand nice things which they would never be able to do if they were not taught, and which it was immensely jolly to be able to do, when the teaching was once over'. The traditional hierarchical moral of the story is, however, applicable to all ages, and in a quite different tone of voice: 'Animals under man – servants under masters – children under parents – wives under husbands – men under authorities – nations under rulers – all under God'. Gatty's hierarchy is similar to Wollstonecraft's and Trimmer's here, except for the inclusion of 'wives under husbands'. The story of the colt is by analogy applicable to children, like the education of Trimmer's robins, or Tuppy the donkey, or Neptune the dog. But the story to the child also contains messages for the adult: for instance, 'judgements

---

17 Gatty, *Parables*, p. 246.
18 Gatty, *Parables*, p. 247.

formed by the lesser intelligence concerning a greater which it cannot comprehend
– what rebellion and ruin have they not caused!'[19]

We could talk here about a 'hidden polemic', in Bahktin's term, with an adult
doubter, behind an overt address to children, but in other stories the address to
adults is quite overt, and the doubts are given expression. As we have seen, 'Inferior
Animals' addresses itself to adult readers, inviting them to recover their childhood:

> Reader ... shall you and I become children in heart once more? Come! own with me how
> hateful were the lessons which undeceived us from our earlier instincts of faith and sweet
> companionship with all created things; and let us go forth together and for a while forget
> such teaching.[20]

The story which follows is a comic parody of evolution, using the child-like device
of talking animals to mock a very adult debate. In all her stories, the notions of
the child and the child-like are cleverly deployed to aid the polemic against the
adult doubter. Using both child-like vision and adult wisdom, Gatty can come at her
targets from several directions. Moreover, her understanding of nature involves both
child-like sympathy and adult scientific knowledge, leaving no room for contrary
opinions.

Some of her procedures in this battle against scientific materialism and loss
of faith can be seen in a story called 'A Lesson of Hope' (1855),[21] which is a
fairly straightforward rebuttal of Tennysonian doubt, using the device of talking
animals. Tennyson became a friend of the Gattys, and several of the *Parables* give
the impression of a very particular argument with him. In 1857, a mutual friend
wrote to Gatty with a message from Tennyson, saying how much he admired one
of her Parables. Gatty then sent Tennyson the complete volume, and a friendship
developed between the Gattys and the Tennysons, with frequent letters and a number
of visits. Alfred Gatty lectured and wrote on Tennyson's poetry.[22] In his long elegy
In Memoriam, Tennyson expressed his doubts and fears following the premature
death of his friend Arthur Hallam. The poem explores not only personal grief, but
the poet's fear of the loss of faith consequent on scientific materialism. The poem
is pre-Darwinian, but alludes to earlier theories of evolution. The poet eventually
overcomes his doubts, through a combination of religious faith and evolutionary
hope.

---

19 Gatty, *Parables*, pp. 257, 268, 260.

20 Ibid., p. 196.

21 Gatty's *Parables* are difficult to date. As Rauch explains, 'There were five "series",
each of which included additional stories, although each individual series was reprinted.
The stories themselves had often appeared in separate publications' (Rauch, 'Parables and
Parodies', p. 150, note 2). The position is complicated by the paucity of first editions of any of
the series. 'A Lesson of Hope', however, belongs to the first series, so can reasonably be dated
to 1855.

22 Maxwell, pp. 126–7; Alfred Tennyson, *Letters*, eds Cecil Y. Lang and Edgar F.
Shannon Jr, (Oxford, 1987), vol. 2, pp. 193 fn, 255 fn.

Tennyson's resolution was perhaps too heterodox for Gatty, and his doubts expressed in too lengthy and heartfelt a manner. Her story 'A Lesson of Hope' carries an epigraph from *In Memoriam*: 'Oh yet we trust that, somehow, good/ Will be the final goal of ill!' (LIV). The 'yet', implying preceding contrary evidence, and the 'somehow', implying desperation, undercut the hopeful message. Gatty's story is designed to confirm the trust, by seeing things through to a 'final goal'. While in *In Memoriam* the speaker's voice moves to and fro between doubt and faith, Gatty's dramatic technique gives voices – trees, birds – to the different positions Tennyson fluctuates between, and right from the start her speaker's doubts are countered by a strong voice from nature itself. This speaker, we find out at the end of the story, is male, when he tells us of 'the children of my love, and the sweet mother who has borne them'.[23] The voice of the human doubter in Gatty is always male, while she takes on the position of the female guardian of faith.

The safe and happy haven, with wife and children, that the narrator reaches at the end of the story, only arrives after a time of solitary doubt and despair, following his parents' death: 'Father and mother lost, swept suddenly away, and I, with straitened means, left alone to struggle through the world!' The story, then, recapitulates in a simple form the trajectory of *In Memoriam* itself, from the death of the beloved (Hallam) to new life (Tennyson's sister's wedding). In between, nature, as in the poem, seems to sympathise with the mourner's dark mood. But in Gatty's story, the trees, the owl and the raven all speak, debating hope and despair with the human narrator, who in this story is able to understand the voices of nature (this convention varies in different stories). The main action of the story takes place on one significant night, 'when, having wandered out one gloomy autumn night to muse on nature and her laws, I found myself contemplating, in the deep recesses of the wood, the progress of a violent storm.' The trees lament their destruction, and the Raven preaches his gloomy message: 'destruction is the law of life.' But this is countered by the authoritative voice of the Owl, who draws attention to the reappearances of the Moon, the 'Moon that shone in Paradise'. The doubter voices his despair: 'order and peace seem meant, but death and ruin come to pass'; the Owl replies, 'Oh, miserable doubter, do you ask? Must the brute beasts and mute creation rise to give an answer to your fears? Look in the heaven above, and in the earth below, and in the water deep beneath the earth. One only law is given – the law of order, harmony, and joy.'[24]

The Owl it seems has looked forward to *In Memoriam* stanza XCV, where Tennyson has a vision of deep universal order:

---

23 Gatty, *Parables*, p. 60.
24 Ibid., pp. 55–8.

The deep pulsations of the world
Aeonian music measuring out
The steps of Time – the shocks of Chance –
The blows of death ...

But, instead of this vision being attained through long struggle, it is here from the first page. The doubter's recovery is paralleled by the return of spring: 'And to me also came a spring! From me, too, passed away the winter and its chill!' Though, at the end of the story, the narrator tells us how he now brings his children into the woods, and tells them of the Owl's message and the moon's promise, the tale is addressed to an adult, male consciousness, someone who 'muses on Nature and her laws'. The children are in the story as the means to this adult's recovery, as is the child-like device of talking trees and birds. But the authoritative voice that contradicts the doubter is also grown-up and male, the wise old Owl. The female moon, the sign of hope, is predictably silent and 'patient': 'the patient moon is never weary of her task of shedding rays of hope and promise on the world.'[25] Gatty, as female story-teller, keeps silent, dramatising her argument through male speakers.

This is not to say, however, that children and childishness are irrelevant to the story. The narrator's despair is occasioned by the loss of his parents. In the all-knowing Owl and the patient moon, he could be said to have recovered them, in Nature. In a sense, he is infantilised, as the Tennyson of *In Memoriam* also is, casting himself as 'An infant crying in the night:/ An infant crying for the light ...' and 'a child that cries,/ But, crying knows his father near' (CXXIV, LIV). The child, for Tennyson, figures his lack of knowledge, helplessness and innocent trustfulness. Gatty builds on this reduction of male authority to cast adult males as children, in the face of an all-knowing, all-providing parental Nature. Just as much as children are they in need of moral tales like this one to keep them on the right track. The hidden authority behind the voices of the story is of course the female story-teller herself.

Gatty's concern in this story to justify the structure and meaning of Nature as benevolent, well-designed and divine, is, like Trimmer's or Barbauld's, in the tradition of Natural Theology. These writers describe Nature's workings in order to show that they must have been made by an intelligent designer, and use evidence from Nature to demonstrate God's benevolence. These arguments are certainly part of Gatty's purpose, but in her stories, Natural Theology is juxtaposed with a different set of overlapping traditions: parable, allegory, emblem, analogy and typology. In these traditions, Nature functions as a metaphor for hidden spiritual and/or moral meanings. Typology originally meant the way Old Testament stories could be read as foreshadowings, or 'types' of New Testament stories, but it was often extended in the nineteenth century to cover natural symbols of supernatural events.[26] A properly devout mind is needed to 'read' nature symbolically. Typological and

---

25 Ibid., p. 60.
26 George P. Landow, *Victorian Types, Victorian Shadows* (Boston, MA, London and Henley, 1980), pp. 7, 31, 113, 215.

analogical readings are then rather different from the evidential readings of natural theologians.

Analogy was a favourite mode of thought among the High Church Tractarians. It is what Keble means when he starts *The Christian Year* (1827) with the line 'There is a Book, who runs may read.' Newman was also in favour of analogical readings of nature, while at the same time being fiercely against Natural Theology. It was *revealed* rather than natural religion that he valued:

> That the new and further manifestations of the Almighty, made by Revelation, are in perfect harmony with the teaching of the natural world, forms indeed one subject of the profound work of the Anglican Bishop Butler; but they cannot in any sense be gathered from nature, and the profound silence of nature concerning them may easily seduce the imagination, though it has no force to persuade the reason, to revolt from doctrines which have not been authenticated by facts, but are enforced by authority. In a scientific age, then, there will naturally be a parade of what is called Natural Theology, a widespread profession of the Unitarian creed, an impatience of mystery, and a scepticism about miracles.[27]

But, as the reference here to Butler's *Analogy* (1736) suggests, Newman was very much in favour of analogical thinking, and what he called 'the Sacramental system; that is, the doctrine that material phenomena are both the types and the instruments of real things unseen'.[28]

Gatty was very suspicious of the Tractarian movement, especially when it led to Rome.[29] But interestingly her admired friend Tennyson, Broad Church if Christian at all, like Newman differentiated between two different ways of finding God in Nature. Towards the end of *In Memoriam*, he repudiates the arguments of natural theology:

> I found him not in world or sun,
>   Or eagle's wing or insect's eye
>   Nor through the questions men may try,
> The petty cobwebs we have spun. (CXXIV)

On the other hand, typological thought is essential to the resolution of his poem, as physical evolution typifies moral evolution, and Hallam is a 'type' of the higher beings to come. Landow points out that typological thinking was popular with both low and high churches.[30] Perhaps because she was a scientist, Gatty, unlike Newman, Keble, or Tennyson, wants to hold on to Natural Theology. As John Hedley Brooke has pointed out, Natural Theological ways of thought had proved immensely useful and productive for science, and Darwin was extensively influenced by Paley's *Natural*

---

27 John Henry Newman, *The Idea of a University*, ed. I. T. Ker (Oxford, 1976), pp. 190–93.

28 *Apologia Pro Vita Sua*, ed. Martin Svaglic (Oxford, 1967), p. 29.

29 Maxwell, pp. 86–9.

30 Landow, p. 20.

Theology, even if he took Paley's evidences to quite different conclusions.[31] At the same time, Gatty's analogical thought comes from the same kind of seventeenth-century tradition as Newman's.[32] The different connotations of Natural Theology, analogy, and moral allegory, clash in her work in rich and charming ways. Maybe because she was writing for children, Margaret Gatty felt no need to be intellectually consistent on these points.

Being content with one's station in life is the moral of many of Gatty's stories. Here she is no different from many of the animal autobiographers, especially when they deploy the 'servant' analogy. But, mixed with typology and moral allegory, references to class sometimes create confusion in her stories. She is very fond of the analogy of metamorphosis – the caterpillar changing into the butterfly. She uses it not as an analogy of evolution, but, as was standard among Victorian writers and painters, following Coleridge's example, as a 'type' of the soul's immortality, our translation after death into a higher and different spiritual world.[33] But in her story 'A Lesson of Faith', the caterpillar is given a humble, worthy working-class character, while the butterfly is frivolous, stupid and upper-class.[34] Why the caterpillar should be so pleased to find out it will become a butterfly is unclear, as is the politics of the implied change in *class* terms. The parable has escaped from its moral. All the parts of Gatty's multiple hierarchy – 'Animals under man – servants under masters – children under parents – wives under husbands – men under authorities – nations under rulers – all under God' – do not always work smoothly together. She is keen to assert hierarchy, but also to some extent also undermines it, suggesting in particular that animals may be better than humans, and children than adults. In many of her stories, the ironies she uses, together with the mixture of genre and method, threaten to escape control, and lead to more subversive readings than the overt message, overturning the hierarchies she has set up. The perspectives of animals, plants and children are valorised above those of arrogant male thinkers. We have already seen, in stories by Barbauld and Trimmer, how taking an 'animal's-eye' perspective can implicitly challenge human domination.

These effects can be best illustrated in the story 'Whereunto', where comedy and irony threaten to destabilise the order and hierarchy Gatty is ostensibly committed to.[35] The perspective here is that of the small creatures of the sea, who speak back in answer to an adult doubter. He is reduced to an ignorant 'creature', unable to understand their complex relationships to their environment. At the same time, their perspectives are ironised, and put in a larger context by the voice of the sea. By

---

31   John Hedley Brooke, *New Interactions between Theology and Natural History* (Milton Keynes, 1974).

32   Wendy Katz, *The Emblems of Margaret Gatty* (New York, 1993), pp. 235–9.

33   See Michael Wheeler, *Death and the Future Life in Victorian Literature and Theology* (Cambridge, 1990).

34   Gatty, *Parables,* pp. 1–6.

35   This story appears in the third series, the third edition of which is dated 1864. See note 21 above for the difficulties of dating Gatty's stories.

setting this story on the sea-shore, Gatty puts it into her territory – sea-life is what she has studied and published on. The centre of the story is in fact a knot of seaweed.

The story carries another tentatively hopeful epigraph from *In Memoriam*: 'I see in part/ How all, as in some piece of art/ Is toil co-operant to an end' (CXXVIII). When juxtaposed with the epigraph, the story's project seems to be to firm up this tentative insight. It begins with a starfish and a crab speaking. As the tide recedes, the crab scuttles to shelter in the rocks, but the starfish, unable to move, lies suffering in the sun; 'as for the jellyfish, who had shared a similar fate, they had died almost at once from the shock, as the wave cast them ashore.' Gatty is brisk and unsentimental about suffering in Nature, and does not shield a potential child audience from death. However, though the talking animals and plants are comic and childlike, the moral is not primarily directed at children, but at the adult figure who now appears on the shore. He and his companion are only referred to as 'two creatures': 'what the creatures were who came up to this place and stopped to observe it, I shall not say.'[36] This way of describing them serves to keep us in the animals' point of view, and also reduces their human pretentions. The idea of man as only an animal is comic in Gatty's story, while the same idea causes despair in Tennyson's *In Memoriam*:

> Be near me when my faith is dry
>   And men the flies of latter spring,
>   That lay their eggs, and sting and sing
> And weave their petty cells and die. (L)

Gatty's lack of either sentimentality or melodramatic despair over the deaths of the jellyfish in her story, together with her comic equation of human and animal, positions her differently from both Tennyson, and the stereotypical female guardian of the faith with her tears over 'drowning flies'.

One of the human 'creatures' is holding forth about the wastefulness and uselessness of Nature: '"Here again, you see; the same old story as before. Wasted life and wasted death, and all within a few inches of each other! Useless, lumbering plants, not seen half-a-dozen times in the year; and helpless, miserable sea-creatures, dying in health and strength, one doesn't know why."' The 'creature' then turns the scene into a simile for human life: '"And so we go up, and so we go down, ourselves…with no more end in life, and of no more use, than these vile useless seaweeds."'[37] Nature, as for Tennyson, is a scene of purposeless destruction and waste, a gloomy type of all life. The 'creature's' state of mind is hardly one likely in children: the story's polemic is directed against this adult doubter. But it is the child-like voices of the small creatures that answer him back, though he does not hear them. Their message combines science and religion, as they rejoice in the perfect adaptations of their environment. The doubter's inability to hear suggests his limitations and ignorance, and also the superior wisdom of a childlike perspective.

---

36 Gatty, *Parables*, p. 155.
37 Ibid., pp. 155, 156.

Comically, the doubter, poking about in the seaweed with his stick, has managed to 'chuck the unhappy starfish into the air, who, tumbling by a lucky accident under the shelter of the tangle, was hid for a time from sight'. This is just as the doubter is saying despairingly 'so we go up, and so we go down'. He is unaware of this ironic juxtaposition, which undercuts his words. For, from the starfish's point of view, purposeful intervention has occurred: '"Why, he said he was as useless as these vile useless sea-weeds, and had come into the world, like them, for nothing; whereas, don't you see, he was born to save me."'[38] The sea-weed tangle, too, is there for the purpose of sheltering her. Other sea-creatures dispute this:

'If the tangle had come into the world for nothing but to shelter you, there would have been a fuss to very little purpose, indeed! Can't your advantages tell you there are other creatures in the world quite as important as yourself, if not more so, you poor helpless Lilac-legs? Do you know who is speaking? It is the blue-eyed limpet, I beg to say – the Patella pellucida, if you please'.[39]

The limpet goes on to give a short natural history lesson, in the same comic style, informing us of its appearance and habits, and the importance of the tangle to its race as home and food. Other creatures join in the argument, urging their own claims: '"Oh, the narrow-mindedness of people who live under a shell! ... Talk of the useless tangle indeed! Yes, the creature was ignorant indeed who said so. Little he knew that it was the basis of the lives of millions."'[40]

Lessons on the interdependence of sea-life are being conveyed, from an expert on the subject. The narrator can see from the perspectives of sea-creatures not just because she is a woman talking to children, but because she is a marine scientist, and in possession of superior knowledge. A natural theological message about the perfect adaptations of Nature is also being conveyed. But at the same time, the creatures' voices are heavily ironised. Gatty elsewhere declares herself a believer in hierarchy: if these voices were not undercut, a carnivalesque inversion might get out of hand. Gatty is always very keen to emphasise the limitations of everyone's perspective, and to urge that there may be larger explanations and forces at work which we are not capable of understanding. This has the effect of making fun of those men who pretend to philosophical certainty, like the doubter, and elevating the perspectives of 'creatures' lower down the hierarchy (animals, plants, women, children).[41] She must emphasise that these are not authoritative voices.

But, by doing this, she makes possible yet another reading: the perspectives of the sea-creatures, narrowly self-centred, could be all entirely mistaken, like the beliefs of the ant community in Barbauld's 'Travelled Ant'. The human creature's stick was obviously not created to save the starfish. Could the sea-creatures' views be a

---

38 Ibid., pp. 156, 157.

39 Ibid., p. 158.

40 Ibid., p. 159.

41 For a similar technique deployed by another woman naturalist, see Stephen Jay Gould, 'The Invisible Woman', in Gates and Shteir, p. 37.

parody of human self-centredness in believing in divine care? A radical relativism, rather than the natural theological acceptance Gatty usually urges, would then be a possible effect of the text (though surely not intended by Gatty). It is interesting here to make further intertextual comparisons, and read this story together with Browning's poem (also set on a sea-shore) 'Caliban Upon Setebos', and Darwin's famous closing image in *The Origin of Species* of Nature as an 'entangled bank'. In Browning's poem, Caliban is theorising about the nature of his god, Setebos, who turns out to be remarkably similar in character to Caliban himself, in his arbitrary savagery. Caliban's blinkered perspective invents a god in his own image. The poem's subtitle, 'Natural Theology on the Island', presents it as a satire on natural theological thinking. The nature Caliban describes is cruel and destructive, like him. Gatty's is benevolent and well-designed, but only from the self-centred perspectives of her shellfish. Her story too could be read as a satire on the complacency and circular argumentation of Natural Theology. I do not think that such a reading was her intention, but it is an effect, or indicator, of the unwitting instabilities of her position, speaking as woman/scientist, child/adult, animal/human.

Darwin's 'entangled bank' image works differently, without irony, to convey a scientific delight in Nature's self-evolving complexity and inter-relatedness:

> It is interesting to contemplate an entangled bank, clothed with many plants of many kinds, with birds singing on the bushes, with various insects flitting about, and with worms crawling through the damp earth, and to reflect that these elaborately constructed forms, so different from each other, and dependent on each other in so complex a manner, have all been produced by laws acting around us.[42]

Gatty's story could also be, perversely, read as an analogue to Darwin: the Divine is nowhere mentioned, but is left to be inferred (or not), by both writers. Her tangle of seaweed echoes his entangled bank as an image of self-sustaining symbiosis. Despite her opposition to Darwin, an unintentional Darwinian meaning could be read into her image.[43]

There is a sense in this story, as in some of her others, that things are getting out of control, and the narrative must be shut down quickly. The sea-creatures' voices are cut off in mid-sentence by the returning tide, and two authoritative voices from higher up the hierarchy close the matter. The doubter's companion gets to speak, praising the seaweed as a type of human goodness: "'there is not one of them but what gives shelter to the helpless, food to the hungry, a happy home to as many as desire it.'" At the same time, the sea-water transforms the weeds, in a sensuous descriptive passage: 'the huge fronds surged up like struggling giants, as the waves rushed in below ... as the tide rose higher and higher, their curved stems unbent, so

---

42　Charles Darwin, *The Origin of Species* (Harmondsworth, 1982), p. 459.

43　It is reasonably certain that this story was written after the *Origin* was published in 1859 (see notes 21 and 35 above), especially as 'Inferior Animals', which both Beer and Rauch take to be a satire on Darwin, was also published in the third series. In this case Gatty may be intentionally alluding to Darwin's tangle.

that they resumed their natural position, till at last they were bending and bowing in graceful undulations to the swell of the water.' Once the human creatures have gone, the sea itself speaks up, berating the other creatures: '"poor little worms and wretches, who have been talking your small talk together, as if it were in your power to form the least idea of anything an inch beyond your own noses"'. The real purpose of the seaweed is to keep the sea '"pure, sweet and healthy"'.[44] Predictably, the sea is male, and the story ends by making fun of the female starfish, Lilac-legs, who still insists on seeing everything as centred on her experience and her providential escape from the sun. The return of the sea acts like the end of carnival, as proper authority is restored. But the subversive possibilities of the carnivalesque remain: readers could ask, why should the sea be right?

More carnivalesque confusions ensue when Gatty subjects evolutionary thought to complex mockery in her story 'Inferior Animals', involving a debate among a gathering of rooks.[45] Rooks had already featured in *Evenings at Home*, in a dialogue on 'The Rookery', between Francis and his father, Mr Stangrove. Mr Stangrove points out and relates many features of rook behaviour, in answer to Francis' questions. At the same time, the rooks are lightly anthropomorphised: Mr Stangrove agrees with Francis' idea that 'a rookery is a sort of town itself', and describes the rooks' 'sense of the criminality of thieving', when the whole rook community fall 'in a rage' upon a 'lazy' pair of rooks who have been stealing nest material. The conversation moves on to social animals in general: 'the societies of animals greatly resemble those of men; and that of rooks is like those of men in a savage state, such as the communities of the North American Indians.' More 'civilised' communities are represented by the beavers, who work together on building projects. The conversation comes round to those exemplary social animals, the bees, and moves into fabular mode with a moral: 'The principle upon which they all associate, is to gain some benefit for the whole body, not to give particular advantages to a few.'[46] Gatty's parable is written against this background of the moral, social and political meanings that have been read into the behaviour of social animals.

Gatty's story, unlike 'The Rookery', takes the form of a debate among the animals, not a dialogue about them by humans. Animal debates have a long history, dating back at least to Chaucer's *Parliament of Fowles*. More recently, the device featured in 'The Council of Quadrupeds' in *Evenings at Home*, the papillonade 'The Lion's Parliament, or The beasts in Debate', and the Topsy-Turvy poem 'The Hogs' Court of Inquiry'. This last is perhaps a direct source for Gatty, as the hogs' debate concerns a possible evolutionary link with man, and the idea is used to mock man's pretensions. Both the 'Council of Quadrupeds', and 'The Hogs' Court of Inquiry', like Gatty's parable, turn the tables on man: instead of men debating

---

44 Gatty, *Parables*, p. 162.

45 For tentative date, see note 43 above. For a fuller discussions of this story, see Beer, *Darwin's Plots*, pp. 140–41.

46 Barbauld and Aikin, *Evenings at Home*, pp. 36–7.

the characteristics of animals, animals debate the characteristics of men. This is a particularly effective way to parody scientific debate. In 'Inferior Animals', man's characteristics, as observed by the rooks, are interpreted as a degeneration from his original rook-like form – his arms are vestigial wings, his clothes the remains of feathers. Man, they argue, is attempting to become a rook again, as evidenced for instance by his predilection for black:

> '*Black* also the usual colour of the coverings with which men protect their heads from the outer air. *Black* even the clumsy boots which cover their feet. *Black* pretty nearly everything, everywhere', Mr Ravenwing positively declared.
> And on another occasion, in some parts of the country, he came upon whole races of men who left their homes every morning at an early hour, *white*, but returned to them every evening *black*, having accomplished this transformation during the course of the day.[47]

The rook-evolutionist is talking about coal-mines, as soon becomes clear.

All through the rooks' debate, the narrator as observer interjects. She makes authoritative comments designed to put the rooks in their place and point the moral: 'But I – the transcriber of this arrant nonsense – am ready, as I listen to their senseless caws, to throw down my tablets in despair. Oh! to think of finding the false glozings of philosophical conceit among the birds of the air'; or, later, 'Am I then half-convinced? – Yet for an imperfect being to hope to fathom the higher nature? Bah! what balderdash of folly!' This is a recurring moral in many of Gatty's parables: the 'lower' (animals, children, or man in relation to God) do not possess the faculties to understand the 'higher' nature, and must submit to the authority of those wiser and better endowed. While the rooks are being mocked as 'inferior', because they label man as 'inferior', at the same time they are acting as a parody of human scientific behaviour and pretensions; so, in a further twist, the story *is* also about human 'inferiority'. Some words the narrator used in the opening frame of the story, mocking human language, are now spoken by the rooks: 'There is, in fact, "*neither sweetness nor sublimity, neither melody nor majesty, in the shouting, and piping, and whistling, and hissing, and barking of closely intermixed human voices and laughter*".' Hearing them, the narrator becomes quite giddy: 'Where am I? – where am I? – what am I about? Is some mocking echo repeating my former words?'[48] Her pretension of adult, and human, authority is undercut. She finally extricates herself from the situation by turning it all into a dream.

The convolutions of this story are quite daunting. What seems to be happening is that on the one hand a hierarchy of inferior and superior animals, rooks and men, is being asserted, but on the other, man is being debased from his 'superior' status, and a rook's-eye view of him is given a degree of truth. At the same time, the child's-eye view, which delights in an improbable fable, is given priority over the prideful grown-up evolutionists who do not know all the answers, though the adult voice of

---

47 Gatty, *Parables,* p. 208.
48 Ibid., pp. 199, 207, 211.

the narrator is needed to point the moral for us. Carnivalesque propensities are once more emerging: the narrator seems all too aware of the need to frame and restrict carnival to a special period of licence, belonging here to the child and to the dream.

'Inferior Animals' is the only story in which Gatty reflects on actual animal language, and what it might mean, as well as the human propensity to attribute language to animals. In other parables, she cheerfully attributes speech not just to animals, but to trees, flowers and inanimate objects, making it clear by this undiscriminating attitude that the speech is only an arbitrary imaginative device. But 'Inferior Animals' opens like this: 'What do they say? – What do they say? – What do they say? – What can they *have* to say, those noisy, cawing rooks?' The narrator then moves from the idea that animal language only exists in the imaginations of children, to serious thought about natural facts: 'That they do understand each other's song is clear', she says, judiciously. The problem of knowing what they say is *mutual* unintelligibility: 'we are altogether as ignorant' of their language 'as they would be of ours round a large dinner table'. This idea is then used to mock human pretensions: 'As to the noises, there is not much to choose between them in the manner of agreeableness. Nay, of the two, perhaps the din produced by human voices is the more discordant and confused'. Scientific and satirical speculations about animal language are then replaced by a return to Romantic valorisation of childhood imagination: 'hand in hand, in the dear confiding way in which only children use, let us go forth into the fields, and read the hidden secrets of the world.' This passage could stand as an apologia for all her parables: the child-like frame of mind allows a temporary regression to the primitive and poetic anthropomorphic vision of talking Nature. Valuing the child-like allows the narrator to attack 'the great philosophers', who cannot explain or translate the rooks' behaviour, and so prove themselves inadequate as guides to the Creator's larger purposes and proceedings. Preferable is the child-like vision, which works like magic, but also to dispel magic: 'the spell is broken at last, and language, language, resounds on every side!'[49]

The story of Gatty's that Tennyson admired 'as much as anything he has ever read' was 'The Unknown Land', an unexceptional and unexceptionable parable about the hope for a future life, delivered in the sweet voice of a mother sedge-warbler.[50] There is no evidence that he read anything else in the copy of *Parables* that Gatty sent him: he writes that he will give it to his boys when they are old enough to read. It is in keeping with his stereotype of the sweet-hearted, childish female guardian of faith that this is the story he would have liked, whereas the others that engage more closely, fiercely, ironically and scientifically with his doubts are ignored. The editor of the Everyman edition also has no problem in assimilating Gatty back into the sweet-hearted stereotype. But her stories are much more complex and tough-minded than this, and her position as a woman scientist writing for children about animals and plants gives her rhetorical advantages that she does not fail to exploit. At the same

---

49 Gatty, *Parables*, pp. 193–4, 196–8.
50 Tennyson, *Letters*, vol. 2, p. 193.

time, Gatty's position as a woman who adopts the perspectives of children and small animals, who attacks misguided male philosophers, but who nevertheless subscribes to a rigid hierarchy and an ultimate male authority, produces contradictions that give the best of her stories a potential carnivalesque quality, as the voices of the marginalised take over the centre, and comic inversion privileges the unprivileged.

Charles Kingsley (1819–75), like Margaret Gatty, was a naturalist. While Gatty was a clergyman's wife, Kingsley was a clergyman: both pursue science in a religious context, though, as we will see, they had different ideas about the religious implications of Darwin's theory. Both Gatty and Kingsley had a particular interest in the seashore. During the mid-Victorian period, marine natural history became a popular pastime, as an offshoot of the development of seaside holidays. Many books were published providing information and advice on this hobby, by writers such as Edmund Gosse and G. H. Lewes. Kingsley's own book, *Glaucus or, the Wonders of the Shore* (1855) was addressed to a representative wealthy middle-class father, urging him to escape the boredom of his holiday, and provide his sons with useful amusements, by taking up an interest in marine life. Kingsley may be trying here to establish marine natural history as a masculine pursuit, suitable for a respectable paterfamilias and his sons: his daughters, we read, are already setting an example with their craze for ferns. Girls' 'crazes' are differentiated here from serious science. In *The Water Babies*, it is young ladies who are criticised for their failure to look after their pet sea-creatures properly: an aquarium craze 'swept through Great Britain between 1853 and 1860'.[51] The grown-up male reader, on the other hand, is quite anxiously assured in *Glaucus* not to think that 'Natural History is a pursuit fitted only for effeminate or pedantic men.' He and the narrator are referred to as 'two plain sportsmen', as they survey together the geology of a mountain tarn, which the narrator explains in plain language.[52]

Despite this affectation of a masculine plainness, however, Kingsley is also keen to stress the 'wonderful' aspect of 'the Wonders of the Shore'. Sea-animals, rightly understood, exhibit 'a certain charm of romance, and feed the play of fancy'. It is this fanciful aspect that is given free rein in *The Water Babies*, excused by its status as a fairy-tale for children. In *Glaucus* we find Kingsley anthropomorphising the creatures he describes, just stopping short of letting them speak. The whelk is a 'cunning fellow', the soldier crab is provided with 'a stout leather coat', the sea-urchins are described as 'babies' heads, covered with prickles, instead of hair', anticipating the water babies, and Tom's punishment, when he grows prickles. Other comparisons point forward to the social satire enacted by the talking animals in *The Water Babies*: the Pyrogama 'having sown its wild oats', 'settled down in life, built itself a good stone house, and became a landowner'. These anthropomorphic descriptions are teaching tools, to convey the appearances and behaviours of the

51 W. H. Brock, '*Glaucus*, Kingsley and the Seaside Naturalists', *Cahiers Victoriens et Edouardiens* (1976): 25–36.

52 Charles Kingsley, *Glaucus* (Boston n.d.), p. 20.

sea-creatures more vividly and enticingly. There is also the implication that they could convey moral and scientific lessons, if they could speak: 'if the House of Commons would but summon one of the little Paramecia from any Thames sewer-mouth, to give his evidence before the next Cholera Committee, sanitary blue-books, invaluable as they are, would be superseded for ever and a day.' *The Water Babies* goes one step further, and allows the sea-creatures to speak. As a fairy-story, it can actualise the longing, expressed in *Glaucus*, 'to walk on and in under the waves … and see it all'.[53]

But while in *Glaucus* Kingsley appears from the beginning as the advocate of science (though in a plain, sportsmanlike form), in *The Water Babies* he takes a different tack, casting himself as an anti-didactic Romantic. His epigraphs are mostly from Wordsworth; there is also one from Coleridge's *Ancient Mariner*, one from Spenser, and two from Longfellow. These quotations set the story in a Romantic context that emphasises the relationship between an idealised childhood and an idealised Nature. The Spenserian passage is about God's love for all his creatures, a theme taken up in the moral to the *Ancient Mariner*, 'He prayeth best who loveth best / All things both great and small: / For the dear God who loveth us, / He made and loveth all.' The Wordsworthian epigraph to Chapter Four opposes science, art, books and our 'meddling intellect' to 'the lore which Nature brings', that is available to 'a heart / That watches and receives'. The quotations from Longfellow link this simple understanding of Nature to childhood:

> Come to me, O ye children!
> For I hear you at your play;
> And the questions that perplexed me
> Have vanished quite away …
>
> For what are all our contrivings
> And the wisdom of our books,
> When compared with your caresses,
> And the gladness of your looks?[54]

Kingsley seems to be placing himself in the anti-scientific position of Charles Lamb when he attacked contemporary children's literature for its instructional and scientific bias. Kingsley even subtitles his book '*A Fairy Tale* for a Land Baby' (my emphasis), echoing Lamb's preference for 'wild tales' and 'old wives fables' (see p. 27 above). Moreover, all through *The Water Babies*, he parodies and attacks two made-up stereotypes of children's authors whom he refers to as 'Cousin Cramchild', with his 'Conversations', and 'Aunt Agitate', with her 'Arguments' on political economy. 'Cramchild' is clearly related to Dickens' 'MChoakumchild' in *Hard Times*, and 'Aunt Agitate' could easily be part of the 'cursed Barbauld crew' that Lamb attacks.

---

53 Ibid., pp. 18, 34, 51, 77, 63.
54 Longfellow, 'Children', verses 1 and 8.

Kingsley allies Cramchild and Agitate with the unimaginative men of science, who insist there are no fairies, and no water babies.

But what differentiates Kingsley from Lamb, Wordsworth and Longfellow, is that he insists that true scientists are open-minded, and realize how wonderful and unpredictable Nature is. It is only Cramchild, Agitate, and dull popular lecturers who use phrases like 'cannot exist' and 'contrary to nature'. In the same way, Gatty attacks materialist 'philosophers' who claim to know all the truth. Kingsley's implied aim is to reinstate religious ideas that, like fairies and water babies, cannot be disproved. In particular, immortality is hinted at in the many instances of metamorphosis among the water creatures that Tom the water baby meets. There is a parallel here with C. S. Lewis' later project to open children's minds to the possibilities of the supernatural through his Narnia stories, which, like *The Water Babies*, are full of religious allegory. Both writers find the children's book and the child audience congenial to their purpose. But Kingsley is also concerned to use science and its discoveries as part of his purpose: the scientific 'facts' turn out to be wonderful and mysterious. So the 'lore that Nature brings', and the 'story book' of Nature are not opposed to science, but *are* science. Science and fairy-tale are brought together. His version of natural theology works by showing the 'magic' of the natural world: as he says, scientists used to deny the existence of flying dragons, but now science has brought us 'Pterodactyles'.[55] Rather than emphasising the rational efficiency of Nature as a system, he points to its 'wonders'.[56] Here is his conclusion to a description of a lobster: 'for all the ingenious men, and all the scientific men, and all the fanciful men, in the world … could never invent, if all their wits were boiled into one, anything so curious, and so ridiculous, as a lobster.' Metamorphosis is one of these natural 'wonders', that points to further, spiritual, developments. The trope works not only as an emblem or religious analogy, but also as a type of evidence: 'Does not each of us, in coming into this world, go through a transformation just as wonderful as that of a sea-egg, or a butterfly? and do not reason and analogy, as well as Scripture, tell us that the transformation is not the last?'[57]

The Water Babies begins in the 'real' world of the Victorian social problem novel. Tom is a much-abused boy chimney sweep, with a violent Master, Mr Grimes. Tom is not sentimentalised: he is looking forward to growing up and being like Mr Grimes, and abusing his own apprentices. The Wordsworthian epigraph to this first chapter opposes 'what man has made of man' to the 'fair works' of Nature: society has corrupted Tom away from any childhood innocence he once had. Tom and Grimes are summoned to sweep the chimneys at Hartover Place, and as they walk along the power and beauty of Nature is contrasted with, and begins to impinge upon them. The architecture of Hartover Place itself is described as if it were a natural object,

---

55 Kingsley, *Water Babies*, p. 72.

56 Naomi Wood, 'A (Sea) Green Victorian', *The Lion and the Unicorn*, 19 (1995): 233–52.

57 Kingsley, *Water Babies*, pp. 143–5, 75.

in line with Ruskin's theories of the organic qualities of the Gothic, except that this house is a curious accretion of every kind of historical style: 'the house looked like a real live house, that had a history, and had grown and grown as the world grew.' This quaint and unlikely house is a little like the lobster, and also foreshadows the evolutionary theme of the novel. Hartover, housing the squire Sir John, comes to seem like the curious shell or casing of one of the animals Tom is to meet under the water. Tom himself is also loaded with animal imagery: as overworked and beaten apprentice, he is like a donkey. When he accidentally comes down a chimney into Miss Ellie's room, he sees himself in a mirror as a 'little black ape'. When the whole household subsequently chase him across the moors, he is compared to a fox, a gorilla, a squirrel and a stag. Escaping the pursuit, he finally slips under the water of a stream, thinking 'I will be a fish.'[58] A blurring of the animal/human divide is being set up.

This blurring is rather different from the carnivalesque inversions we have seen in other texts, which depend for their effect on there being clear boundaries between the hierarchical oppositions that are inverted. It is true that *The Water Babies* is full of carnivalesque allusions and devices. Rabelais is one of Kingsley's models (see p. 118 below) – Rabelais was the inspiration for Bakhtin's theory of the carnivalesque. Kingsley loves to use absurd Rabelaisian lists, describing his 'doctrine' as:

orthodox,   *inductive,*
rational,   *deductive,*
philosophical,   *seductive,*
logical,   *productive*
irrefragable,   *salutary,*
nominalistic,   *comfortable,*
realistic,
and on-all-accounts-to be-received.[59]

His story is playful and chaotic, and hierarchies are sometimes inverted, as when Mrs Bedonebyasyoudid punishes all the adults who have mistreated children by making them undergo similar treatment. For instance, 'she called up a whole troop of foolish ladies, who pinch up their children's waists and toes; and she laced them all up in tight stays, so that they were choked and sick, and their noses grew red, and their hands and feet swelled.' Doctors, nurserymaids and schoolmasters are similarly punished. But this episode of topsy-turvydom is carefully controlled and contained: the authoritative Mrs Bedonebyasyoudid is always in charge, and is meting out natural justice. While adults are put in the place of children, children are not elevated to adult status, and neither are animals included. Children may have the power of uncontaminated Wordsworthian vision, but only when Kingsley the adult narrator has lectured them into it: 'You must not say that this cannot be, or that is contrary to nature … It is only children who read Aunt Agitate's Arguments, or

---

58 Ibid., pp. 20, 2, 26, 31, 35, 56.
59 Ibid., p. 85.

Cousin Cramchild's Conversations ... who talk about "cannot exist" and "contrary to nature".'[60] The child narratee may have had the feeling he has lived before, but needs the narrator to quote Wordsworth's *Immortality Ode* to him to explain and justify his feelings. Ellie, with her Keatsian belief in the beautiful as true, falls over and is knocked unconscious just as the Professor catches Tom in his fishing net: she cannot give evidence against scientific unbelief. The animals speak only to explain natural facts, or as satirised mouthpieces for human class snobbery: they are not given a perspective that challenges human centrality.

There is an episode of true topsy-turvydom when Tom visits the Island of Polupragmosyne, where he sees 'ploughs drawing horses, nails driving hammers, birds' nests taking boys, books making authors, bulls keeping china shops, monkeys shaving cats', but the list moves into social satire: 'blind brigadiers shelfed as principals of colleges, play-actors not in the least shelfed as popular preachers; and, in short, every one set to do something which he had not learnt, because in what he had learnt, or pretended to learn, he had failed'.[61] Here, topsy-turvydom is just an image of the stupidity of social arrangements, a place that Tom rightly flees, aided by the natural instincts of his dog. Kingsley's tale does not work to invert hierarchies: its challenge to hierarchy works differently. By accepting the principles of evolution and degeneration, on both a social and biological level, the hierarchy becomes permeable – something to be travelled, up or down. At the centre of this vision is Tom the water baby, a creature who is both human and animal (he grows gills when he enters the water), and who puts both categories in doubt. In his ambiguous status, he is related to Kipling's Mowgli, who also has affinities with both the animal and human worlds. Significantly, both children are male: the girl Ellie in *The Water Babies*, dressed all in white and visiting Tom in his water world from somewhere above, is placed between human and angel, rather than animal and human. In their double natures these male animal/child heroes embody both an evolutionary view in which the child is 'nearer' to our animal origins, and a Romantic view in which the child is 'nearer' to Nature.

There is then a significant contradiction in the meanings Kingsley assigns to Tom's transformation from chimney sweep to water creature: on the one hand, his transformation into an animal mirrors his degraded nature: 'he is but a savage now, and like the beasts which perish; and from the beasts which perish he must learn.' Tom has to work his way back up the evolutionary ladder to humanity. On the other hand, the watery world into which he plunges is an image of the purifying power of Nature, which washes off the soot of his degraded human condition. Theological meanings attach to both interpretations: on the one hand, Tom's 'evolution' is a kind of purgatory; on the other, his plunge into the water is a baptism, a re-birth. Kingsley is quite happy with contradictions, however, which are licensed by the child-audience and the fairy-tale genre: 'Am I in earnest? Oh dear no! Don't you know that this is a fairy tale, and all fun and pretence; and that you are not to believe one word of

---

60 Ibid., pp. 199, 69–70.
61 Ibid., p. 290.

it, even if it is true?'[62] This repeated injunction from the narrator stands in marked contrast to Trimmer's 'earnest' contract with her young readers: 'I will never tell you anything but truth.'[63] Both Kingsley and Gatty have a multi-layered and evasive quality quite different from the directness and explicitness of earlier writers. Part of their brief is to reintroduce ideas of wonder and mystery into science and natural history. For Kingsley, the 'magic' of fairy-tale is an obvious way to introduce the supernatural to a child audience.

The contradiction in *The Water Babies* between Nature as 'beastly' in a negative sense, and Nature as pure is managed by assigning different values to different parts of Nature. On the whole, it is animals who must embody the 'beastly', while plants and inanimate Nature are pure. A significant exception is Tom's faithful water-dog, who leads him unerringly in the right direction: domestic animals illustrate the right use of animal qualities. The most beastly creatures are a race called the Doasyoulikes, who degenerate from humans back into apes. This process is described in explicitly Darwinian terms by Mrs Bedonebyasyoudid:

'Folks say now that I can make beasts into men, by circumstance, and selection, and competition, and so forth. Well, perhaps they are right; and perhaps, again, they are wrong ... But let them recollect this ... if I can turn beasts into men, I can, by the same laws of circumstance, and selection, and competition, turn men into beasts.'[64]

Darwin himself did not extend his theory to mankind in *The Origin of Species*, though it became immediately known as the 'ape hypothesis'. Kingsley, writing a children's story, can dare to suggest human evolution as a fanciful idea, and link it to moral progress by the reverse analogy of degeneration. His account of the Doasyoulikes' degeneration includes some elements of volition and the inheritance of acquired characteristics – non-Darwinian explanations that help speed up the process and relate it to morality. But he also includes the operation of sexual selection, a process which Darwin only went into in detail in *The Descent of Man* in 1872, when he finally applied evolutionary theory to humans. So, as the Doasyoulikes change from humans into apes, 'it was only those who could use their feet as well as their hands who could get a good living; or, indeed, get married', and once a hairy individual appears, 'this hairy chief had had hairy children, and they hairier children still; and every one wished to marry hairy husbands, and have hairy children too; for the climate was getting so damp that none but the hairy ones could live.'[65] Kingsley is doing a good job of simplifying Darwinian evolution into a children's story.

The final animalisation of the Doasyoulikes is signified by their inability to speak: the last survivor is shot by M Du Chaillu, a noted hunter of gorillas, because he cannot articulate the old abolitionist slogan, 'Am I not a man and a brother?' It is not clear whether or not Kingsley is making a racist joke here: earlier on,

---

62 Ibid., pp. 58, 76.
63 Trimmer, *Easy Introduction*, p. 157.
64 Ibid., pp. 237–8.
65 Ibid., pp. 234–5.

in his chimney-sweep days, Tom's own degradation has been signalled when he catches sight of himself in the mirror in Ellie's room, when he has come down the wrong chimney. He sees 'a little black ape ... with bleared eyes and grinning white teeth', whom he does not at first recognise as himself, and the illustration gives him Negroid features. Kingsley is certainly open to animalising human 'races', as when he parallels the Doasyoulikes' degeneration with that of the Irish: 'when people live on poor vegetables instead of roast beef and plum-pudding, their jaws grow large, and their lips grow coarse, like the poor Paddies who eat potatoes.'[66] What I also want to point out is the hostility to apes here, who have long been reviled because of their similarity to humans, and portrayed as grotesque imitations of the human.[67] This tradition is continued in the evolutionary story, where the ape represents the terrifying borderline between the human and the animal.

Kingsley then gives us two different 'borderline' creatures: Tom as ape, and Tom as water baby. The baby with gills, swimming in the sea, 'the noble rich salt water, which, as some wise men tell us, is the mother of all living things', surely comes from embryology, one of the evidences for human evolution, since the embryo goes through a fish-like phase. It suggests 'upward' development: Tennyson uses foetal development as a 'type' of further evolution in the Epilogue to *In Memoriam*, when his sister's child will be born after it has 'mov'd through life of lower phase', and will constitute a 'closer link / Betwixt us and the crowning race'. The ape is a less pleasant image from more recent evolutionary history: 'Move upwards, working out the beast, / And let the ape and tiger die' (CXVIII). Though Kingsley does not quote from *In Memoriam* as Gatty does, he is providing a children's version of the more optimistic parts of Tennyson's poem, where the poet parallels evolutionary, moral and spiritual development. For Tennyson as for Kingsley the 'ape' stands for the 'beastly' part of human nature that we must escape from. Interestingly, Kingsley himself unwittingly gives us an explanation for human dislike of apes, in a conversation Tom has with a (talking) salmon. The aristocratic salmon looks down on his near-relation the trout. The narrator comments: 'For you must know, no enemies are so bitter against each other as those who are of the same race; and a salmon looks on a trout, as some great folks look on some little folks, as something just too much like himself to be tolerated.'[68]

We see here, and in the Doasyoulikes' story, Kingsley's multi-layered method of paralleling social comedy, moral instruction and evolutionary parable. The story of the Doasyoulikes is told by Mrs Bedonebyasyoudid, who personifies the workings of natural cause and effect, and can turn men into beasts, beasts into men. The story is both an explanation of evolutionary theory, and a moral exhortation. Similarly, the salmon's story contains both natural fact (the biological kinship of salmon and trout), moral criticism of the degenerate ways of the trout, and social criticism of

66 Ibid., pp. 236, 26, 233.

67 Susan Wiseman, 'Monstrous Perfectibility', in Erica Fudge, Ruth Gilbert, and Susan Wiseman (eds), *At the Borders of the Human* (Houndmills, 1999).

68 Kingsley, *Water Babies*, pp. 136, 126.

the salmon's snobbery. This technique can be seen at its best in the longest piece of animal speech in the book, the autobiographical story of the Gairfowl. The Gairfowl, the last of her race, lives on the Allalonestone. Like the Dodo, she faces extinction because she cannot fly. She is presented as like an 'old Highland chieftainess', full of the pride of ancestry, and prejudiced against the modern desire for wings:

> It is quite refreshing nowadays to see anything without wings. They must all have wings, forsooth, now, every new upstart sort of bird, and fly. What can they want with flying, and raising themselves above their proper station in life? In the days of my ancestors no birds ever thought of having wings, and did very well without; and now they all laugh at me because I keep the good old fashion. Why, the very marrocks and dovekies have got wings, the vulgar creatures, and poor little ones enough they are; and my own cousins too, the razor-bills, who are gentlefolk born, and ought to know better than to ape their inferiors.[69]

Kingsley manages here to satirise the aristocracy, and the idea of a fixed social hierarchy, as well as providing an example of extinction at work in nature. The message of sticking to your 'proper station in life', so often emphasised in the 'autobiographies' of domestic animals, is here cast aside. Evolution undoes fixed hierarchies, and Kingsley seems to be using nature to promote fluidity between social classes. On the other hand, it is always clear in the story that humans are 'above' animals, especially apes. There is a hierarchy, but individuals, and races, can aspire to move up it into a different class or species.

Water creatures are also repeatedly shown aspiring upwards through metamorphosis, suggesting a spiritual dimension to the processes of change. But, as in Gatty's caterpillar story, Kingsley also attaches satirical social messages to the trope: the transformed and beautiful dragonfly is conceited and short-sighted, 'and never could see a yard before his nose; any more than a great many other folks, who are not half as handsome as he' (97). Another insect despises his origins: 'So you live under the water? It's a low place.' In his new shape, 'he had grown as dry and hard and empty as a quill, as such silly, shallow-hearted fellows deserve to grow' (100, 102). In both these cases, the animal's failings are paralleled immediately to human examples: 'a great many other folks'; 'such silly, shallow-hearted fellows'. This device is repeated again and again by Kingsley, almost every time an animal speaks. The sand-pipes are 'rude and selfish, as vain people are apt to be', the otter is sentimental, 'like a good many people who are both cruel and greedy'.[70] The human moral of the comic, satirical characterisation of the animals is always immediately apparent. But the animals are not just stand-ins for humans: putting 'people' on a continuum with animals fits in with the idea of an evolutionary kinship that Kingsley develops elsewhere. Kingsley is here adapting the social satire of the animals' speech in the 'papillonades' for his own purposes.

---

69 Ibid., p. 249.
70 Ibid., pp. 97, 100, 102, 89, 109.

The underwater worlds visited in *The Mermaid at Home* (1809), *The Water-King's Levee* (1808), *The Fishes Grand Gala* (1808) and *The Lobster's Voyage to the Brazils* (1808) must surely have influenced *The Water Babies*. *The Water-King* begins by inviting the readers to enter the world below the lake, fulfilling the desire expressed in *Glaucus* 'to walk on and in under the waves … and see it all', in very similar language: 'So follow! – and into the lake walk with me/ And the crystalline dome at the bottom we'll see', 'And now open your eyes and attend to the show.'[71] The readers are provided with a spell to allow them to breathe below water: Kingsley goes one better in *The Water Babies* by providing Tom with gills. Also similar to Kingsley's technique are the accurate, beautiful, but also anthropomorphic descriptions of the water creatures, such as the 'Muscle' in the *Lobster's Voyage*, 'At his two folding doors / Which the purple of Morn, in her beautiful hue / Had just painted with crimson, with gold, and with blue.'[72] In *The Water Babies*, Tom breaks a caddis' 'house-door', 'which was the prettiest little grating of silk, stuck all over with shining bits of crystal' (92). A dolls' house aesthetic of miniaturisation prevails in such passages, combined with the close observation of the naturalist. Both the poems and *The Water Babies* are concerned to impart accurate natural historical information. Kingsley's Sir John Hartover opines 'If they want to describe a finished gentleman in France, I hear, they say of him, "*Il sait son Rabelais*" But if I want to describe one in England, I say, "*He knows his Bewick.*"'[73]

Kingsley here puts himself into a tradition of English natural history. While mocking Cramchild and Agitate, his contemporaries, he acknowledges a debt to the observational and experiential natural history of earlier children's books: Barbauld is not in fact one of his targets. In the Preface to *Madam How and Lady Why* (1869), a children's book on natural history (mostly geology), he praises a story from *Evenings at Home* called 'Eyes and No Eyes', a dialogue which contrasts an observant boy with a bored, careless one. They have taken the same route home, but one has seen nothing, while the other has gained a wealth of facts from his observations of nature. It is not true, then, that Kingsley's 'approach to children in the literature he wrote for them was new', in seeking 'to call out their powers of observation' in an entertaining way, as he openly acknowledges his debt to Aikin and Barbauld.[74] Kingsley approves of their moral, but is apologetic about their style: the story is 'old-fashioned, prim, sententious … solemn'.[75] Clearly, he thought of his own style as less 'prim' and serious, more comic and enticing. Unlike his predecessors, he makes fun of the cumbersome system of nomenclature that had sprung up, following the

---

71 Kingsley, *Glaucus*, p. 63; *Water-King*, p. 8.

72 *Lobster's Voyage*, p. 3.

73 Kingsley, *Water Babies*, pp. 92, 119–20. Thomas Bewick, wood-engraver and naturalist, published *A General History of Quadrupeds* in 1790, and *British Birds* in 1797.

74 John C. Hawley, 'The *Water Babies* as Catechetical Paradigm', *Children's Literature Association Quarterly*, 14/1 (1989): 19.

75 Charles Kingsley, *Madam How and Lady Why* (London, 1890), pp. viii–ix.

Linnean system of classification.[76] Here he differs from the earlier texts, especially the papillonades, which give long Latinate names for their creatures in completely serious footnotes. But when the Professor catches Tom in his net, he would have liked to have

> … given him two long names, of which the first would have said a little about Tom, and the second all about himself; for of course he would have called him Hydrotecnon Ptthmllnsprtsianum, or some other long name like that; for they are forced to call everything by long names now, because they have used up the short ones.[77]

And when Tom first becomes a water baby, we are told he has 'round the parotid region of his fauces a set of external gills (I hope you understand all the big words)'.[78] Later in the book a tax on long words is proposed. As a populariser, Kingsley sees the need to simplify the language of science.

But like his eighteenth-century predecessors, Kingsley also feels the need to explain and excuse his use of talking animals. He introduces the topic like this: 'Now you must know that all things under the water talk; only not such a language as ours; but such as horses, and dogs, and cows, and birds talk to each other; and Tom soon learned to understand them and talk to them.'[79] When Grimes and some other men appear on the river bank, Tom cannot understand what they say, as he has moved into animal language. As in the *Jungle Books*, the animal speech needs a special sort of half-animal child to understand it. But what the animals say is so very human, as we have seen, and constantly referred to human social snobberies, that there is no consistent pretence that this is how animals communicate: the device is obviously comic and improbable. This is not 'what [they] would say for [themselves] if able to speak', and the animals' speech is never used to arouse sympathy or pity for their feelings.[80] There are a few instances when animals are given a type of speech that accords with their assumed characteristics, as when the 'happy stupid' sea-snails talk like this: 'Whence we come we know not; and whither we are going, who can tell? We float out our life in the mid-ocean, with the warm sunshine above our heads, and the warm gulf-stream below; and that is enough for us.'[81] This language of living in the moment is like the limited intelligence given to the cows in *Sable and White* (see p. 72 above).

At the same time as crediting his animals with language, Kingsley also insists, like Trimmer, that the possession of language is one of the dividing lines between the human and the animal. As we have seen, the Doasyoulikes become fully animal once they have lost the power of speech. Kingsley also stresses the importance of this

---

76 See Harriet Ritvo, *The Platypus and the Mermaid* (Cambridge, 1997) for the history of systems of classification.

77 Kingsley, *Water Babies*, p. 157.

78 Ibid., p. 67.

79 Ibid., p. 91.

80 Trimmer, *Story of the Robins*, p. 151.

81 Kingsley, *Water Babies*, p. 140.

dividing line in his parody of the 'hippocampus' controversy. This was an argument between Professors Huxley and Owen, in 1861, in which Owen held that humans were distinguished from apes by the presence of an organ called the 'hippocampus minor' in their brains. Owen was trying to disprove human evolution by finding an irreducible physical difference between men and apes; Huxley opposed him, arguing for Darwin and similarity. Kingsley mocks the debate as the 'hippopotamus' controversy, and comments ironically to the reader,

> You may think that there are other more important differences between you and an ape, such as being able to speak, and make machines, and know right from wrong, and say your prayers, and other little matters of that kind. But that is a child's fancy, my dear. Nothing is to be depended on but the great hippopotamus test.[82]

Language goes together with tool-making and spirituality as the mark of the human. Kingsley refuses any purely material or physical explanation of the difference between men and animals, insisting always that 'Your soul makes your body, just as a snail makes his shell', not the body the soul 'as if a steam engine could make its own coke'. [83] By mocking the hippocampus controversy, Kingsley opens the way for evolutionary kinship between animals and humans on the physical plane, while reserving the spiritual, including language, for men.

This means that he has no problem with using a mechanistic model for the workings of the physical world. Mrs Bedonebyasyoudid represents both natural justice and natural cause and effect. She says, 'I work by machinery, just like an engine; and am full of wheels and springs inside; and am wound up very carefully, so that I cannot help going.' She is a speaking variant of the 'watch' analogy, used so often by natural theologians (see p. 18 above). Her justice is severe and impersonal: 'if you don't know fire burns, that is no reason that it should not burn you; and if you don't know that dirt breeds fever, that is no reason why the fever should not kill you.' The epigraph to the chapter in which this speech appears is from Wordsworth's 'Ode to Duty', in which the 'stern lawgiver', duty, is equated with natural as well as moral law: 'Thou dost preserve the stars from wrong; / And the most ancient heavens, through Thee, are fresh and strong.' The 'Ode to Duty' is a poem about adulthood and responsibility, as opposed to the nostalgia for an idealised childhood in the 'Immortality Ode'. Kingsley's story contains both these Wordsworthian phases, and could be called a story about growing up, as Tom 'evolves' into a 'great man of science'. Mrs Bedonebyasyoudid's kindly sister, Mrs Doasyouwouldbedoneby, represents the maternal, nurturing aspect of nature, and also its playfulness. This maternal quality is stressed from the beginning, when Tom, fleeing Hartover Hall, sees a vixen playing with her cubs. Later, the river he falls into sings a song with a repeated refrain 'Play by me, bathe in me, mother and child.'[84] At the end of the book, Tom realises the two sisters are one, and are also the same as Mother Carey, the

---

82 Ibid., p. 154.
83 Ibid., pp. 86, 85.
84 Ibid., pp. 197, 196, 174, 44.

source of all life, who does not make creatures, but, in accordance with evolutionary theory, makes them make themselves.

Kingsley gives considerable authority to this multiple nature-goddess figure, who first appears as a strange Irishwoman on the road to Hartover, and who seems to know all about Tom and Grimes. In her various forms, she is in charge of the action, and she speaks for nature and natural processes. The speech of the various animals is secondary, a pleasant joke, compared to the serious messages of Mother Carey and her avatars. Together, the women speak to both the adult trying to retain child-like faith and wonder, and the child, trying to grow into an effective adult. The processes they represent – evolution, cause and effect, maternal nurture – hold together the various quaint, comic, idiosyncratic, separate creatures that Tom meets on his journey.

Kingsley's personification of nature as mother is part of a long tradition, which had some particular inflections in the Victorian period. Darwin found himself unable not to personify nature, with 'her' powers of selection; and Tennyson's famous image of 'Nature red in tooth and claw', is part of a maternal personification – in this case, as James Adams argues, nature as bad, uncaring, destructive mother, an especially horrific image for a male poet who casts himself as 'an infant crying in the night'. Adams reads into this image a Victorian male fear of independent female action and intellect, a fear which Tennyson elaborates on further in *The Princess*, a poem about women who attempt to set up a female-only university.[85] This terrifying, destructive mother-figure is the shadowy obverse of the innocent, caring female guardian of faith. The implication is that if women are not kept innocent and uneducated, they may become uncaringly intellectual. Both Gatty and Kingsley negotiate their way around these implications. Gatty shows that an intellectual, informed woman can still be a guardian of faith. Moreover, protected by her fierce attacks on materialism and doubt, she is able defend, make use of, and even identify herself with a very uncaring image of nature, who (like the female narrator) cares nothing for the deaths of the jellyfish, and who (again like the narrator) often puts childish male philosophers in their place.

Kingsley's Mother Nature figures, like Gatty's narrator, are quite fierce and sometimes pitiless. Mother Carey just sits unmoving, while creatures make themselves; Mrs Bedonebyasyoudid runs by clockwork, and cannot help visiting the consequences of their actions on those who do wrong, or make mistakes. But their fierceness is mitigated by the nurturing figure of Mrs Doasyouwouldbedoneby, and also by Kingsley's insistence on the justice, however harsh, of the way nature acts. Here his image of nature bears a resemblance to Huxley's slightly later personification of Nature as (male) chess-player against man: 'his play is always fair, just and patient. But … he never overlooks a mistake, or makes the smallest allowance for

---

85 James Eli Adams, 'Woman Red in Tooth and Claw', *Victorian Studies*, 33/1 (1989): 7–27.

ignorance.'[86] A source for both Kingsley and Huxley could be Wordsworth's image of Duty as (female) 'stern lawgiver', operating in both social and natural realms: the concept of scientific 'law' gives order and meaning to what Tennyson sees as a random process. Kingsley's personifications also bear a resemblance to the fiercely instructional female narrators and teachers of earlier children's literature – Mrs Mason, Mrs Benson, Mrs Teachwell, and their ilk. Gatty's narrator is also of course a development from this tradition. The 'wild' animal stories of my next chapter offer instead a more masculine vision of Nature, in which powerful carnivorous animals act as instructors and exemplars.

---

86 Thomas Huxley, 'A Liberal Education' (1868), *Collected Essays* (London, 1893–94), vol. 3, p. 302.

Chapter Five

Wild Animal Stories

In Sarah Trimmer's *Story of the Robins*, 'wild' animals are a slightly puzzling and unpleasant part of the Creator's scheme, to be avoided or destroyed, as Mrs Benson explains:

> 'Some animals, such as wild beasts, serpents, &c, are in their nature ferocious, noxious, or venomous, and capable of injuring the health, or even of destroying the lives of men and other creatures of a higher rank than themselves; these, if they leave the secret abodes which are allotted them, and become offensive, certainly may with justice be killed.'[1]

While the birds of Trimmer's story could be thought of as wild animals, here she means something else by the term – powerful and destructive animals, who live far from mankind in remote and inaccessible areas. These are the creatures who are often the heroes of Rudyard Kipling's and Ernest Thompson Seton's animal stories. If we are looking for their antecedents, they would be in updated fables such as the African 'Council of Quadrupeds' in *Evenings at Home* (1792–96); the wild animal stories in *Sandford and Merton* (1783); accounts of 'wild' children; and the adventures of faithful dogs in wild places, such as Martha Sherwood's *The Little Woodman and his Dog Caesar* (1818) and R. M. Ballantyne's *The Dog Crusoe* (1860). What all these have in common is their 'wild' setting, often geographically distant and exoticised, and increasingly moving into colonial spaces that offer scope for masculine adventure and violence. I will briefly discuss Kipling's and Seton's relation to their predecessors, and then pause to investigate the way Victorian science constructed the evolutionary child, a development highly relevant to both sets of stories.

The colonial context of the wild animal story is clear in 'The Council of Quadrupeds', where the animals are presented as an analogue to the natives of Southern Africa, in their persecution by the white invaders, while their social structure is a more general analogy to the weakness of human solidarity and the failures of revolution. Both these analogies are used and revised in the *Jungle Books*. Kipling turns the colonial analogy around: the craven natives are the object of the animals' revenge in 'Letting in the Jungle', and the offstage imperial power is implicitly their friend. His animals' social structure is a hierarchy that is offered as a model to human society. In the *Jungle Books*, there is no vestige of the kindness-to-animals message that is so strongly present in Trimmer's and other eighteenth-century talking animal stories, and in the ongoing tradition of the animal autobiography. Neither is

---

1   Trimmer, *Story of the Robins*, p. 205.

Kipling overtly interested in the detailed and accurate natural historical information purveyed by Kingsley, Gatty and their eighteenth-century predecessors. Instead he gives us mythic and legendary accounts of animal origins, customs and relations with mankind – a tendency pushed to comic extremes in his *Just So Stories*.

Through the presence of the wild child Mowgli, he also brings into question the interconnected relations between the animal and the human, the child and the adult. Here there is an obvious debt to Kingsley, as Mowgli, like Tom, grows up from animal to adult: but for Kipling the beasts Mowgli at first identifies with are not 'beastly' but noble. They do not need any humanoid presences, like Mrs Bedonebyasyoudid, in order to teach Mowgli effective practical and moral lessons. Kipling himself suggests a debt to Gatty's talking animal stories, writing that as a boy he 'imitated' the *Parables*, 'and thought I was original'.[2] 'Inferior Animals' could have provided a model for animal community and debate on the animal/human relationship, though Kipling takes his animals more seriously than Gatty's comic rooks. Like Gatty and Kingsley, Kipling is interested in the parabolic, analogical and fabular possibilities of animal stories, but not in a Christian context. Instead, his use of myth and fable is a self-conscious return to the supposed thought-patterns of 'primitive' men, while at the same time rejecting the 'superstitious' elements of the 'primitive'. In common also with Kingsley and Gatty, and the animals of 'The Council of Quadrupeds', Kipling allows his animals to talk.

Here he differs from the adventure stories by Day, Sherwood and Ballantyne, which also have less of an allegorical or fabular dimension than Kipling. These stories seem to lead on into a parallel tradition of non-speaking wild animal stories, often centred biographically, rather than autobiographically, on individual animals. Grenby remarks that the fight between the dog and wolf in Sherwood's *The Little Woodman* (1818), places it 'in a tradition of animal stories which was not yet fully under way ... but which would reach its zenith with Jack London's *The Call of the Wild* (1903) and *White Fang* (1906), and Eric Knight's *Lassie Come Home* (1940)'.[3] Ernest Thompson Seton is a key figure here, moving deliberately from talking to non-talking animals in stories set in the wild spaces of North America. Seton is deeply invested in the natural historical truth of his stories, which embroiled him in a bitter controversy. Like Gatty and Kingsley, he was an amateur naturalist. He also purveys an anti-cruelty message, through his attempts to give us the animal's-eye perspective. This message is in the service of a conservationist creed: for Seton, the 'wild' and its animals are to be preserved as a heritage for humanity. Like Kipling's, his animal characters are for the most part noble, embodying the highest human virtues. Both writers also have a strongly didactic, educational element in their stories: Mowgli is taught by wise, older animals, while Seton repeatedly shows us animals teaching their young, and emphasises what we can learn from them. It is perhaps not surprising, then, that both Kipling and Seton were involved in the Boy Scout

---

2   Rudyard Kipling, *Something of Myself* [1937] (London, 1964), p. 32. See also J. M. S. Tompkins, *The Art of Rudyard Kipling* (London, 1959), pp. 59–60.

3   Grenby, Introduction.

movements, which took ideas and imagery from their animal stories. A complex of assumptions about children, gender, animals and the wild can be unpacked here.

Before embarking on a closer examination of Kipling's, and then Seton's animal stories, I want to look at the way Victorian science was constructing the child in relation to language and to animals, and reinterpreting the Rousseau-inspired connection between child, animal and savage in the light of evolutionary theory. In 1877, the journal *Mind* contained a translation of an article, first published in 1876, by Hypolite Taine, on 'The Acquisition of Language by Children'. In the next number, there followed an article by Darwin, 'Biographical Sketch of an Infant', corroborating much of what Taine had said, though, typically of Darwin, without formulating as many conclusions. Taine both compares the child's language to animal noises, and differentiates it from them: 'she takes delight in twitter like a bird', but 'if I compare her to animals ... I find that ... she far surpasses them in the delicacy and abundance of her expressive intonations.' Nevertheless, the child's speech is given a natural origin – for.instance, her word 'Ham' for 'eat' is described as 'the *natural vocal gesture* of a person snapping up anything'.[4] Darwin's article rather differently also suggests a natural origin for language – the musical intonations of the child support the theory 'that before man uttered articulate language, he uttered notes in a true musical scale as does the anthropoid ape Hylobates'.[5]

As well as comparing the child to animals, both Darwin and Taine compare her (or him, in Darwin's case) to primitive peoples. For Taine, 'the mental state of a child' is in many respects 'that of primitive peoples at the poetical and mythological stage'.[6] For Darwin, less positively, the child's fears may be 'the inherited effect of real dangers and abject superstitions during ancient savage times'.[7] This connection is put in a larger framework by Taine, using one of the staples of Victorian evolutionary thinking – recapitulation theory: 'the child presents in a passing state the natural characteristics that are found in a fixed state in primitive civilizations, very much as the human embryo presents in a passing state the physical characteristics that are found in a fixed state in the classes of inferior animals.'[8] Ontogeny recapitulates phylogeny here – that is, the development of each individual parallels and is causally connected to, the development of the race as a whole.

Recapitulation theory reappears insistently in writing on child psychology in the 1880s. For instance, James Crichton-Browne in an essay on 'Education and the Nervous System' (1883), sees children as 'diamond editions of very remote ancestors, full of savage whims and impulses, and savage rudiments of virtue', and James Sully exclaims in an Introduction to a book on early childhood (1885), 'How curiously do the naïve conceptions of nature, the fanciful animistic ideas of things,

---

4   Taine, pp. 252, 257.
5   Charles Darwin, 'Biographical Sketch of an Infant', *Mind*, 2/7 (1877): 293.
6   Taine, p. 258.
7   Darwin, 'Biographical Sketch', p. 288.
8   Taine, p. 259.

and the rude awe and terror, which there is good reason to attribute to our earliest human ancestors, reflect themselves in the language of the child!'[9] Here we can see the Romantic child being reconstituted as the evolutionary child, more primitive and more fanciful, literally closer to animals, than adults. This fanciful or poetical propensity in the child is applied by Taine specifically to the phenomenon of talking animal stories:

> If we speak to her of an object ... her first question always is – 'What does it say?' – 'What does the rabbit say? – 'What does the bird say?' – 'What does the horse say?' – 'What does the big tree say?' Animal or tree, she immediately meets it as a person and wants to know its thoughts and words; that is what she cares about; by a spontaneous induction she imagines it like herself, like us; she humanises it. This disposition is found among primitive peoples, the more strong the more primitive they are; in the Edda, especially in the Mabinogion, animals have also the gift of speech.[10]

Talking animal stories, while no longer proper to civilised man, are appropriate to both children and savages.

While the child in recapitulation theory appears almost as a 'missing link' between animal and human, primitive and civilised, at the same time a hierarchy is assumed, inferior/superior animals, primitive/civilised man, a hierarchy which has implications for the colonisation of less 'civilised' nations. If the 'primitive' is constructed as a 'child', as well as the child as primitive, this licenses the imperial power to take on the colonial role of 'parent'. So 'the studious and insistent infantilization of the primitive enacts and legitimates a practice of domination', producing 'the familial trope of a world in which mother England would be caretaker to lesser children of imperial Gods'.[11] These are the frameworks of belief within which Kipling is writing. Recapitulation theory was already important to both Tennyson and Kingsley, but they used it to figure the possibility of a moral and spiritual ascent from the animal, the ape and tiger, to the human, within every individual. Kingsley also implies that there are 'degenerate' human types or races who slip down the scale of evolution. Kipling puts these ideas into a full-blown colonial context, removing any religious analogies. At the same time, he differentiates between good and bad versions of the 'primitive', as we shall see: the poetic and mythic, and the degenerate and superstitious. In the process, hierarchy is upset, in that noble talking animals are often better than abject natives. On the other hand, animal society itself preserves a strict hierarchy among its members.

---

9 Sally Shuttleworth and Jenny Bourne Taylor (eds), *Embodied Selves: An anthology of psychological texts* (Oxford, 1998), pp. 340, 343, quoting James Crichton Browne, 'Education and the Nervous System', in M. A. Morris (ed.), *The Book of Health* (London, 1883), pp. 379–80, and James Sully, Introduction to Bernard Perez, *The First Three Years of Childhood* (London, 1885), pp. v–ix.

10 Taine, p. 258.

11 Don Randall, *Kipling's Imperial Boy* (Houndmills, 2000), p. 44; Zoreh T. Sullivan, *Narratives of Empire* (Cambridge, 1993), p. 2.

In his story 'Tiger, Tiger', from the first *Jungle Book*, Kipling draws attention to the newness, the modernity, of his animal stories as opposed to the old, superstitious kind. Mowgli, brought up in the Jungle by wolves, has returned to the human village, and he listens to old Buldeo, the village hunter, telling 'wonderful' stories 'of the ways of beasts in the Jungle'. Mowgli, who 'knew something about what they were talking of, had to cover his face not to show that he was laughing'. Buldeo explains that the tiger known by Mowgli as Shere Khan 'was inhabited by the ghost of a wicked old money-lender', who limped, and this is why the tiger limps. Mowgli intervenes to pour scorn on this superstition: 'Are all these tales such cobwebs and moontalk? … That tiger limps because he was born lame, as everyone knows. To talk of the soul of a money-lender in a beast that never had the courage of a jackal is child's talk.'[12]

The use of 'child' as a term of abuse here is interesting, associating it with fantasy and myth-making. In contrast, Kipling is implicitly claiming that *his* stories about Mowgli and the Jungle are 'grown-up', demystified, accurate. And yet they are not. In 'How Fear Came', Hathi the Elephant tells the story of how the Tiger got his stripes, as 'the trees and creepers marked him' on the orders of the Elephant god Tha, 'and made him the striped thing that we see'.[13] This is for some reason an acceptable kind of mythologising, while Buldeo's is not. And of course the Mowgli stories in the *Jungle Books* are also premised on an acceptance of the 'childish' device of talking animals. In the only Mowgli story addressed to adults, 'In the Rukh', the animals do not talk. It is the line Kipling draws between acceptable and unacceptable myth-making that I am going to investigate in what follows.

Kipling's attitude to 'primitive' people like Buldeo in 'Tiger, Tiger' resembles Darwin's to the 'abject superstitions' of savages. On the other hand, Taine implies that the child can reclaim as fiction what the adult has to lose as primitive superstition. Sandra Kemp, discussing the importance of the 'childlike' in Kipling's work, sees a 'correspondence between the animistic eye of the small child and certain supernatural beliefs', while 'Kipling attributes the same kind of paranormal or even magical powers to the Indians.' This attribution is in line with the pervasive colonial equation of native equals child.[14] Achar, however, points out that natives in Kipling's fiction are presented as both child-like, and childish.[15] In reclaiming the primitive power of myth for children's fiction, Kipling carefully distinguishes between these two aspects, rewriting, reformulating and framing the old 'primitive' traditions within a modern, anthropological understanding. As Dieter Petzold says of Kipling's *Just So*

---

12 Rudyard Kipling, *The Jungle Book* [1894] (London: 1961), pp. 96–7.
13 Rudyard Kipling, *The Second Jungle Book*.[1895] (London: 1962), p. 28.
14 Sandra Kemp, *Kipling's Hidden Narratives* (Oxford, 1988), p. 18.
15 Radha Achar, 'The Child in Kipling's Fiction', *The Literary Criterion*, 2/4 (1987): 46–53

Stories, these are not just parodies of folktales, but 'sophisticated ... recreations of the form'.[16]

Some of this procedure of recreation can be illuminated by a comparison of the *Jungle Books* with *Beast and Man in India*, written by John Lockwood Kipling, Rudyard's father, and published three years before the first of the *Jungle Books*. There are many intertextual connections between the two men's work: the epigraphs to most of the chapters in *Beast and Man* are poems by Rudyard, while the *Jungle Books* are illustrated by John Lockwood. *Beast and Man* is a compendium of folktale, observation and myth. Interestingly, it is introduced by a discussion of cruelty to animals in India, in which John Lockwood argues against sentimentalised Western accounts of Indian religions that forbid the taking of animal life. John Lockwood sees the Indians, despite their official religions, as just as 'human' as the rest of the world. Kindness to animals is just as much a 'modern' idea in India as it is elsewhere. Westerners too do not always take their religion seriously. The Indians, in his argument, have the advantage, in that there is no casual cruelty of the stone-throwing, bird-nesting variety: perhaps this is why Rudyard's children's stories never take up the issue. John Lockwood does, however, criticise the Indians, in that 'the High Gods described in the works one may call "official" may not be quite dead, but they are practically superseded in favour of witchcraft, demonolatry, and fetishism.'[17] These are the kind of beliefs represented in the *Jungle Books* by Buldeo, and the cruel villagers who want to burn Mowgli's adoptive mother as a witch, and kill him as a Demon. The natives are constructed as both primitive and degenerate. A Western scholar, like John Lockwood, may know more of their 'real', original religion than they do: and indeed in Rudyard's novel *Kim*, the keeper of the museum in Lahore (John Lockwood's own position) is able to give the Lama information about the texts and places of his religion that the monk himself does not have.

As well as distinguishing between original and degraded beliefs, John Lockwood also distinguishes between accurate natural history, and inaccurate or superstitious reports. In the main text of *Beast and Man*, as well as reporting native beliefs about animals, he often rates them as to accuracy, and emphasises where they are attested to either by his own observation or by European witnesses. For instance, speaking of the mongoose, he pours scorn on the 'fixed' native belief that 'the mongoose knows a remedy for snake-bite – a plant which no-one has seen or can identify.' Instead he insists that 'the mongoose has only its quickness of attack and its thick fur for safeguard.' Both these points are repeated almost verbatim in 'Rikki-Tikki-Tavi' in *The Jungle Book*. Similarly, John Lockwood relates the native belief that 'wild elephants assemble together to dance!' Colonel Lewin, who told the story, himself discovered 'a large beaten place in the forest, the floor beaten hard and smooth, like that of a native hut', which the 'men' said was an elephant's ballroom. In the face of this white man's testimony, John Lockwood concedes, 'there is no reason why

---

16 Dieter Petzold, 'Fantasy out of Myth and Fable: Animal Stories in Rudyard Kipling and Richard Adams', *Children's Literature Association Quarterly*, 12/1 (1987): 15–19.

17   John Lockwood Kipling, *Beast and Man in India* (London, 1891), p. 7.

he [the elephant] should not dance', and confesses envy of 'the Assam coolie who said he had been a hidden unbidden guest at an elephant ball'. This story forms the basis of 'Toomai of the Elephants' in *The Jungle Book*, where little Toomai witnesses the dance, and his report is vouched for when Petersen Sahib, the white man in charge of the elephants, goes next day and discovers the 'ballroom' in the forest. John Lockwood also discusses the 'supernatural' belief that Indian ascetics have a power over wild creatures. He supplies instead a naturalistic explanation of why this may appear to be so: 'a bored hermit … might amuse himself with the easy feat of taming a wild animal; but here surely, the miracle would end.'[18] Kipling's story 'The Miracle of Purun Bhagat', in *The Second Jungle Book*, takes up this point, developing it much more sympathetically, as Purun Bhagat's stillness attracts the animals, and enables him to read their warnings when a landslip is imminent. But for both Kiplings the 'miracle' is a natural one.

What I am arguing here, is that a comparison with *Beast and Man* reveals some of the ways in which the *Jungle Books* purge and modernize 'primitive' beliefs, setting them in a framework of Western scientific naturalism. The 'Darwinism' of Kipling's view of nature has often been remarked. John Lockwood spells out how this world-view can be reconciled with Indian beliefs:

> Does the survival of respect for monkeys, amounting at times to a definite acknowledgement of kinship, indicate the early arrival of Hindu philosophers at the latest conclusion of European Evolutionists? … the Hindu respect for life, the admission of the essential unity of the life-spark, whether in man or moss, and the special regard for the ancestral monkey, its deification, and the traditions of its aptitude for speech, labour and war, [are] proofs that the philosophy of the East has for ages sat in tranquil occupation of a peak of discovery to which the vanguard of Western science has but now attained.[19]

This respect for Hindu philosophy does not extend to any spiritual content. It is interesting that Rudyard Kipling in the *Jungle Books* excludes or ridicules any belief in transmigration of souls, reincarnation, or even the question of the 'soul' in man or beast at all. This is an aspect of Eastern and Western religion that he dismisses here as superstition. The religion of the Mowgli stories encompasses Law and Myth, but not an immaterial or transcendental dimension. Significantly, in *Kim*, though the Lama's beliefs are respected (unlike Buldeo's), his religious experience is also given a naturalistic explanation – falling into a brook during an epileptic fit.

If we see Kipling as purging native beliefs of their superstitious content, and aligning them with a more scientific, Western approach, it seems at first anomalous that he makes his animals talk. But here too he frames the phenomenon with scientific and pseudo-scientific explanations, both accounting for, and showing up the fictiveness of what he is doing. Again Buldeo stands for native superstition, when he 'embroidered the story of his adventures in the Jungle, till he ended by

---

18 Ibid., pp. 350, 229–30, 397.
19 Ibid., pp. 81–2.

saying that Akela stood up on his hind legs and talked like a man'.[20] Paradoxically, of course, the animals do talk *like* man, but it is always emphasised that it is a different kind of language. In *The Second Jungle Book*, as the animals encircle Buldeo, they talk unconcernedly, 'for their speech began below the lowest end of the scale that untrained human beings can hear.'[21] In order for the readers to understand animal speech then, they must accept that what they are being offered is a 'translation'. This idea had been used before, on the original title page of *Black Beauty* for instance, but Kipling takes the device further, inventing a narratorial persona as 'editor'. The 'editor' appears explicitly as translator in a headnote to one of the interspersed poems: 'Just to give you an idea of the immense variety of the Jungle Law, I have translated into verse (Baloo always recited them in a kind of sing-song) a few of the laws that apply to the wolves.'[22] How, then, does the editor know this language? The very tongue-in-cheek Preface claims that the stories come from many animal informants: the editor, as a man who understands animal language, seems to be a forerunner of Hugh Lofting's Doctor Dolittle.

Distinct from this 'editor', the first-person narrator of 'Her Majesty's Servants' (1894), can only understand some kinds of 'beast language'. He overhears the talk of a number of animals in the service of the British Army, and can understand them because 'I knew enough of beast language – not wild-beast language, but camp-beast language, of course – from the natives.' The assumption here that the natives are more likely to know animal language is interesting. In the 'Mowgli' stories, the animals' speech is interspersed with Indian words, and the 'editor' intervenes to put in brackets a translation, for instance, 'the *Gidur Log* [the Jackal People]'.[23] In the story 'Quiquern', which concerns Inuit (Eskimo) people, terms in their language are translated in a similar way: '"Aua! Ja aua!" (Go to the right). "Choiachoi! Ja choiachoi!" (Go to the left). "Ohaha!" (Stop)'.[24] Of course, this is a redundant convention, in that Kipling's 'editor' is 'translating' the rest of what the animals or Inuit are saying – the 'native' words are sprinkled in to give a flavour of authenticity. But these words reveal that Kipling is treating the animal language as if it were a 'native' dialect, translated by a Western scholar (like his father). The connection between native speech and animal speech is also suggested in another way. In the Mowgli stories, the animals speak in a heightened, archaic form of English, in line with their primitive and poetic status: '"Out!" snapped Father Wolf. "Out and hunt with thy master. Thou hast done harm enough for one night." "I go," said Tabaqui quietly. "Ye can hear Shere Khan below in the thickets. I might have saved myself the message."'[25] It is significant that in *Kim*, native speech is also in this archaic register.

---

20 Kipling, *Jungle Book*, p. 93.
21 Kipling, *Second Jungle Book*, p. 68.
22 Ibid., p. 29.
23 Kipling, *Jungle Book*, pp. 251, 4.
24 Kipling, *Second Jungle Book*, p. 188.
25 Kipling, *Jungle Book*, p. 8.

As well as intervening in order to translate 'foreign' words, the editor also explains phrases that result from the different cultural perspective of the animals: 'the stinging fly that comes out of white smoke [Hathi meant the rifle]'.[26] Here, the animals invent metaphors for objects made or controlled by man. Fire is called 'the Red Flower'. This device has a history dating back at least to Barbauld's 'Travelled Ant', and father robin's attempts to describe guns and ovens in Trimmer's *Fabulous Histories*. There is an attempt here to make animal speech 'realistic', in that it has no words for the man-made, and to use it to inhabit a more 'primitive' type of consciousness. In 'Her Majesty's Servants', each animal has a different perspective on battle, dependent partly on whether they have the ability to imagine consequences or not. The unimaginative buffaloes are braver than the imaginative Elephant. The animals in this story, however, speak in an everyday colloquial register: '"It's disgraceful," he said, blowing out his nostrils. "Those camels have racketed through our lines again – the third time this week. How's a horse to keep his condition if he isn't allowed to sleep."' The difference between this type of language, and the heightened diction of the Mowgli stories could be explained by the camp beast/wild beast dichotomy, except that the wild seals in 'The White Seal' are just as colloquial. In this story, animal language is used at times for social satire, very much in the manner of Kingsley in *The Water Babies*: '"The beach is disgracefully crowded this season. I've met at least a hundred seals from Lukannon Beach, house-hunting. Why can't people stay where they belong?"'[27]

While Kipling did later publish all the Mowgli stories together, in the original *Jungle Books* they are interspersed with stories such as 'The White Seal' and 'Her Majesty's Servants', that use animal language in quite different ways, and also, as we shall see, play the animal/man relationship in quite different ways. In 'Toomai of the Elephants', 'The Miracle of Purun Baghat' and 'Quiquern', the animals do not speak at all. In 'The Undertakers' they parody 'native' speech: '"It is anything the Protector of the Poor pleases. I am his servant – not the servant of the thing that crosses the river"', says the jackal, fawning on the crocodile.[28] This variety of different types of animal speech, and mixture of talking and non-talking animal stories is reminiscent of the medley in *Evenings At Home*, and also in the later *Aunt Judy's Magazine*, edited by Margaret Gatty, which similarly mixes all kinds of naturalistic and fabular animal stories. Kipling wrote of his attachment to *Aunt Judy's*.[29] The effect here is to reveal animal speech as a fictional device, which can be used in a variety of different ways. Kipling's procedures both 'clean up' the talking animals device, making it more 'realistic' and 'scientific', and undermine it as ultimately fictional, a form of play.

This does not mean that the Mowgli stories don't also use animal language as part of a serious and often painful investigation of the hero's ambivalent status

---

26 Kipling, *Second Jungle Book*, p. 26.
27 Kipling, *Jungle Book*, pp. 252, 130.
28 Kipling, *Second Jungle Book*, p. 128.
29 Kipling, *Something of Myself*, p. 2.

between and among the hierarchical categories man/animal, adult/child, sahib/native, sometimes questioning and inverting these hierarchical relationships. By choosing to write a 'wild child' story, Kipling inevitably raises taxonomical questions about the definition of 'man' and the status of language in that definition. In *Beast and Man*, Lockwood Kipling mentions that 'India is probably the cradle of wolf-child stories, which are here universally believed and supported by a cloud of testimony, including in the famous Lucknow case of a wolf boy the evidence of European witnesses.'[30] As in other cases, European testimony seems to make this event acceptable to Rudyard Kipling as the basis for his stories. There had been several widely reported accounts of European wild children in the eighteenth century, which had been used by a variety of thinkers to debate the relation of man and animal, some natural historians actually placing the children in a newly invented category, *Homines feri*, between man and ape. Others saw them as evidence of human degeneration. Enlightened believers in human progress and the developmental possibilities of childhood were disappointed when attempts to educate the children, and especially to teach them language, ended in failure. On Rousseau's theory, a natural upbringing isolated from human society should have produced superior beings. As Julia Douthwaite points out, the wild children, like other subjects of Rousseau-inspired experiments, 'made a poor showing, revealing human frailty and limitations instead of confirming notions of unlimited progress'.[31] This also seems to have been true of the Wolf Boy of Lucknow, who was discovered in 1844. He never learnt language, though he was able to understand and obey signs. At any opportunity, he tried to escape back to the jungle.

The chief details that Kipling seems to have taken from the Lucknow story are the friendship between the boy and several wolves who come to visit him and play with him in his captivity; and his recognition as her stolen son by a native woman. Kipling ignores the linguistic limitations consistently reported of wild children, and makes Mowgli not only fluent in animal language, but also able to pick up native language with ease. In his stories, language is not an important distinguishing mark between animal and man, or between 'wild' man and civilised man. This could be part of Kipling's Darwinism: we have seen that Darwin placed human language on a continuum leading from the sounds made by animals. The most important characteristic of Mowgli seems to be his adaptability, his ability to know all the animal languages and ways, as well as those of men, and to move between the two worlds, while being at home in neither. He is an 'amphibian', Mowgli being the Hindu word for frog. We can read this either as a comment on man's divided nature, his literal 'kinship' with the beasts as stressed by Darwin, or as the coloniser's frustrated desire to blend into the culture he rules.

As a comment on 'man', the 'frog' image contrasts with the 'metamorphosis' trope so often used by earlier writers like Gatty and Kingsley. The transformation

---

30 John Lockwood Kipling, *Beast and Man*, pp. 313–14.

31 Julia V. Douthwaite, *The Wild Girl, Natural Man and the Monster* (Chicago and London, 2002), pp. 12, 135.

of tadpole to frog, caterpillar to butterfly, was for these writers a natural sign and a metaphor of man's transforming spiritual potential, his animal nature and his immortal soul. But Kipling's 'frog' remains a dual-natured frog. Mowgli does use animal imagery that hints at human evolution via recapitulation: '"Mowgli the Frog have I been," said he to himself; "Mowgli the Wolf have I said that I am. Now Mowgli the Ape must I be before I am Mowgli the Buck. At the end I shall be Mowgli the Man."'[32] Notice however that the progression is not clear – it is not from Ape to Man, Buck intervenes. This is because Mowgli is talking about his tactics in misleading the Red Dogs to their deaths: first he needs to climb through the trees like an Ape, and then leap down the rocks like a Buck – adaptability is what is being stressed. It is never clear that Mowgli ends up unequivocally as Man, or that he wasn't Man all along. Susan Walsh has pointed out the way in which the Mowgli stories cannot deliver a difference between human and animal 'that is not implied by and dependent upon its other'.[33] More than this, the stories seem to proliferate ambiguities and contradictions around this point, which are further emphasised by the context of the other stories with which they were published in the *Jungle Books*.

So, in *The Jungle Book*, the first three stories, which all concern Mowgli and his wild friends, contrast with the last three, 'Rikki-Tikki-Tavi', 'Toomai of the Elephants' and 'Her Majesty's Servants', which all deal approvingly with animals in the service of man, though in 'Toomai' we see a serving animal returning briefly to his life in the jungle. But the middle story, 'The White Seal', casts man the hunter as the villain, and the white seal leads his people to a man-free paradise. This story follows on immediately from 'Tiger, Tiger', which celebrates Mowgli's hunting of Shere Khan. In *The Second Jungle Book*, 'How Fear Came', which tells of violence and dissension among the animals, is followed by 'The Miracle of Purun Bhagat', where wild animals are helpful messengers to the hermit, and save the villagers from the landslide: nature and man are in harmony. This is however followed by 'Letting in the Jungle', where the wild animals destroy the native village: nature and man are at variance. The next story, 'The Undertakers' takes this theme to an extreme, focusing on a man-eating crocodile and his scavenger friends. But 'The King's Ankus' depends on a contrast between the innocent, jungle-bred.Mowgli, and the destructive passions of civilisation, as the jewelled ankus that Mowgli throws away causes the deaths of five men. 'Quiquern' then shows primitive man as seal-hunter, reversing the perspective of the earlier 'White Seal'. 'Red Dog' again emphasises violence and conflict within Mowgli's jungle, and 'The Spring Running' ejects Mowgli from an animal world that longer pays him attention. It is hard not to see the contrasts between these stories, and the different ways they play the animal/ man relationship as deliberate, particularly in the light of the different uses of animal language that I have already discussed. Kipling is running through all the different ways in which human and animal can relate and be defined.

---

32 Kipling, *Second Jungle Book*, p. 242.

33 Susan Walsh, 'Untheming the Theme: The Child in Wolf's Clothing', PhD Thesis, University of Reading, 2001, p. 49.

Within the Mowgli stories, one of the chief ways in which Mowgli's difference from the animals is asserted is through his gaze, rather than his possession of, or potential for language. This difference is present right from his first introduction to the Jungle: 'he discovered that if he stared hard at any wolf, the wolf would be forced to drop his eyes, and so he used to stare for fun.'[34] Later on, Mowgli uses this power more deliberately: 'Once more Mowgli stared, as he had stared at the rebellious cubs, full into the beryl-green eyes till the red glare behind their green went out like the light of a lighthouse.'[35] Bagheera, out-stared like this, drops his head in submission, but Mowgli immediately whispers 'Brother – Brother – Brother', and consoles him. Here, we come across a contradiction that runs right through these stories, and is intimately involved with the deployment of animal language. There is a persistent ambiguity as to whether knowing animal language means an admission of kinship, or a means to mastery. Mowgli is taught the 'Master Words' of the Jungle, in the speech of different species – the bird-people, the snake-people – so that he will be able to say 'We be of one blood, you and I' in any language. Human and animal are related, but knowing the words is also a kind of trick, by which Mowgli compels the animals to do his will. The stories chart not only Mowgli's painful division between his animal and his human natures – 'I am two Mowglis' he sings – and his inability to be accepted into either community, Jungle or village, but also his gradual rise to dominance in the Jungle, so that he ends up acknowledged 'Master of the Jungle', recognised as such by both Hathi the elephant and Kaa the python, previously the wisest and most powerful.

This rise to dominance by Mowgli might suggest that as he grows from boy to man, he becomes less 'animal' and more 'human'. But, as I have said, he possesses the power of the gaze from the beginning. Kipling also, unobtrusively, makes him a biped from the start. The wolf-boy of Lucknow had 'hardened marks upon his knees and elbows, from having gone on all fours', and had to be beaten to make him stand and walk.[36] But Mowgli's marks are only from wolf-bites, and when he first approaches the wolves, it is as 'a naked brown baby who could just walk'. As a child, he is able to wield fire, 'the Red Flower', another of man's prerogatives. And yet when he goes to the village, it is his animal nature that predominates, and he fears houses as 'traps'.[37] The stories relate a to-and-fro process by which Mowgli is alternately rejected by Jungle and village: he belongs to both, and to neither. These two worlds are also not clearly distinguished: sometimes the Jungle is purer and more innocent than the corrupt village; sometimes it is traversed by dissension and violence. The story 'How Fear Came' relates a Jungle version of the Fall: a peaceful animal kingdom is destroyed when the First Tiger kills a buck, and then goes on to kill man. Man is ambiguously placed here: he is named as 'Fear', and at first he

---

34 Kipling, *Jungle Book*, p. 25.

35 Kipling, *Second Jungle Book*, p. 85.

36 W. H. Sleeman, *A Journey Through the Kingdom of Oude 1849–1850* (London: 1858).

37 Kipling, *Jungle Book*, pp. 10, 33–4, 92.

is naked, helpless and frightened before the Tiger. But after the first man has been killed, men return with weapons, and embody 'Fear' in a different way.

The Jungle is also always hierarchical. Walsh points out how Mowgli's innocence and scorn of the caste-system in the village is belied by his knowledge of the hierarchies of the Jungle.[38] In the Jungle, Tabaqui the jackal is despised as a lesser being; the monkeys are taboo outcasts whom the other animals ignore; and the Red Dogs are particularly disliked not only because of their destructiveness, but 'because they did not smell like the Free People, because they did not live in caves, and, above all, because they had hair between their toes while he and his friends were clean-footed'.[39] The 'Free People' are the wolves, but they lose this status when they become rebellious and leaderless. Only when there is a Chief Wolf who imposes the Law can they be 'Free'. This Jungle hierarchy is also apparent in that Mowgli, as a child, is under the tutelage of three especially wise animals, Bagheera the panther, Balou the bear and Kaa the snake. These three have been seen as an allegory of the trinity, Love, Strength and Wisdom.[40] Balou in particular is full of didactic and useful advice. Animal language is the voice of the parent or educator, a voice from 'above', not from the bottom of the hierarchy.

The final *Jungle Book* story, 'The Spring Running', seems to send Mowgli finally out, as a grown-up, to join the human world, but it ends with his return to the Jungle for a last farewell. The story is full of ambiguities, that question and belie Mowgli's role as 'Master', and his difference from the animals. The animals' language has changed, because of the Spring, 'the Time of New Talk', and they no longer pay Mowgli any attention, as 'they were busy hunting and fighting and killing and singing.'[41] The unspoken subtext is that this is all to do with *mating*, and that it is sex, too, that drives Mowgli back to humankind. As Darwin says, 'The sexes of many animals incessantly call for each other during the breeding-season; and in not a few cases the male endeavours thus to excite the female.'[42] This 'new talk' excludes Mowgli, and threatens to upset the ordered hierarchy of the Jungle and its language. Mowgli rebukes Bagheera the panther for his childish behaviour: '"*is* it well for the Black Panther so to mouth and cough, and howl and roll? Remember, we be the Masters of the Jungle, thou and I."' Bagheera answers,

'Indeed, yes; I hear, Man-cub … We be surely the Masters of the Jungle! Who is so strong as Mowgli? Who so wise?' There was a curious drawl in the voice that made Mowgli turn to see whether by any chance the Black Panther were making fun of him, for the Jungle is full of words that sound like one thing, but mean another. 'I said we be beyond question

---

38 Walsh, pp. 32, 35.

39 Kipling, *Second Jungle Book*, p. 227.

40 Juliet McMaster, 'The Trinity Archetype in The Jungle Books and The Wizard of Oz', *Children's Literature*, 20 (1992): 90–110.

41 Kipling, *Second Jungle Book*, p. 291.

42 Charles Darwin, *The Expression of the Emotions in Man and Animals* (London, 1904), p. 85.

Masters of the Jungle,' Bagheera repeated. 'Have I done wrong? I did not know that the Man-cub no longer lay upon the ground. Does he fly, then?'[43]

Bagheera's irony, and the notion, first introduced here in the last Mowgli story, that the Jungle language could have double meanings, undercut Mowgli's pretensions to be Master. Once animals have been allowed language of any complexity, irony can creep in, and upset fixed animal/human hierarchies. The child, who is identified with the animals and their speech, participates in these inversions. 'Child', as we have seen, is a pivotal term in the relationship of man and animals: the link to the 'primitive' and 'poetic' world of talking animals, and the 'primitive' who must be civilised in order to become an adult. In 'The Spring Running', the sexuality that unbalances Mowgli's relation of dominance to the animals, and sends him out to humankind, is paradoxically seen as 'childish' behaviour on the animals' part, their very 'animality'. Sexuality is Mowgli's unruly animal nature that he cannot fully master, as well as being the sign of his grown-up humanity.

Whether we read Mowgli as leaving behind the 'animal' and moving on to the 'human' as he grows up depends also on how we read the story 'In the Rukh', written and published before the *Jungle Books*, but dealing with the end of Mowgli's story. At the end of 'Tiger, Tiger', the last of the Mowgli stories in the first *Jungle Book*, we are told that Mowgli 'was not always alone, because years afterward he became a man and married. But that is a story for grown-ups.'[44] This comment has been taken to refer to 'In the Rukh', a story about the grown-up Mowgli, written for grown-ups. In this story, sex and then marriage act to integrate Mowgli safely into human organisations, as he takes a job, with a pension, as a ranger under Gisbourne Sahib of the Department of Woods and Forests. The most notable difference between this story 'for grown-ups' and the stories for children is that the animals do not talk. Mowgli speaking animal language is observed from outside, from an adult human point of view: 'He put out his hand to sign for silence, and still lying on his back called aloud thrice – with a deep gurgling cry that was new to Gisbourne.'[45] The narrator/translator, who could speak to animals because he was speaking to children, has disappeared.

Mowgli's equality with the animals is also not evident: his four wolf-brothers appear here more like performing dogs. Mowgli is seen 'playing upon a rude bamboo flute, to whose music four huge wolves danced solemnly on their hind legs', confirming Buldeo's (false) claim in 'Tiger! Tiger!' that Akela stood on his hind legs. In *The Second Jungle Book*, as the animals encircle Buldeo, they talk unconcernedly, as the pitch of their speech cannot be heard by humans. The sort of 'gurgle' that Gisbourne hears is not evident: animal language is a silent secret; and of course there is no question in the *Jungle Books* of the animals 'standing on their hind legs'. The animals are diminished in this grown-up story, and Mowgli is

---

43 Kipling, *Second Jungle Book*, pp. 265–6.
44 Kipling, *Jungle Book*, p. 121.
45 Kipling, *Many Inventions* (London, 1893), p. 205.

reduced to a government employee. He is 'placed' in history and literature: 'He's like the illustrations in the Classical Dictionary', thinks Gisbourne. Mowgli appears 'in the very form and likeness of that Greek god who is so lavishly described in the novels'.[46]

But these descriptions, and the fact that he remains in the Jungle, in contact with the wolves, despite entering the service of the empire, gives him a numinous, superhuman rather than human quality, something that is also hinted at in 'The Spring Running': 'As he stood ... strong, tall and beautiful, his long black hair sweeping over his shoulders, the knife swinging at his neck, and his head crowned with a wreath of white jasmine, he might easily have been mistaken for some wild god of a jungle legend.'[47] Moreover, if we take the stories in the order of composition, rather than the order of the plot, we can construct a different picture. The *Jungle Book* stories themselves are not arranged in chronological order, but often ask the reader to 'remember' a previous point in the telling, as the start of a new story. In the reading suggested by Jane Hotchkiss, Kipling begins with 'In the Rukh', which places and contains Mowgli, but then moves on to open up and complicate the story: 'reading the Jungle Book stories, it is hard to imagine the Mowgli we encounter there ever growing up to be Gisbourne's loyal subordinate.'[48] In Hotchkiss' version, the end-point is Mowgli's return to his 'mother' Messua in 'The Spring Running'. Messua, like the woman in the story of the boy of Lucknow, has claimed Mowgli is her long-lost son. But the tiger Shere Khan has earlier claimed to have eaten Mowgli's woodcutter parents in the jungle. It is Messua who first tells Mowgli he is 'beautiful' and gives rise to the god-like description I have quoted. Hotchkiss' reading then ends with this semi-incestuous return to the mother who isn't really the mother. But actually 'The Spring Running' does not end here – Mowgli leaves Messua again ("'Mother, I go'"), and returns to the Jungle again, to say farewell to his friends and teachers. We leave him again about to leave ("'I would not go; but I am drawn by both feet'").[49] This is his characteristic position: always leaving either the Jungle or the village, never in his right place. There is no clear development from the animal to the human: Mowgli, like Darwinian man, is always, painfully, both.

Much Victorian debate on 'Man's' place in nature centred on the notion of the 'missing link'. For the most part, representations of or allusions to this figure in adult literature are monstrous and terrifying: the hairy animalistic Mr Hyde (1886); the tormented half-animal, half-human creatures in Wells's *Island of Dr Moreau* (1896); the atavistic Caliban in Browning's 'Caliban upon Setebos' (1864). All these figures provide comment on existing human nature, and its repulsive 'animal' component. In the domain of children's literature, however, such hybrids can appear charming and enjoyable: the wolf-boy Mowgli, the water baby Tom in Kingsley's novel, and the

---

46 Ibid., pp. 218, 216, 198, 215.

47 Kipling, *Second Jungle Book*, p. 283.

48 Jane Hotchkiss, 'The Jungle of Eden: Kipling, Wolf Boys, and the Colonial Imagination', *Victorian Literature and Culture*, 29/2 (2001): 442.

49 Kipling, *Second Jungle Book*, pp. 287, 293.

talking animals themselves. Somehow, the grown-up Mowgli of 'In the Rukh' also retains his charm – with help from the Classical Dictionary, and by his unambiguous human (or divine) dominance over the animals: he is not half-animal. The child Mowgli, however, often seems so, and is not monstrous; perhaps partly because his type of hybridity is contrasted with another, disgusting, mixture of animal and human in the monkeys, the *Bandar-log*.

As we have seen, prejudice against monkeys as 'aping' humans, too close for comfort, has a long history. Unlike the other animals in the *Jungle Books*, Kipling's monkeys have no language of their own, and no law or leader. On one level, their community is a satire on America: 'What the *Bandar-log* think now the Jungle will think later', they claim.[50] But their status as almost-human is also in question: the monkeys are outcast, they are 'dirt', calling up notions of taboo and the abject. They are so disgusting because they are not human and not animal – they are what these categories define themselves against. So while the stories deal with the ambivalence of Mowgli's animal and human natures, the outcasting of the monkeys preserves a barrier across the obvious evolutionary connection between man and apes. The lawless, parodic behaviour of the monkeys, who steal animal speech and mimic human actions, is extremely carnivalesque. Their defeat and punishment places a limit on the free-play, the inversion of hierarchy, that is allowed in Kipling's use of the talking animal convention. On the other hand, because the monkeys are also used as a parody of certain human societies, the analogy between monkeys and men creeps back in.

Read allegorically, the monkeys have been taken to be both a satire on democracy, and a representation of the degenerate Indian natives . The imperial allegory is the one that has dominated recent criticism of Kipling. Mohanty points out that the *Jungle Books* 'invite an allegorical reading, with the jungle representing the political stage of colonial India'.[51] In these readings both the animals and Mowgli himself provide sites of ambiguous and contradictory readings, sometimes appearing as the natives, sometimes as the colonisers. Perhaps it is this very plasticity that gives them their power as a way of investigating the complex relations between colonised and colonisers. For instance, in Hotchkiss' reading, mentioned above, the contented grown-up Mowgli of 'In the Rukh' is the loyal native, uniting Darwinian and imperial paradigms, 'an evolutionary "missing link" that would obviate the problem of the Mutiny and its possible future re-eruptions; with sepoys like Mowgli, the Mutiny would never have happened'.[52] The *Jungle Book* Mowgli is, however, a much more recalcitrant character, and 'Letting in the Jungle' is read by Hotchkiss as an allegory of the Mutiny, with Mowgli and the animals as the mutineers, though 'paradoxically' they destroy a Hindu village. On the other hand, Don Randall also reads the stories

---

    50 Kipling, *Jungle Book*, p. 53.

    51 Satya P. Mohanty, 'Drawing the Color Line: Kipling and the Culture of Colonial Rule', in Dominick LaCapra (ed.), *The Bounds of Race* (Ithaca, NY, 1991), p. 321.

    52 Hotchkiss, p. 242.

as an allegory of the Mutiny, but he sees the animals as the English exacting revenge on the natives. Particularly persuasive here is his reading of the violence done by the villagers to Messua, which is Mowgli's main reason for revenge. British reports of the Mutiny dwelt on the violence done to British women. But of course this interpretation depends on us taking Mowgli uncomplicatedly as representing the white colonisers, something that several critics have no problem with.[53]

In these readings, Mowgli's 'mastery' of the Jungle represents the white sahib's rule of India, or the fantasy of mastery that sustained that rule. Mowgli is able to 'blend in', to know the natives, as well as to rule them. His mastery is sustained by spying and surveillance: as Brantlinger points out, it is no accident that the spies in *Kim* disguise their activities as an ethnographic survey.[54] Mohanty remarks on the way 'colonial rule consolidated itself through a phenomenal increase in its "scientific" knowledge of the various populations of India as well as the land itself.'[55] So Mowgli's, and the 'editor's', quasi-anthropological understanding of animal language is a form of surveillance and control. But of course Mowgli, unlike Kim, is not white: he is a 'brown baby', son of native woodcutters. Here Robert Young's concept of 'colonial desire' can be invoked: 'the many colonial novels in English betray themselves as driven by desire for the cultural other, for forsaking their own culture.'[56] As Hotchkiss puts it, the 'Mowgli tales offer the vicarious satisfaction of the desire to *be* the other.'[57] Not only can the white reader identify with the brown Mowgli, but Mowgli himself enacts the colonial desire to belong, to be both brother and master, in his conflicted relationship with the Jungle. Such a reading would explain the confusing way in which the Jungle animals duplicate the villagers as representatives of the 'natives'. The animals can then stand for the desirable qualities of the 'primitive', and the villagers are their degenerate negative. At other times, the animals can become the British, just as Mowgli hovers between native and British identities. The Jungle is a liminal space in which opposed identities can mix and exchange themselves. Young mentions the usefulness of language as a metaphor for this kind of hybridity, figured in, for instance, 'creolization'.[58] It is interesting that the animals' language in the *Jungle Book* Mowgli stories is a mixture of heightened, poetic English, and Indian words.

Randall has pointed out the importance of the adolescent boy hero to the liminality of Kipling's Jungle. Boys can hold 'subject positions between opposed categories' such as animal and human, childhood and adulthood, nature and culture, white and dark. He refers to the important influence of recapitulation theory, which places the child with the primitive, and also the primitive as a child, in need of

---

53 Mohanty; John A. McClure, *Kipling and Conrad* (Cambridge, MA and London, 1981); John McBratney, 'Imperial Subjects, Imperial Space', *Victorian Studies*, 35/3 (1992): 277–93; Mark Pafford, *Kipling's Indian Fiction* (Houndmills, 1989).

54 Patrick Brantlinger, *Rule of Darkness* (Ithaca, NY and London, 1988), p. 163.

55 Mohanty, p. 327.

56 Robert J. C. Young, *Colonial Desire* (London, 1995), p. 3.

57 Hotchkiss, p. 242.

58 Young, p. 5.

colonial rule. The white child will of course grow beyond his primitive status, and so 'stands between the European adult and the "primitive" cultural other', enabling mergings and boundary transgressions.[59] Brantlinger also sees the importance of both adolescence and masculinity to the imperial imaginary:

> Yet the 'benighted' regions of the world, occupied by mere natives, offer brilliantly charismatic realms of adventure for white heroes, usually free from the complexities of relations with white women … As against the tame, monotonous realm of domestic routines and responsibilities emerges an alternative – daring, distant, charismatic, but somehow also irresponsible and immature.[60].

Consequently, 'an adolescent quality pervades imperialist literature.'[61] Mowgli as boy hero exemplifies both liminality and aggressive masculine adventure. All the animals he encounters are male, apart from the fierce mother wolf, Raksha 'The Demon'. The animals Mowgli defines himself with are powerful carnivores: wolves, bears, panthers, pythons. As McClure says, 'had he been adopted by the antelopes, for instance, it would have been harder for Kipling to ignore the degree of anxiety and the amount of carnage licensed by his Social Darwinian Jungle Law.'[62] Mowgli, like his mentors, eats meat from animals which he has killed, and almost every story contains a fight. Where we are, briefly, given the perspective of the prey, the hunt is seen as 'life and death fun' by the young bucks.[63] Karen Davis argues that 'animals summoning forth images of things that are "natural, wild, and free" accord with the "masculine" spirit of adventure and conquest idolised by our culture.'[64] However, Kingsley has no problems in associating his male hero with weak and powerless water creatures. Kipling by contrast allies his animals with a new, imperial masculinity.

This masculine violence is, as McClure suggests, part of Kipling's Darwinian view of nature. His father also sees violence as 'natural' and scientifically justified. In a chapter on beast fights, in *Beast and Man*, John Lockwood attacks 'false phrases such as "unnatural strife" and the like, used in denunciation of one of the central instincts of life'. In fact, 'war is always natural to man and beast. The next best thing to fighting is to see others fight.' Some of the 'beast fights, promoted by men … are simply developments of the beneficent principle described by modern science as the survival of the fittest'.[65] Rudyard's representation of wild animals in natural surroundings combines a Darwinian struggle for survival with a boisterous, imperial

---

59 Randall, pp. 3, 16, 45,

60 Brantlinger, pp. 11–12.

61 Ibid., p. 190.

62 McClure, p. 59.

63 Kipling, *Second Jungle Book*, p. 8.

64 Karen Davis, 'Thinking like a Chicken', in Carol J. Adams and Josephine Donovan (eds), *Animals and Women* (Durham, NC, 1995), p. 196.

65 John Lockwood Kipling, *Beast and Man*, p. 384.

masculinism. In presenting the Jungle like this, Kipling is being 'realistic': his tales are not wholly mythological and fabular, but contain natural historical verisimilitude – as when he echoes his father in debunking native myths about mongoose behaviour in 'Rikki-Tikki-Tavi' (see above). Ernest Thompson Seton is often credited by contemporary and current critics with inventing the 'realistic' animal story, and his project is defined by a contrast with Kipling, whose work is seen as fabular: 'Bagheera and Baloo and Kaa are simply delightful variants of Prince Charming and Jack the Slayer of Giants.'[66] Robert Macdonald counters this trend by arguing that Kipling and Seton are both 'mythic'.[67] Similarly, they are also both 'realistic'. Kipling consulted Robert Sterndale's *Natural History of the Mammalia of India and Ceylon* in writing his *Jungle Books*.[68] Pafford notes how the description of Kaa the snake mesmerising the monkeys is 'both convincing natural history and an image of India's dire fascination', while 'the descriptions of the native village and its inhabitants have the important function of insisting that the jungle is not entirely mythical, since the village itself is clearly not.'[69] It is not Kipling's project to provide natural historical information in the manner of Gatty, but he participates in the same enlightened, modernising tradition, and his stories are grounded in a realistic world.

Ernest Thompson Seton was born in England in 1860, and emigrated with his family to Canada in 1866, performing a reverse journey to Kipling, who was born in India and sent to England at the age of six.[70] Most of Seton's wild animal stories are based on his experiences in Canada as a boy and a young man, as various members of his family tried homesteading in the wilderness. Later, he moved to the United States, and some of his stories are set in wild places like New Mexico, or the newly designated Yellowstone Park. He did not, however, relinquish his British citizenship until 1933, and I am including him here as a British writer of the colonial experience, though others see him as primarily American, or quintessentially Canadian. His work provides a link in a chain that leads on to later more 'realistic' animal stories that claim not to be anthropomorphic and that utilise the generic characteristics of biography, rather than autobiography.

Seton's collections of stories, such as *Wild Animals I Have Known* and *Lives of the Hunted,* have an ambiguous relationship with the developing scientific disciplines of animal behaviour and animal psychology. After early attempts at a painting career, Seton's main ambition was to be recognised as a naturalist. Like Kingsley and Gatty, he did produce a recognised work of natural history, *Life Histories of Northern Animals* (1910). He is always keen to stress the 'scientific' and truthful nature of

66 Edward B. Clark, 'Roosevelt on the Nature Fakers' (1907) in Ralph H. Lutts (ed.), *The Wild Animal Story* (Philadelphia, PA, 1998), p. 167.

67 Robert H. Macdonald, 'The Revolt Against Instinct: The Animal Stories of Seton and Roberts' (1980), in Lutts, p. 232.

68 Harry Ricketts, *The Unforgiving Minute* (London, 1999), p. 82.

69 Pafford, pp. 94, 95.

70 Seton was born Ernest Thompson. Later he claimed descent from the aristocratic Setons, and added the name. He was variously known as Seton Thompson and Thompson Seton.

what he writes; at the same time, the 'anecdotal' methods used by Darwin and his follower George Romanes in their observations on animal behaviour read like fiction, and are deliberately anthropomorphic, in order to stress the continuity between animals and man. Seton and Romanes have much in common in their representation of animals. But the beginnings of more experimental and behaviourist approaches, and the remains of an older, more 'mechanical' view of animals, led to conflicts over Seton's credentials. Ironically, some critics now see him as more in tune with later developments that involved a return to the study of animal behaviour in the wild, and reappraisals of animals' capacities for learning and communication.[71]

Large claims have been made for Seton's stories as something entirely new. 'He was the first to produce stories in which the animals were not given human traits to make them more interesting, the first to write "true" stories about individual specimens in their wilderness habitat, and the first to promote conservation and ecological concepts within a popular framework', writes Keller.[72] But the commitment to 'truth' has been there from the first children's animal stories – as Sarah Trimmer's protagonist promises her children, 'I will never tell you anything but truth.'[73] Natural theology itself can be seen as a way to convey ecological concepts. Gatty and Kingsley were naturalists who based their parables and fairy-stories on natural historical facts, and Trimmer's *Fabulous Histories* shows us the birds in their natural habitat. Seton's work is 'part of a chain going back to the seventeenth century, a continuing effort to incorporate science, the culture's authoritative source of knowledge, into the nature-myths of society'.[74] What is different about Seton's work is its use of realist and biographical conventions, the ways human and animal characters interact, the presentation of animal language, and the wild 'frontier' setting.

Seton's first collection of animal stories is entitled *Wild Animals I Have Known* (1898). The personal pronoun, and the verb, are both significant. Nearly every story includes an appearance by a first-person narrator, who testifies to the truth of its events, from personal experience, and who often claims special intimate knowledge of the ways of wild creatures. He observes, he hunts, he tracks, he does experiments, he collects testimony from other witnesses. A story like 'Lobo' may begin as 'gathered from the cowboys', and then the narrator will come on the scene, at a precise date: 'in the fall of 1893, I made the acquaintance of the wily marauder, and at length came to know him more thoroughly than anyone else.'[75] In this story, it is the narrator who eventually traps the wily wolf Lobo; in other stories such as 'Wully' or 'The Pacing Mustang', he plays less of a part, but still records the particular date when he himself sees the animal in question. In 'Johnny Bear', we find him hidden in a garbage heap, taking pictures of the bears; in 'Silverspot', he watches the crows through a telescope; in 'The Kangaroo Rat' he cages the animal for a while, digs up

71 Macdonald, 'The Revolt Against Instinct'; Lutts.
72 Betty Keller, *Blackwolf* (Vancouver, 1984), p. 14.
73 Trimmer, *Easy Introduction*, p. 157.
74 Thomas R. Dunlap 'The Realistic Animal Story', in Lutts, p. 244.
75 Ernest Thompson Seton, *Wild Animals I Have Known* (Toronto, 1991), p. 27.

its burrow, and records its behaviour in the cage (though this is uncharacteristically interventionist behaviour). In order to bring us objective information about nature, a human observer has to be present. Where we seem to be getting an omniscient view, as with the infancy of 'Krag, the Kootenay Ram', Seton explains in his 'Note to the Reader': 'of course we know nothing of the lamb-days of Krag. I have constructed them out of fragments from the lives of many mountain-lambs.' But, he insists, 'the latter parts, the long hunt and the death of Scotty MacDougall, are purely historical. The picture of the horns is photographically correct.'[76] In the same way, photographs of pets attest to their real existence in the animal autobiographies.

Seton's desire seems to be to take animals out of natural history, and put them into history, that is, into human time and human tradition. The other witnesses of the stories – cowboys, farmers, vagrants – not only testify to their scientific truthfulness, they turn the story into a tradition, the animal becomes a famous local character, spoken about if unspeaking. Scotty, the human hunter who kills Krag, 'is forgotten, but the Ram's head hangs enshrined on a palace wall'.[77] A notable feature of all Seton's tales is their focus on a named individual animal, capable of attaining fame. This animal is not representative of its species, but is outstanding in some way, an animal hero or genius, like the great man of human biography, 'an animal who is stronger or wiser than his fellow, who becomes a great leader, who is, as we would say, a genius, and if he is bigger, or has some mark by which men can know him, he soon becomes famous in his country'. The mark is important, to verify the individual's identity – scars, spots, size, colouring, all feature in these stories as distinguishing signs. The animals in his stories, Seton claims 'were all real characters. They lived their lives as I have depicted, and showed the stamp of heroism and personality'. Nevertheless, he admits an inconsistency, in that he has 'pieced together some of the characters', but that is because of 'the fragmentary nature of the records'. While 'Lobo' is 'substantially true', 'Wully' conflates the stories of two different dogs and other animal protagonists have 'ascribed to them the adventures of more than one of their kind'.[78] Individuality and representivity are blurred here. What we are being given are ideal animal superheroes, who are being made 'more interesting' by ascribing a consistent personality and life story to them.

The naming of the animals is a human device, again to give them individuality. Their names are not, like the names of the autobiographical animals, used to 'call' them in any way. Neither are the names a sign of human possession in a crude sense. They serve instead as recognition devices, a sign that these animals are 'known' by humans. The names sometimes are sometimes arbitrary – 'Lobo', 'Krag' – and sometimes refer to appearance or characteristics – 'Silverspot', 'The Pacing Mustang', 'Redruff', 'Saddleback', 'the Wise One'. Of this last, the narrator says, 'the sheep think of this leader, not as one *to be obeyed*, but as one *safe to follow*, the one who is always wise; and though they do not give each other names, they have

---

76 Ernest Thompson Seton, *Lives of the Hunted* [1901] (London, 1924), p. 10.
77 Ibid., p. 104.
78 Seton, *Wild Animals*, pp. 47, 13, 14.

this idea; therefore I shall speak of her as the Wise One.'[79] This narrator apparently knows how sheep think. Despite the commitment to external, verifiable observation, the narrator often gives us an animal's perspective, by using inferences from their behaviour. Knowledge leads to insight: the narrator claims the ability 'to really know [a wild animal] for a long time while it is wild, and to get an insight into its life and history'.[80] He acts as a mediator, explaining the motives and ideas behind animal behaviour to us from his privileged position of knowledge. This manoeuvre is especially evident in the matter of animal language.

In his 'Note to the Reader' in *Lives of the Hunted*, Seton explains that in his early work, he 'used the archaic method, making the animals talk'. But 'since then I have adhered to the more scientific method.'[81] This suggests that there will be no animal language in these stories, but this is not in fact so. Seton includes 'Why the Chickadee Goes Crazy Once a Year' as an example of his 'early work', and so we can try to work out what 'the archaic method' and 'the more scientific method' mean for him. The 'early' story is rather like one of Kipling's *Just So Stories*, an origin myth. The chickadee only has one speech, in which it refuses to migrate like the other birds, or to believe in frost and snow. There is no pretence that any individual real bird said these words. In other, later stories, however, great use is made of the 'translation' convention: the narrator interprets for us particular instances of animal communication – bird-song, coyote howls, rabbits thumping on the ground. Seton's is a more limited and particular use of the convention than either Sewell's or Kipling's, and without any humorous or metafictional element. He is not transparently 'translating' something he himself has made up, as when Kipling translates Baloo's songs. Instead, he is claiming he can decode real signs that animals make.

Here are some examples: in 'Silverspot', various 'caws' made by the crows are set out, in musical notation, and translated as '*All's well, come right along*' or '*Be on your guard*' or '*Danger*', or '*Great Danger – a gun*'. In 'Bingo', the narrator learns a new word from his dog: 'I studied the dreaded track and learned that in Bingo's language the half-terrified, deep-gurgled "*grrr-wff*" means "*timber wolf*".'[82] Similarly, in 'Raggylug', the narrator explains:

> Truly rabbits have no speech as we understand it, but they have a way of conveying ideas by a system of sounds, signs, scents, whisker-touches, movements, and example that answers the purpose of speech; and it must be remembered that though in telling this story I freely translate from rabbit into English, *I repeat nothing that they did not say*.[83]

This is quite different from Trimmer's purpose to tell us 'what they would say if they could'.

---

79 Seton, *Lives of the Hunted*, p. 37.
80 .Seton, *Wild Animals*, p. 47.
81 Seton, *Lives of the Hunted*, pp. 10–11.
82 Seton, *Wild Animals*, pp. 50–51, 115.
83 Ibid., p. 69.

How 'scientific' is Seton being here? His kind of interpretation is in line with Lloyd Morgan's in *Animal Behaviour*, when he quotes a witness who saw wild pigs giving different cries that organised the herd for flight or for defence: "'I imagine that the first assailant was a tiger, and the case was at once known to be hopeless, the cry prompting instant flight, while in the second case the cry was for defence. It can scarcely be doubted that in the first case each adult pig had a vision of a tiger, and in the second of a leopard or some minor foe.'"[84] However, Morgan refuses to credit animals with language, which he takes as characterised by sentences, and not just words. His predecessor, Romanes, appears more credulous, and relays several accounts of crow and rook assemblies, in which malefactors are judged and punished, crediting animals with ideas of morality and justice as well as means of communication.[85] These anecdotes are very similar to those that were told to children in *Evenings at Home* in the eighteenth century. While Seton too credits his animals with a moral sense, he can be more cautious than Romanes: 'It is hardly possible that sparrows have refined ideas of justice and retribution, but it is sure that things which look like it do crop up among them.'[86] His crow assembly in 'Silverspot' has the social purpose of training the young crows, not of punishing malefactors.

Behind Romanes stands Darwin, who has no difficulty in attributing both emotion and reason to animals, with the purpose of creating an evolutionary continuity between man and animal. In *The Descent of Man*, Darwin writes:

Most of the more complex emotions are common to the higher animals and ourselves. Everyone has seen how jealous a dog is of his master's affection, if lavished on any other creature; and I have observed the same fact with monkeys ... Animals manifestly feel emulation. They love approbation or praise; and a dog carrying a basket for his master exhibits in a high degree self-complacency or pride.[87]

He goes on to find shame, modesty, magnanimity and a sense of humour in dogs, and in the Zoological Gardens, he sees a baboon who invents 'imaginary offences'. As to reason, 'only a few persons now dispute that animals possess some power of reasoning. Animals may constantly be seen to pause, deliberate, and resolve ... the more the habits of any particular animal are studied by a naturalist, the more he attributes to reason and the less to unlearnt instincts.'[88] Seton's stories are full of examples of animals learning, and laying cunning plans to outwit their enemies. His purpose is to demonstrate 'our kinship with the animals by showing that in them we can find the virtues most admired in Man'. The list that follows sounds allegorical or emblematic, but Seton means it literally: 'Lobo stands for Dignity and Love-Constancy; Silverspot, for Sagacity; Redruff, for Obedience; Bingo, for Fidelity; Vixen and Molly Cottontail, for Mother-love; Wahb, for Physical Force; and the

---

84 C. Lloyd Morgan, *Animal Behaviour* (London, 1900), p. 196.
85 George J. Romanes, *Animal Intelligence* (London, 1883), pp. 322–5.
86 Seton, *Lives of the Hunted*, p. 128.
87 Charles Darwin, *The Descent of Man*, in Shuttleworth and Taylor, p. 305.
88 Ibid.

Pacing Mustang, for the Love of Liberty.'[89] These virtuous and reasoning animals function in a Darwinian nature which is full of violence and competition, where the weakest are removed by 'inexorable law', and a wild animal's story is always 'tragic'.[90]

My purpose in juxtaposing Seton and Darwin here is not to prove that Seton had necessarily read Darwin, but to show that, by certain lights, Seton's procedure is 'scientific', and also to show how 'anecdotal', and similar to children's animal stories is this part of Darwin's text. For Darwin and Romanes, 'anthropomorphism' is not unscientific, but is part of their scientific approach: once you have a theory that admits no significant gap between man and animal the term loses much of its negative meaning. Nevertheless, Seton was attacked in 1903 by John Burroughs, another naturalist and nature writer, in an article called 'Real and Sham Natural History'. What is interesting, is that for Burroughs the issue does not revolve around talking animals, as it seemed to do for Seton with his contrast of the 'archaic' and the 'scientific'. Burroughs quotes approvingly another nature writer, who describes a trapped possum like this: 'he blinks at you inquiringly, and says, "Please, sir, if you will be so kind as to shut the door and go away, I will finish my nap."' Burroughs himself, disputing the accuracy of the description of a porcupine, puts words into the creature's mouth: 'Now come on, he says, if you want to.' What Burroughs objects to is the animal behaviour that Seton claims to have witnessed: 'such dogs, wolves, foxes, rabbits, mustangs, crows, as he has known, it is safe to say, no other person in the world has ever known.'[91] As Lutts points out, the dispute was not just about the details of animal behaviour, but involved different interpretative frameworks: Burroughs believed in instinct as the sole basis of animal behaviour, while Seton credited animal with reason, and in particular the ability to learn, both in infancy from teaching by parents, and in adulthood from their own experience.[92]

Theodore Roosevelt joined in the dispute, on Burroughs' side. Seton himself did not engage directly in the argument, though he claimed later to have converted Burroughs to a belief in his scientific credentials. But Jack London, who had also been attacked, defended himself as more scientific than his critics: the view that we are the only animals capable of reasoning, he claims, 'makes the twentieth-century scientist smile. It is not modern at all. It is distinctly medieval.' He brands this view as 'homocentric', and refers to both Darwin and Romanes in his defence.[93] We can then see Burroughs either as subscribing to an outdated theory of animals as instinctual machines, or as a supporter of the soon-to-be-dominant behaviourist approach to animal psychology. Edward Thorndike, for instance, criticises Romanes

---

89   Seton, *Lives of the Hunted*, p. 9.
90   Seton, *Wild Animals*, p. 218.
91   John Burroughs, 'Real and Sham Natural History', in Lutts, pp. 130–31.
92   Lutts, p. 9.
93   Jack London, 'The Other Animals' (1908), in Lutts, pp. 200–201, 206.

for his 'anecdotal' method, and promotes his own, experimental and laboratory-based method.[94]

Recently, however, the methods of Darwin and Romanes have been revalued. A collection investigating this development significantly numbers Seton himself among its dedicatees.[95] Contributors revalue both anecdotalism and anthropomorphism as valuable tools in the study of animal behaviour, and point up the limitations of behaviourism: 'how intelligent scientists bought whole-hog into behaviourism for most of this century is still hard to understand.'[96] 'Mechanomorphism' is seen as just as unverifiable an assumption as anthropomorphism.[97] In her book, *Images of Animals*, Crist defends Darwin's and Romanes' use of anecdote – to exclude anecdotal evidence is to exclude 'exceptional or unique information', which can reveal the extent of variation within a species.[98] Seton's focus on the exceptional individual is vindicated. An article in the *Chronicle of Higher Education* claims that 'Scientists Rethink Anthropomorphism'. One of the examples given is a researcher who solved a problem in snake behaviour by imagining himself as the snake: '"This is something I don't think I would ever have done if I didn't imagine myself in that situation."'[99] Similarly Seton asks us to imagine ourselves into the lives of his animal heroes. Seton's purpose is not just scientific, but also ethical – he is using a reversal strategy to be found also in eighteenth-century animal stories. Significantly, the article ends with scientists agreeing that a more anthropomorphic and empathetic approach to animals implies a concern for their welfare: science cannot exclude ethics.

In present-day terms then, there is a case to be made for Seton's stories as scientifically sound, but in his own time the significant point is the terms of the debate. Just as much as for Trimmer and Fenn, the accuracy and truth of the animal story is at issue, and especially so in that *children* were involved as potentially gullible and malleable readers. Burroughs insists that 'there should be nothing equivocal about sketches of this kind; even a child should know when the writer is giving him facts and when he is giving him fiction.'[100] Clark writes of Roosevelt's 'alarm and indignation that some school boards are adopting for the use of children these fantastic animal stories that the writers claim are true'. He quotes Roosevelt: 'as for the matter of giving these books to children for the purpose of teaching them the facts of natural history – why, it's an outrage. If these stories were written as fables, published as fables, and put into the children's hands as fables, all should be

---

94 Edward Thorndike, *Animal Intelligence* (New York, 1898).

95 Robert W. Mitchell, Nicholas S. Thompson and H. Lyn Miles (eds), *Anthropomorphism, Anecdotes, and Animals* (New York, 1997).

96 Bernard E. Rollin, 'Anecdote, Anthropomorphism, and Animal Behavior', in Mitchell et al., p. 129.

97 Mitchell et al., p. 3.

98 Eileen Crist, *Images of Animals* (Philadelphia, PA, 1999), p. 41.

99 McDonald, Kim A., 'Scientists Rethink Anthropomorphism', *Chronicle of Higher Education*, 41/24 (1995): A8.

100 Burroughs, p. 135.

well and good.' Roosevelt's point is not just that children should be told the truth, and scientifically educated, but also that the preservation of nature depends on their intelligent interest: 'the preservation of the useful and beautiful animal and bird life of the country depends largely upon creating in the young an interest in the life of the woods and fields. If the child mind is fed with stories that are false to nature, the children will go to the haunts of the animal only to meet with disappointment.'[101] As in *Beautiful Joe* and *The Adventures of a Donkey*, human behaviour towards animals is to be altered by an address to children, though here it is preservation of the wild, rather than kindness to domestic animals that is being taught.

Seton's aim is in the same tradition. In the 'Note' at the beginning of *Lives of the Hunted*, he writes:

> My chief motive, my most earnest underlying wish, has been to stop the extermination of harmless wild animals; not for their sakes, but for ours, firmly believing that each of our native wild creatures is in itself a precious heritage that we have no right to destroy or put beyond the reach of our children.
>   I have tried to stop the stupid and brutal work of destruction by an appeal – not to reason: that has failed hitherto – but to sympathy, and especially the sympathies of the coming generation.[102]

Though he claims here that, 'I do not intend primarily to denounce certain field sports, or even cruelty to animals', his appeal to sympathy often means he takes up a rhetoric of animal rights, as near the end of 'Redruff': 'have the wild things no moral or legal rights? What right has man to inflict such long and fearful agony on a fellow creature, simply because that creature does not speak his language?' He also practises the reversal strategy that was so prevalent among eighteenth-century writers trying to awaken children's sympathies for animals. In 'Bingo', the narrator is caught in a wolf trap, and thinks, 'This is how a wolf feels when he is trapped. Oh! What misery have I been responsible for! Now I'm to pay for it.' He hears the approach of wolves, 'wondering if it would not be strictly just that they should come and tear me to pieces'.[103] Sympathy in these stories is with the hunted animal and not the human hunter. Seton replies to criticisms of the distressful nature of Lobo's story like this: 'In what frame of mind are my hearers left with regard to the animal? Are their sympathies quickened toward the man who killed him, or toward the noble creature who, superior to every trial, died as he had lived, dignified, fearless, and steadfast?'[104]

Despite Seton's declaration of his intent to work on the sympathies of the 'coming generation', and the heavily didactic nature of the stories, there is no direct address to children in them. But the emphasis in many of them on the training of young animals by their parents, the lessons of obedience they learn, and the lessons a human

---

101 Clark, pp. 165, 171.
102 Seton, *Lives of the Hunted*, p. 13.
103 Seton, *Wild Animals*, pp. 245, 124.
104 Seton, *Lives of the Hunted*, p. 12.

observer can learn from watching this process, can all be seen as an educational message, one that took on institutional form in the creation of Seton's Woodcraft Indians, a forerunner of the Boy Scouts.[105] 'Woodcraft' itself features in the stories as something possessed both by animals and by the naturalist who tracks and observes them – it is a skill transferable from animals to man, and especially mastered by the native American 'Indian'. The association of child/animal/primitive in recapitulation theory is central here: both Seton and Baden-Powell were heavily influenced by the reiteration of recapitulation theory in Hall's book, *Adolescence,* 'the most popular contemporary theory of male adolescent development, which stated that if only civilized boys could be trained to duplicate the savage life, then they might have everything that the savage had not yet lost – virility, hardiness, martial spirit'.[106] As Anderson puts it, 'the whole woodcraft scheme has been summed up as a culmination of Rousseau's child-centred education theory, incorporating G. Stanley Hall's theory of recapitulation.'[107] The other main difference from Rousseau is the emphasis on group activity, as opposed to the isolated child. The model for the group is a 'tribal' one for Seton; and for Baden-Powell, the military 'patrol'. But Macdonald stresses that imagery from the imperial and the American 'frontiers', the primitive warrior and the colonial police forces, was conflated in the creation of a powerful myth of 'frontier' masculinity. I would add that the 'wild animal' also features in this complex of ideas.

Baden-Powell did not himself write animal stories, but when he decided to form an organisation for younger boys, modelled on the Scouts, he went to Kipling's *Jungle Books* for the rituals and imagery of the Wolf Cubs. He had previously used material from *Kim* for the Scouts, and Kipling himself had written them a 'Patrol Song'. Though Gillian Avery has criticised Baden-Powell's 'drab re-telling' of Kipling's stories, which picks out the 'moral patches' and slides over all the rest, it is indisputable that Kipling did lend his approval to the Scouting movement.[108] At the first Scout camp in 1907, Baden-Powell divided the boys into patrols with animal names, Ravens, Wolves, Curlews and Bulls.[109] Significantly, both he and Seton had given themselves the nickname 'Wolf', independently and well before founding their respective youth movements. At the first meeting of Seton's Woodcraft Indians, Seton took the role of 'Medicine Man', under the name of 'Black Wolf', associating animal name with 'primitive' tribe, just as Baden-Powell claimed his Wolf name was bestowed by an African tribe. Seton himself was known for his 'animal' appearance and behaviour, his 'wild, shaggy locks and slouchy hat', his strong, unwashed odour,

---

105 Seton's movement still continues, in the form of the Woodcraft Folk, an alternative youth organisation.

106 G. Stanley Hall, *Adolescence* (New York, 1904); Robert H. MacDonald, *Sons of the Empire* (Toronto, 1993), p. 132.

107 H. Allen Anderson, *The Chief* (College Station, TX, 1986), p. 137.

108 Gillian Avery, 'The Children's Writer', in John Gross (ed.), *Rudyard Kipling, the man, his work and his world* (London, 1972), pp. 116–17; Hugh Brogan, *Mowgli's Sons* (London, 1987).

109 Macdonald, *Sons of the Empire*, p. 118.

and his habit of breaking into a wolf-howl to impress his guests.[110] Kipling gave the Wolf Cubs advice on how to produce a communal wolf-howl.[111] Baden-Powell cultivated not so much an animal persona as a boyish one, with his shorts and his 'Peter Pan' personality.[112] Boy/man, man/animal, savage/civilised boundaries can be transgressed within the framework of the youth movements. A philosophy of kinship with the animals leads here to humans taking on animal names and animal behaviours: not talking animals, but howling boys.

In Beatrix Potter's *Tales* and Kenneth Grahame's *Wind in the Willows*, the subjects of the next chapter, self-sufficient worlds of animals in human clothing also blur the human/animal distinction, but to quite different effects. For Potter, animals share occupations and qualities with the human inhabitants of the English countryside, while for Grahame they represent an idyllic holiday existence dreamed of by suburban man.

---

110 Anderson, p. 110.
111 Brogan, p. 44.
112 Macdonald, *Sons of the Empire*, p. 206.

Chapter Six

Arcadias?

Beatrix Potter's *Tales* and Kenneth Grahame's *The Wind in the Willows*, like Kipling's Mowgli stories, concern a separate animal 'world' in a special space. Their settings, however, are not the colonial space of the Jungle, or Seton's frontier world, but the English countryside. Here they create an area that critics have called 'Arcadian' or 'idyllic', inhabited by small animals, without the emphasis on action and violence of Kipling and Seton's wild nature. It is hard to imagine an effective Scout Patrol in which the participants are called Mole, Rat, Toad and Badger, or even Peter Rabbit and friends. Potter's fox, Mr Tod, is as carnivorous as Kipling and Seton's wolves, but he is definitely not to be admired. To some extent, Potter and Grahame represent a feminine and domestic take on the natural world, as opposed to the strenuous masculinism of Kipling. But, as we will see, the domestic is not without its dangers in Potter's tales, and Grahame's world has a misogynistic aspect. Both Potter and Grahame hark back to earlier literature. Potter has links with Trimmer, Barbauld and the papillonades; Grahame's text is full of allusions to the Romantic poets, and deploys the romanticised view of nature that can be found in Kingsley and Gatty. Potter's illustrations show the attention to natural historical detail of Gatty, and her texts blend the realism of Trimmer with the fantastic of the papillonades. Grahame has no scientific pretensions, though his work is grounded in the knowledge of a particular landscape. As in the papillonades, their animals engage in human activities, and sometimes wear clothes.

Another earlier animal world in which dressed animals behave like humans is Alfred Elwes' 1857 *Adventures of a Dog*. Unlike other animal autobiographies, this book situates its hero in a separate dog world, Canneville, which operates in all respects just like a human world. Potter and Grahame complicate this device, by presenting creatures who are sometimes animal, sometimes human. Another new departure is the way their animals can change size when they encounter the human world – subtly in Potter and blatantly in Grahame. In both texts, the language spoken by the animals can at times be understood by human characters, going against a long-standing tradition in children's animal stories. These devices blur the animal/human distinction even more than the hybridity of Mowgli. Like Kipling, Potter and Grahame are not interested in purveying an anti-cruelty message. Their stories do not have a clear moral: both Peter Rabbit and Toad pay for their transgressive behaviours, but readerly sympathy is on their side. Grahame ends by upholding hierarchical social arrangements, but Potter has no such message. Both their texts, however, have been put to conservationist uses. If not Arcadias, they represent anti-urban, anti-industrial enclaves that provide a critique of the modern. In this respect, their descendants are Richard Adams's *Watership Down* (1972) and Colin Dann's *The Animals of Farthing Wood* (1979), while their dressed, semi-human animals anticipate texts like Jean de Brunhoff's *The Story of Babar* (1934), in which the animality of the protagonists is no longer a real issue.

Beatrix Potter, like Margaret Gatty, Charles Kingsley and Ernest Thompson Seton, was an accomplished naturalist. She was, however, born in an age when the increasing professionalisation of science meant that there was no longer a place for the unqualified amateur, especially if she was a woman. Her meticulous work on fungi and algae, involving hundreds of detailed and accurate drawings, was not taken seriously by either the botanists at Kew, or the Linnaean Society, to whom she tried to present it. Lurie claims that if Potter had been born into 'this [twentieth] century', or born a man, she would have been a well-known naturalist, but Gates points out that 'at an earlier juncture in the history of natural history', her discoveries would have 'qualified her as an expert', much as Gatty's work on seaweeds gave her authority and recognition.[1] Even Seton, as a man writing at the same time as Potter, had difficulty in establishing his scientific credentials. Though it may have been that lack of scientific recognition made Potter turn to writing animal stories for children, she could well have combined the two careers if she had been born earlier. Peter Hollindale presents her combination of 'traditional fantasy and modern natural history' as a new departure for children's literature. By 'modern' here he means twentieth century, and he compares her way of writing about animals to Konrad Lorenz. But, as we have seen, this combination is a feature of children's animal stories from the mid-eighteenth century, and Hollindale's description of her works as 'miniature post-fabulist comedies for children born into an age of science' could well describe stories by Barbauld, Trimmer, Dorset, Gatty or Kingsley, who all went beyond the simplicity of the Aesopian fable.[2]

Carpenter has commented on the Regency affiliations of Potter's work – she was fascinated by the reminiscences of her paternal grandmother. Jane Austen clearly influenced Potter's style.[3] The eighteenth-century setting of *The Tailor of Gloucester* is clear: 'the time of swords and periwigs and full-skirted coats with flowered lappets – when gentlemen wore ruffles, and gold-laced waistcoats of paduasoy and taffeta'.[4] In other stories, the costumes are eighteenth-century, or timeless traditional country wear. Jemima Puddle-duck's 'poke bonnet' belongs to the early nineteenth century, as well as being suitable for her long duck face. There are also some specific parallels with earlier children's texts. In Potter's story, *The Tale of Two Bad Mice*, there is an illustration of the mouse Tom Thumb explaining a mouse-trap to his children, echoing

---

1   Alison Lurie, *Not in Front of the Grown-Ups* (London, 1991), p. 108; Barbara Gates, *Kindred Nature* (Chicago, IL, 1998), p. 84.

2   Peter Hollindale, 'Aesop in the Shadows', *Signal* 89 (May 1999): 115–32.

3   Humphrey Carpenter, *Secret Gardens*, 139; M. Daphne Kutzer, *Beatrix Potter, Writing in Code* (London, 2003), p. 11.

4   Beatrix Potter, *The Complete Tales* (London, 2002).p. 39.

Barbauld's 'The Young Mouse' from *Evenings At Home*, in which the mother mouse explains the trap to her over-enthusiastic child. The text in Potter's tale merely reports the human intentions: 'But the nurse said – "I will set a mouse-trap!"', while it is the illustration that gives us the sympathetic mouse's-eye view.[5] Barbauld and Aikin's story, 'The Dog and His Relations', starts off with the fox and the wolf assuring the dog that they are related to him. The naïve dog allows his 'relations' freedom of the farm. We follow his puzzled thoughts and questions until he realises their true natures, and why the geese have been disappearing. Potter's Jemima Puddle-duck similarly trusts the plausible fox, till rescued by a more knowing farm dog. Behind both tales lurk the medieval stories of Reynard the Fox and his wiles.

The 'papillonades' also provide an ancestry for Potter's work, with their animals dressed up in human clothing, and, specifically, the way in which the clothing device is varied, blurring the human/animal divide: some of the animals are clothed, some not, and in some cases their 'natural covering' is presented as clothing, like the hen's long yellow stockings or the lambs' woolly coats in Potter's *Mrs Tiggy-winkle*. The food in *The Peacock at Home*, 'Wasps *a la sauce piquante*' and 'Flies *en croute compote*', 'Worms and Frogs *en friture*' and barbecued Mouse, compares with Jeremy Fisher's 'butterfly sandwich', and 'roasted grasshopper with ladybird sauce' (see p. 56 above).[6] At the same time, the animal protagonists themselves are possible food for predators and humans: Peter Rabbit's father was famously 'put in a pie by Mrs McGregor', while the Partridge, as we have seen, declines the Peacock's invitation, because 'a Neighbour hard by /Had engaged a snug party to meet in a Pie'. The Wheatear, remembering a 'feast' from which none of her friends returned, does not want 'to appear in a costume of vine-leaves or paste', showing more foresight than Potter's Jemima Puddle-duck when invited to dinner by the fox and asked to bring along the sage and onions for the stuffing.[7] The grotesque image of Tom Kitten rolled up in pastry in Potter's *Samuel Whiskers* also comes to mind here.

Both Dorset and Potter are playing with a combination of the natural historical and the anthropomorphic. While the accurate natural historical reference of the papillonades is buttressed by the weighty informational footnotes, in Potter's stories it is often the illustrations that do this work, more unobtrusively. Catherine Golden has revealed how much Potter drew on her earlier natural history studies for her book illustrations, which, compared to the idealisations of other illustrators, are 'more akin to … the paintings of specimens from nature used to illustrate natural history books'.[8] At the same time, anthropomorphic details are inserted into these pictures, the animals sometimes appearing in natural poses, sometimes on their hind legs in

---

5   Beatrix Potter, *The Tale of Two Bad Mice* (London, 1904), pp. 54–5.

6   Dorset, *Peacock at Home*, p. 14; Beatrix Potter, *The Tale of Mr Jeremy Fisher* (London, 1906), pp. 26, 59.

7   Beatrix Potter, *The Tale of Peter Rabbit* (London, 1902), p. 10; Dorset, *Peacock at Home*, p. 5.

8   Catherine Golden, 'Beatrix Potter: Naturalist Artist', in Bill Katz (ed.), *A History of Book Illustration* (London, 1994), pp. 633–5.

human poses. Whether they are clothed or not, or using tools and furniture, or living in human houses, does not necessarily correspond to their animal/human poses, nor do all these features work together consistently. For instance, the illustration of Peter Rabbit unable to get out of the door of Mr McGregor's garden shows an anatomically correct, unclothed rabbit in a human posture of grief. In *The Tale of the Pie and the Patty-Pan*, Ribby the cat wears a dress, but Duchess the dog is unclothed, in what the text tells us is her 'beautiful black coat'.[9] They are shown in realistic human interiors, but Dr Maggotty the magpie is drawn with complete naturalism, pecking about the yard. In *Squirrel Nutkin*, Old Brown the owl is for the most part drawn as a naturalistic, silent owl. But one picture shows him inside his tree, sitting at table on a carved chair, eating honey off a plate with a spoon. Jemima Puddle-duck is at first depicted as an ordinary farmyard duck, but when she reverts to her 'wild' nature and flies, she is wearing a shawl and a poke bonnet.

Figure 6.1 Illustration by Beatrix Potter for *Peter Rabbit* **(1902).**

The disjunction between and among the various indicators of humanity leads to a blurring of animal/human differences, which are always being reconfigured, in both pictures and text. If we look at the opening of *Peter Rabbit*, a naturalistic picture of the seemingly wild rabbit family outside their home in the sand-bank under the fir-tree is accompanied by a text which names them, three having pet rabbit names and one human name: 'Flopsy, Mopsy, Cotton-tail and Peter'. Here, Potter takes Trimmer's formula, 'Dicksy, Flapsy, Pecksy and Robin', and points up its contradictions: the next illustration shows the family all clothed and upright, Peter separated from his

---

9   Potter, *Complete Tales*, p. 109.

good little sisters who are crowded round their mother, wearing matching red cloaks, while he faces outward, wearing his blue jacket. In the text, Mrs Rabbit is speaking, warning her children not to go into Mr McGregor's garden. Peter's pose already suggests that he will disobey (Figure 6.1).

Figure 6.2 Illustration by Beatrix Potter for *Peter Rabbit* **(1902).**

In the next picture, rabbit features as food, as Mrs McGregor places the pie containing Peter's father onto the table, in front of Mr McGregor's hands, holding knife and fork, and the head of an enthusiastic dog showing above the table (Figure 6.2).[10] A child waving a fork appears in the background. Child, dog and man are all equivalent carnivores, the dog's head and the human hands being right next to each other. At the same time, Mrs McGregor's blue bodice and her pose are very similar to Mrs Rabbit's in the preceding picture, also looking after her family, and the information about who is in the pie is spoken in the accompanying text by Mrs Rabbit, in terms of 'an accident'. On these first three pages, rabbits have featured as wild, natural, pets, clothed, talking, and food.

---

10 This illustration was not included in the original edition. It can be found in Potter, *Complete Tales*, p. 9. Potter was never happy with the way she drew human beings: this may be why she excluded this illustration.

These juxtapositions between the different constructions of the animal/human division have something of the same effect as the contrasts between the different stories in the *Jungle Books,* or the different animal stories and dialogues in *Evenings at Home*, except that for Potter, the contrasts take place within as well as between stories. It is clear that Potter is fictionalising, not claiming that animals can 'really' talk. Her light, ironic tone, like the mock-heroic of the papillonades, helps to establish the animals' humanity as a comic device, while the naturalistic style of the illustrations, which does not vary with their content, smooths over contradictions. At least three critics have used the word 'seamless' to describe her procedure: Kutzer finds text and illustrations 'seamlessly' integrated; Gates sees discourses and genres combined in a 'seamless' art form – scientific knowledge, fables, animal biography and talking animals; and MacDonald comments on the 'seamlessness' of the convergence between animal and human worlds.[11] The ways in which Potter varies her use of animal language is one of her 'seamless' procedures, along with the variations in clothing, housing, scale and perspective.

In *Peter Rabbit*, her first book, there is very little animal speech. It begins with Mrs Rabbit's archetypal warning, 'you may go into the fields or down the lane, but don't go into Mr McGregor's garden.' This imitates the many parental warnings of previous animal stories, as well as referring back to Little Red Riding Hood's mother – allusions to Little Red Riding Hood recur in Potter, with its theme of animals disguised in human clothes. After telling her children about their father's accident, and that she is going out, Mrs Rabbit does not speak directly again, though she reappears at the end of the story to dose the returned Peter with camomile tea. Peter does not speak directly at all – not surprisingly, as he is mostly on his own in the garden, but his speech is at one time indirectly reported: 'Peter asked [the mouse] the way to the gate.' Some friendly sparrows also speak indirectly, as they 'implored him to exert himself' when he is trapped by his jacket in the gooseberry net. Interspecies communication can go on, though the cat says nothing, and the mouse cannot speak because of a pea in her mouth. The formality of 'implored him to exert himself' contrasts with the naturalistic picture of the sparrows. The indirect speech suggests the narrator may be 'translating' sparrow language. Peter's thoughts are also expressed indirectly – a contrast with later tales, when there is a great deal of interior monologue by animal characters. But here, 'Peter thought it best to go away without speaking to [the cat].'[12] This reads as an ironic, euphemistic way of referring to Peter's real fear of cats, based on what he has heard from Benjanim Bunny.

The comparative absence of animal speech is balanced by the importance of clothing in this story. The animals' clothing in Potter's stories, as Carole Scott has pointed out, is not just a matter of decorative illustration, but often plays a decisive

11 Kutzer, p. 1; Gates, *Kindred Nature*, p. 231; Ruth Macdonald, 'Narrative Voice and Narrative View in Beatrix Potter's Books', in Charlotte F. Otten and Gary D. Schmidt (eds), *The Voice of the Narrator in Children's Literature* (New York, 1989), p. 55.

12 Potter, *Peter Rabbit*, pp. 10, 45, 33, 46.

role in the narrative.[13] Here, it is Peter's blue jacket that traps him when its buttons catch in Mr McGregor's gooseberry net. Only by slipping out of the jacket, and reverting to a naked wild animal, can Peter eventually escape. The jacket is associated with his mother's control over him: we see her buttoning him into it as she warns him not to get into mischief: she almost appears to be strangling him in this picture. The connection between clothes, maternal control and socialisation is made more obvious in the later story of *Tom Kitten*, when the kitten and his sisters are dressed up by their socially conscious mother in 'elegant uncomfortable clothes' to meet her friends at a tea-party, with the admonition, 'Now keep your frocks clean, children! You must walk on your hind legs.' Of course the kittens soon dirty and discard their clothes, Tom bursting out of his tight blue costume, 'shedding buttons right and left'.[14] Scott sees the clothes in these stories as a metaphor for conflict between a natural, animal, child self, and adult, human, social confinement.[15]

Squirrel Nutkin, the next story after *Peter Rabbit*, is also rather sparing in the use of animal speech, and what is said is ritualised and formal, quite different from the speech in *Peter Rabbit*. Old Brown the owl never speaks at all: his silence is rather ominous, and erupts into violence at the end. The other squirrels speak in unison, as they offer ritualised propitiation to Old Brown: 'Old Mr Brown, will you favour us with permission to gather nuts upon your island?'[16] Nutkin breaks this ritual, bringing no gifts, playing instead of nut-gathering, and teasing Old Brown with a number of rhyming riddles:

> But Nutkin, who had no respect, began to dance up and down, tickling old Mr Brown with a *nettle*, and singing –
>
> 'Old Mr B! Riddle-me-ree!
> Hitty Pitty within the wall,
> Hitty Pitty without the wall;
> If you touch Hitty Pitty,
> Hitty Pitty will bite you!'[17]

The riddles are as ritualised and traditional as the propitiation ceremony, though in a quite different register. Nutkin's behaviour is childish, as opposed to the grown-up, proper behaviour of the other squirrels, and, initially, the dignified Mr Brown. His childishness, however, is not conveyed through any 'natural' animal behaviour, but through the elaborate riddles, and the very human games of ninepins and marbles he plays with the oak apples and pine cones. No one is clothed in this story, but the responsible squirrels make and use rafts, go fishing, and carry their nuts in sacks. Mr Brown, the authority figure, is once shown using human furniture and implements

---

13 Scott, 'Between Me and the World'.

14 Potter, *Complete Tales*, pp. 151–3.

15 Scott, 'Between Me and the World'.

16 Beatrix Potter, *The Tale of Squirrel Nutkin* (London, 1903), p. 17.

17 Ibid., p. 27.

(see p. 154 above), but at the end it is he who reverts to the 'animal', when he pockets Nutkin, and tears his tail off, in an attempt to skin him. It seems that grown-ups too can become animals, in a much more violent and disconcerting way than the disobedient Peter or Tom: the illustration paralleling the carnivorous Mr McGregor with his dog is relevant here, as well as the polite, seemingly upper-class fox in *Jemima Puddle-duck*, the kitten-eating, clothed rat, Mr Samuel Whiskers, or the cat and dog shopkeepers Ginger and Pickles, who have to restrain themselves from eating their mouse and rabbit customers.

Nutkin ends his story by reverting to animal noises: if you meet him now, says the narrator, taking the tale into the real present of her hearers, he will scold and shout 'Cuck-cuck-cuck-curr-r-r-cuck-k-k!'.[18] Simpkin the cat, in *The Tailor of Gloucester*, the next story to be published, also can only make animal noises, 'Miaw', and 'Mew'. Nevertheless, his master sends him out to the shops with money on an errand, which he performs. When he returns, the illustration shows him standing up, wearing a coat and boots, like Puss-in-Boots. Still, however, the convention that he cannot talk is kept up: 'if Simpkin had been able to talk, he would have asked – "Where is my MOUSE?"' This refers to some (dressed) mice he is supposed to have hidden under teacups. Potter then makes use of the traditional superstition that on Christmas Night the beasts can talk, but what they say is in the form of old rhymes, like Nutkin's riddles. The cocks sing 'Dame, get up and bake your pies!', Simpkin says, 'Hey, diddle, diddle, the cat and the fiddle!', and the mice sing in chorus a number of rhymes about tailors, mice and sewing, as they work on the Tailor's unfinished commission. But at the end it seems they can write as well, as they leave the message 'No more twist', when they run out of thread.[19]

Subsequent tales are more lavish in the matter of animal speech. Benjamin Bunny is positively garrulous compared to Peter: 'It spoils people's clothes to squeeze under a gate; the proper way is to climb down a pear tree', and the Two Bad Mice speak to each other like a farming couple at table: '"It is not boiled enough; it is hard. You have a try, Hunca Munca" … "It is as hard as the hams at the cheesemonger's" said Hunca Munca', as they try to carve the doll's house ham.[20] Mrs Tiggy-winkle has the respectful speech of the lower classes: "Oh yes, if you please'm; my name is Mrs Tiggy-winkle; oh yes if you please'm, I'm an excellent clear-starcher.'[21] The 'gentleman' fox in *Jemima Puddle-duck* speaks in an appropriately upper-class way, belied by his dingy, makeshift house: 'But as to a nest – there is no difficulty: I have a sackful of feathers in my woodshed. No, my dear madam, you will be in nobody's way.' Here, his smart clothes and newspaper, like his speech, serve to disguise him, though his bushy tail gives away his foxy nature. The illustration of him counting Jemima's eggs when she is not there confirms this – he is unclothed and on all fours. Jemima herself hardly speaks, and mostly indirectly, which seems appropriate to her

---

18 Ibid., p. 36.
19 Beatrix Potter, *Complete Tales*, pp. 41, 45, 47, 51.
20 Potter, *Complete Tales*, p. 59; *Two Bad Mice*, p. 25.
21 Beatrix Potter, *The Tale of Mrs Tiggy-winkle* (London, 1905), p. 25.

naïve character. The fox's house of 'faggots and turf', with its 'two broken pails, one on top of another, by way of a chimney', combines suggestions of both an animal's dwelling and the lair of some marginal tramp or poacher. His speech almost gives him away as an animal here: '"This is my summer residence; you would not find my earth – my winter house – so convenient," said the hospitable gentleman.'[22] Samuel Whiskers similarly uses an elevated vocabulary about his plan to eat Tom Kitten: 'We are discovered and interrupted, Anna Maria; let us collect our property – and other people's – and depart at once. I fear that we shall be obliged to leave this pudding. But I am persuaded that the knots would have proved indigestible, whatever you may urge to the contrary.'[23] The reference to 'other people's' gives away his thieving nature. Elevated speech and smart clothes conceal transgressive desires.

The Tale of Mrs Tiggy-winkle introduces another way in which animal speech is represented, animal sound being translated into human words. So Sally Henny Penny clucks 'I go barefoot, barefoot, barefoot!'[24] The words seem meaningless, till Mrs Tiggy-winkle remarks on how Sally is wearing out her yellow stockings, and will soon 'go barefoot'. Sally's sounds are given meaning, in the same way as the marks on the lambs' coats are seen as laundry marks, and the kitten is said to wash her own mittens, which only need ironing. The speech of Dr Maggoty the magpie in *The Pie and the Patty-Pan*, however, seems completely meaningless, as he cries 'Gammon? ha! HA!' and 'Spinach? ha HA!', whatever people say to him. His meaningless cries contrast comically with the polite social speech of Ribby the cat and Duchess the dog, and their faith in Dr Maggoty's pills. Duchess has been trying to disguise her natural distaste for the mouse pie Ribby plans to give her, by an elaborate subterfuge which goes wrong. Her alternative pie is fittingly devoured by the (unclothed) Doctor and some jackdaws in the back yard. This tale also introduces the extensive use of soliloquy or interior monologue by animals, as Duchess makes her plans: '"I am dreadfully afraid it *will* be mouse!" said Duchess to herself – "I really couldn't, *couldn't* eat mouse pie. And I shall have to eat it, because it is a party."'[25] The device is continued in Jeremy Fisher, who comments on his every action: 'I will get some worms and go fishing', 'This is getting tiresome, I think I should like some lunch', 'I will eat a butterfly sandwich', 'I trust that is not a rat.'[26] The most extensive use of this device is in *Mr Tod*, as Mr Tod lays his plans to trick Tommy Brock, the badger who has invaded his house.

Mr Tod begins his commentary in the bedroom, where he has strung up a bucket of water above Tommy Brock, who appears to be sleeping: '"It will make a great mess in my bedroom; but I could never sleep in that bed again without a spring-cleaning of some sort," said Mr Tod. Mr Tod took a last look at the badger and softly left the room.' Is Mr Tod speaking aloud? Unlike Duchess, it is not stated

---

22 Beatrix Potter, *The Tale of Jemima Puddle-duck* (London, 1908), pp. 29, 30.
23 Potter, *Complete Tales*, p. 191.
24 Potter, *Tiggy-winkle*, p. 10.
25 Potter, *Complete Tales*, pp. 115, 117, 103.
26 Potter, *Jeremy Fisher*, pp. 25, 26, 30.

that he is speaking 'to [him]self', though even Duchess could be speaking aloud to herself. As for Jeremy Fisher, it is never specified whether what he says when on his own is speech or thought, though it is represented as direct speech. Since Mr Tod is in the room trying not to disturb Tommy, it would seem strange if he is speaking aloud: maybe the conventions of soliloquy are operating here. Once he is outside, he continues to soliloquize, planning his trick: '"I will wake him up with an unpleasant surprise."'[27] Then when he believes (erroneously) that he has killed Tommy he goes into a long elaborate fantasy about hygiene:

> 'I will bury that nasty person in the hole which he has dug. I will bring my bedding out, and dry it in the sun,' said Mr Tod.
> 'I will wash the table cloth and spread it on the grass in the sun to bleach. And the blanket must be hung up in the wind; and the bed must be thoroughly disinfected, and aired with a warming-pan; and warmed with a hot-water bottle.
> 'I will get soft soap, and monkey soap, and all sorts of soap; and soda and scrubbing brushes; and Persian powder; and carbolic to remove the smell. I must have a disinfecting. Perhaps I may have to burn sulphur.'
>   He hurried round the house to get a shovel from the kitchen – 'First I will arrange the hole – then I will drag out that person in the blanket … .'[28]

Mr Tod's fastidiousness here reads like the soliloquy of an over-anxious housewife – it has similarities with Mrs Tittlemouse's anxieties about the pollution of her home by Mr Jackson the toad. The escalating list of soaps here moves into comic exaggeration. At the same time, Mr Tod's actions characterise him as a child playing a prank with a bucket of water. His childish and feminine aspects introduce a comic element into a very dark tale: Tommy has kidnapped the Flopsy bunnies and is planning to eat them, and Mr Tod's house is surrounded with hellish imagery. It is like a 'cave' or a 'prison'; the setting sun makes the windows 'glow like red flame', there is 'a large carving knife' on the table, and outside are lying 'rabbit bones and skulls, and chickens' legs and other horrors. It was a shocking place, and very dark.' This darker, violent aspect is also present in Mr Tod's speech, in his plans to drag out and bury Tommy Brock in a hole – the hole is actually the opening of the tunnel dug by Peter Rabbit and Benjamin Bunny, who have come to the rescue of the Flopsy Bunnies, and who would be effectively trapped if Mr Tod were to carry out his plan. Animal violence erupts again at the end as Mr Tod and Tommy Brock fall upon each other, 'snarling and worrying', and roll down the hill. But Peter's prim comment on the fight – 'What dreadful bad language!' – introduces some irony and distance. In this story he speaks in elaborate language as a responsible parent-figure: '"My Uncle Benjamin Bouncer has displayed a lamentable want of discretion for his years," said Peter reflectively; "but there are two hopeful circumstances."'[29] The childishness of the two larger animals is thrown into relief by the grown-up rabbits' speech.

---

27 Beatrix Potter, *The Tale of Mr. Tod* (London, 1912), pp. 69, 70.
28 Ibid., pp. 77–8.
29 Ibid., pp. 33, 39, 87, 27.

The soliloquies by Duchess, Jeremy Fisher and Mr Tod do not have the effect of creating sympathy for these characters, or exploring what animal subjectivity might be like. They are not like the narrations of the autobiographical animals, who are addressing a human audience, attempting to persuade them to enter into their plight. Potter's animal soliloquies represent a very 'human' dimension of the characters, comically at odds with their animal forms and instincts – their social pretensions, their scheming, their preoccupation with manmade artefacts like pie-dishes, sandwiches, buckets and soap. The way the animals comment on their own actions also bears a resemblance to the way children, first learning language, go through a phase of commenting aloud on everything they do or are about to do. This is often encouraged by the adult trying to teach language, who adopts the same device and is also adapted in texts teaching children to read. This interpretation fits in with a certain 'childishness' in Potter's adult animals, especially, as we have seen, Mr Tod. Using animal protagonists allows for a child reader to identify both with the animal children – Peter Rabbit, Tom Kitten – and the adult animals. These animals 'play' at being humans, in the same way a child might 'play' at being an adult.

Potter's final tale in my period, *Pigling Bland*, partly reverts to the rhyming language of *Squirrel Nutkin*. The plot is based on the nursery rhymes 'This little piggy went to market', and 'Over the hills and far away', concerning 'Tom, Tom the Piper's Son', who appears as the evil Mr Piperson. The pigs sing verses from 'Over the Hills', and at the end, 'They came to the river, they came to the bridge – they crossed it hand in hand – then over the hills and far away she danced with Pigling Bland!' Earlier, Aunt Pettitoes, sending the pigs to market, gives rhyming advice: 'Mind your Sunday clothes, and remember to blow your nose ... beware of traps, hen roosts, bacon and eggs; always walk upon your hind legs.' This advice proves prophetic, when the hens on Piperson's farm seem to be warning Pigling: '"Bacon and eggs, bacon and eggs!" clucked a hen on a perch. "Trap, trap, trap! Cackle, cackle, cackle!" scolded the disturbed cockerel.'[30] Here, animal noises are interpreted as human words, as with Sally Henny-Penny, or Dr Maggotty. At the same time, the pigs also speak naturalistically, and exchange words with each other and with humans. At the beginning of the story, they are portrayed as naked piglets on all fours, while Aunt Pettitoes their mother is clothed and upright. When she sends them off to market, they are clothed – there is a picture of his mother tying a scarf round Pigling's neck, with the same implication of strangulation that there was in the picture of Peter Rabbit's mother buttoning up his blue coat. As we have seen, they are exhorted to walk on their hind legs, like Tom Kitten and his sisters.

What is interesting here is that when Pigling Bland and Pig-wig escape to the hills at the end of the story, they are still upright, and do not shed their clothes – clothes here are not a consistent image of social control. Social control, however, is a strong theme in the story, as the pigs are continually stopped and asked for their 'licences' by suspicious authority figures. Being 'sent to market' is ambiguous: it obviously means being sent for slaughter, but in the case of these humanised pigs, it

---

30 Potter, *Complete Tales*, pp. 308, 286–7, 292–3.

also means being sent for hire as a labourer: 'the idea of standing all by himself in a crowded market, to be stared at, pushed, and hired by some strange farmer was very disagreeable.'[31] This is the fate the pigs are evading by dancing away over the hills. Their clothes and upright posture indicate that they are not animals, and so they can escape the fate of domestic pigs. There is a similar implication in *Jemima Puddle-duck*. When Jemima is a farm duck, under the control of the farmer's wife, and presumably to be eaten in the end, she is naked. When she decides to act on her own, and find her own nest, she puts on a bonnet and shawl. This story, however, shows her as mistaken: there are greater perils for a duck in the wild, and she is returned to the farm, and loses her clothes.

In *Pigling Bland* another device facilitates human/animal interaction, and that is the changes of scale in the relative sizes of humans and animals. These changes are fairly unobtrusive in this tale, as real pigs on their hind legs are almost human-sized, or at least child-sized. In the last few illustrations, two black and white drawings show the pigs in relation to the wagon-wheel and horse of the suspicious grocer. They are only slightly higher than the centre of the wheel, and the horse's knees. They are upright, in human attitudes of fear and sadness. Pig-wig is crying, and Pigling offers up his licence. In the colour picture that follows, we see the grocer on his cart, reading the piece of paper, and the pigs, their backs turned to us, have grown in relation to wagon and horse. At the beginning of the story there is a similar effect, as Aunt Pettitoes, the pigs' mother, is shown in the dress and posture of the farmer who is looking after them, carrying two buckets. Her human size and status are emphasised by her co-operation with the narrator, who also appears to be charge of the pigs: 'Aunt Pettitoes and I dragged him out by his hind legs.' The two women discuss the sending away of the pigs, and the narrator adds her advice to Aunt Pettitoes': '"And remember," said I impressively, "if you once cross the county boundary you cannot come back."'[32] It is this narrator who has procured the pig-licences, and there is an illustration of her bending down to give Pigling his, in almost the same posture as Aunt Pettitoes tying Pigling's scarf: the female human figure is only slightly taller than Aunt Pettitoes, relative to the piglet.

These changes of scale, and the enlargement of small animals so that they can interact with humans and human objects, are carried much further in Kenneth Grahame's *Wind in the Willows*, where Toad drives a car, rides a horse, or buys a train-ticket. When Potter uses this device, the 'I' who is writing the story is usually involved, signalling her special relationship with the animal world. Mrs Tiggy-winkle the hedgehog/washerwoman appears to Lucie as slightly below her own (child) size. At the end of the story, when the washerwoman reverts to her animal identity, she not only loses her clothes, but shrinks: 'And *how* small she had grown – and how brown – and covered with PRICKLES! Why! Mrs Tiggy-winkle was nothing but a HEDGEHOG.'[33] Surely this is the origin of the incident in *Wind in the*

---

31 Ibid., p. 291.
32 Ibid., pp. 283, 287.
33 Potter, *Tiggy-winkle*, p. 59.

Willows where Toad, disguised as a washerwoman, is eventually recognised by the barge-woman as 'a horrid, nasty, crawly toad'.[34] In Potter's story, a note in brackets follows the revelation of Mrs Tiggy-winkle's hedgehog nature, denying that Lucie dreamt the whole story, since '*I* have seen that door into the back of the hill called Cat Bells – and besides *I* am very well acquainted with dear Mrs Tiggy-winkle!'[35] This claim is similar to the narrator's assertion in *Benjamin Bunny*: 'Old Mrs Rabbit was a widow. She earned her living by knitting rabbit-wool mittens and muffetees (I once bought a pair at a bazaar).'[36]

The combination of changes of scale and the narrator's involvement appears again in *Samuel Whiskers*, where Potter's own house at Sawrey is the model for the illustrations. Here, it is inhabited by a family of cats, with Tabitha Twitchett as housewife. She and her guest Ribby change sizes subtly in relation to the house. Meanwhile, in the walls and under the floors live the rat couple, Samuel and Anna Maria. They are discovered by John Joiner, a little dog with bag of tools, who saws into their hideout, but also 'spent the rest of the morning sniffing and whining, and wagging his tail, and going round and round with his head in the hole like a gimlet'. We learn that he has 'just finished making a wheelbarrow for Miss Potter, and she had ordered two hen-coops'. The 'I' then appears, going to post and noticing 'Mr Samuel Whiskers and his wife on the run, with big bundles on a little wheelbarrow, which looked very like mine … I am sure *I* never gave them leave to borrow my wheelbarrow!'[37] The illustration shows the rats running off with the wheelbarrow along a village street. Either 'Miss Potter' is rat-sized, or they have become human-sized. An earlier picture has shown them about the same height as the rolling-pin they 'borrow'.

Other interventions of the narrator confirm that she is writing and illustrating the books, but this does not break the illusion of reality, as she also claims intimate knowledge of the situation and the animals' experience: 'I cannot draw you a picture of Peter and Benjamin underneath the basket, because it was quite dark, and because the smell of the onions was fearful; it made Peter Rabbit and little Benjamin cry.'[38] Macdonald points out that Potter's appearances as first-person narrator in her stories have the effect not of questioning the perspective, but of confirming the 'truth' of what is being told.[39] The narrator acts as an authoritative mediator between us and the animal world, as Seton does in his 'realistic' stories, except that she steps in to confirm the most fantastic and human-like actions of her animal protagonists. She is more like the 'editor' of Kipling's *Jungle Books*, who claims special knowledge of animal language and a special relationship with animal informants and the animal world.

34 Kenneth Grahame, *The Wind in the Willows* (London, 1969), p. 194.
35 Potter, *Tiggy-winkle*, p. 59.
36 Potter, *Complete Tales*, p. 56.
37 Ibid., pp. 191–3.
38 Ibid., p. 65.
39 Macdonald, 'Narrative Voice', p. 55.

Deirdre Pitts, lamenting the overuse of animal protagonists in 1970s children's literature, praises instead tales by writers like Kipling, Potter and Grahame, which give their animal heroes 'worlds from which man is excluded or in which he is ancillary to the action, or into which he enters at his own risk'. These worlds are 'unified with laws, language, etiquette, even class distinctions among the species'.[40] On the way to Bowness in the Lake District, brown notices direct the visitor to an attraction called 'Beatrix Potter's World', promising a unified imaginary place, though the actual attraction is a disappointing collection of figurines in tableaux. The 'world' that Potter creates has been variously characterised by critics, often using the words 'Arcadian' or 'pastoral'. For Blount, Potter's type of animal story is nostalgic, charming and painless. She recognises the persistent theme of predator and victim in Potter's books, but for her it is somehow cancelled out by the narrator's 'matter-of-fact' attitude.[41] Pennington credits Potter with the creation of a realm outside the industrial world, and the pastoral ideal of a prelapsarian age.[42] Carpenter on the other hand sees an Arcadian setting ironically undercut by 'black comedy', and always incorporating 'threat and fear'.[43] What kind of world, then, does Potter create for her talking animals, and how is it located in time and space? How does it relate to the worlds of human adults and children? To answer these questions, I want to look back first to the world created by Kipling, which Pitts takes as the prototype for later animal worlds that are separate from but parallel to the human world.

Kipling's animal world is a place of learning and danger, rather than a safe enclosed space. The Jungle itself is rarely described, and has very ambiguous characteristics:

> Father Wolf taught him his business, and the meaning of things in the Jungle, till every rustle of grass, every breath of the warm night air, every note of the owls above his head, every scratch of a bat's claws as it roosted for a while in a tree, and every splash of every little fish jumping in a pool, meant just as much to him as the work of his office means to a business man. When he was not learning, he sat out in the sun and slept, and ate and went to sleep again; when he felt dirty or hot he swam in the forest pools ... He would go down the hillside into the cultivated lands by night, and look very curiously at the villagers in their huts, but he had a mistrust of men because Bagheera showed him a square box with a drop-gate so cunningly hidden in the Jungle that he nearly walked into it, and told him it was a trap. He loved better than anything else to go with Bagheera into the dark warm heart of the forest, to sleep all through the drowsy day, and at night to see how Bagheera did his killing.[44]

---

40 Deidre Owen Pitts, 'Discerning the Animal of a Thousand Faces', *Children's Literature*, 3 (1974): 171–2.

41 Blount, pp. 131, 136.

42 John Pennington, 'From Peter Rabbit to *Watership Down*', *Journal of the Fantastic in the Arts*, 10/2 (1991): 68.

43 Carpenter, pp. 144–7.

44 Kipling, *Jungle Book*, pp. 25–6.

The metaphor of the 'businessman' and the 'office' destroys any idea of an Arcadian refuge outside the urban. Commerce and entrepreneurship also operate in Potter's world: Ginger and Pickles keep shop, Peter Rabbit ends up running a nursery garden. In Kipling, the presence of the 'trap' in the jungle attests to the presence of man, infiltrating from the neighbouring village. Human 'traps' are also featured in *Two Bad Mice* and *Pigling Bland*. At the end of the Kipling passage, there is the safe, womb-like 'dark warm heart of the jungle', but this is almost immediately associated with 'killing'. Seemingly cosy domestic spaces also have a less obvious violent quality in Potter's stories, and Mr Tod's house is both trap and killing field. Kipling's stories are distinctly 'postlapsarian': the story of *How Fear Came* relates an animal version of the Fall, that took place in the dim past before the main events of the *Jungle Books*. The story of *Peter Rabbit* itself has often been taken to be a version of the Fall, as Peter disobeys his mother's injunction, enters the garden and eats the forbidden vegetables. He spends much of this tale, and *The Tale of Benjamin Bunny*, half paralysed with fear.

Potter's stories are, unlike Kipling's, themselves set in a past time, eighteenth-century or slightly out-of-date. This by itself, however, does not warrant the charge of 'nostalgia'. Her own later description of the genesis of *Peter Rabbit* plays on the ideas of time and timelessness: 'It seems a long time ago, and in another world. Though after all the world does not change much in the country, where the seasons follow their accustomed course – the green leaf and the sere – and where nature though never consciously wicked has always been ruthless.'[45] This sets the tale in a timeless and pre-industrial world, that is not, however, Arcadian or prelapsarian. The 'ruthlessness' of Nature that for Kipling is part of a Darwinian world-view, and for earlier writers like Trimmer and Kingsley can be explained by variants of natural theology, is here presented as a timeless truth always known in the countryside. Like Trimmer's, Potter's world includes farms where animals are reared to be eaten, and ovens where they are cooked.

The animals in Potter's world are mostly relatively small – the largest are pigs, foxes and badgers, and the second two are always seen as threats from the perspective of smaller animals. This question of size suggests that Gaston Bachelard's ideas in *The Poetics of Space* about the imaginative appeal of 'nests and shells' would be relevant:

> I relived countless aerial or aquatic day-dreams, according to whether I followed the poets into the nest in the tree, or into the sort of animal cave that is constituted by a shell ... I returned to images that, in order for us to live them, require us to become very small, as in nests and shells. Indeed, in our houses we have nooks and corners in which we like to curl up comfortably.[46]

But the only really comfortable space like this is perhaps Mrs Tiggy-winkle's kitchen, child-sized and behind a little door in a hillside. It has been compared to

---

45 Leslie Linder, *A History of the Writings of Beatrix Potter* (London, 1971), p. 92.
46 Gaston Bachelard, *The Poetics of Space* (Boston, MA, 1969), p. xxxiv.

Badger's kitchen in *Wind in the Willows*, a place of safety, comfort and warmth. But the attractions of Mrs Tiggy-winkle's kitchen for Lucie, the child protagonist, are undercut by her growing unease at her hostess's animal qualities:

> They sat before the fire on a bench and looked sideways at one another. Mrs Tiggy-winkle's hand, holding the tea-cup, was very very brown, and very very wrinkly with the soap suds; and all through her gown and her cap, there were hair-pins sticking wrong end out; so that Lucie did not like to sit too near her.[47]

There are distinct echoes here of Little Red Riding Hood and the wolf in grandmother's clothing. Mrs Tittlemouse's hole might seem another cosy miniature domestic world, like the homes of mole or rat in *Wind in the Willows*. But the dormouse hole is continually being invaded by various insects, as well as the slimy toad, Mr Jackson, and cleaning is a constant source of anxiety for Mrs Tittlemouse.

Daphne Kutzer has written persuasively on the perils of domestic space in Potter. Jemima Puddle-duck, looking for a safe place to lay her eggs, finds herself in the fox's feather-filled woodshed, a place of death. Peter Rabbit, back home in his rabbit hole, is confined to bed by his mother, as immobile and smothered as if he, like Tom Kitten, were rolled up in a pudding, or baked in a pie like his father. The illustrations of mothers (Mrs Rabbit, Tabitha Twitchett, Aunt Pettitoes) smothering their children in tight-fitting clothes reinforce the confining nature of domesticity and the maternal. While the mouse-world behind the house walls in *The Tailor of Gloucester* is friendly and supportive, in *Samuel Whiskers* the rat-world inside the walls of Potter's house is malevolent and violent. Ovens and tables are places of violence, where human and animal figures eat or plan to eat smaller animals: Mr McGregor eats Peter's father, and plans to eat the Flopsy bunnies, Tommy Brock imprisons another generation of bunnies in the oven, and lays out a carving knife and a pie-dish on the table, Ribby cooks and Duchess eats mouse pie, Samuel Whiskers and Anna Maria plan to cook Tom Kitten, the fox invites Jemima to a dinner of roast duck.

In contrast to these hot and violent desires, is the cold artificial domesticity of the dolls' house in *Two Bad Mice*. In this story, the mice break into the dolls' house while the dolls are out. The mice are disappointed and then angry to find the dolls'-house food is fake, and cannot be cut and eaten , nor burnt on the fake fire. In a rage, they break up the food – 'bang, bang, smash, smash!' – and start to tear the place to bits.[48] But then the 'frugal' mouse wife, Hunca Munca, decides instead to pillage whatever she needs from the house, and they make off with a feather bed and some furniture and clothes, just as the dolls return. The cold, artificial formality of the dolls' house contrasts with the animal violence of the mice. Autobiographical readings have been made of this tale, with the mice as Potter and Norman Warne, her fiancé, smashing the artificiality of her parents' confining home.[49] The structure and content of the tale also suggest a carnivalesque reading, as the mice run riot while the upper-class

---

47 Potter, *Tiggy-winkle*, p. 46.
48 Potter, *Two Bad Mice*, p. 29.
49 Kutzer, pp. 60–75.

doll, Lucinda, and her servant doll Jane are away. There are attempts by the humans to impose authority at the end: the girl who owns the dolls' house buys a policeman doll, and the nurse installs a mouse trap. Neither of these are effective, however, as the illustrations show the mice quite fearlessly approaching both, and Tom Thumb, the father mouse, explaining the trap to his family. Nevertheless, carnival license is contained at the end, as the mice establish their own domesticity with the items stolen from the dolls, and they also attempt restitution: Tom Thumb pays by giving the dolls a crooked sixpence he found, and Hunca Munca cleans the dolls' house every morning. Domesticity is restored on two fronts.

The eruption of violence in this tale is not the genteel carnivalesque of the papillonades. It is more like one of the Topsy-Turvy poems, in which animals who try rebellion decide it won't work. But with Potter nothing is ever clear-cut: when Hunca Munca is dressed as a cleaning-woman, does this signify the restoration of class hierarchies, or a carnivalesque joke about animals in human dress? Potter's 'seamless' procedures also frustrate any attempt to see her 'world' as a whole as carnivalesque. Rather than creating a topsy-turvy, world-turned-upside-down effect, she proceeds by gradations from animal to human, by means of different kinds of speech, clothing and habitation, as I have shown. Moreover, when the 'naughty' Peter Rabbit enters Mr McGregor's garden and wreaks havoc on the vegetables, he is not like Maurice Sendak's Max entering a liberating play-space of 'Wild Things'. The garden is presided over by a dangerous authority figure. Nutkin's carnivalesque riddles and lack of respect for authority go on at the same time as the responsible behaviour of the other squirrels, and result in a terrible retribution. While the silliness of Mr Tod's prank, and his 'bad language', might suggest he is a carnivalesque figure, he is also dangerous and powerful. In other stories it is *dis*order that is restored at the end, as the kittens continue to riot in the bedroom in *Tom Kitten*, or the pigs evade authority and dance away over the hills in *Pigling Bland*. But in *Samuel Whiskers*, Tom meets his come-uppance, from a rat who is himself marginal and transgressive, and Pigling Bland's aspiration is very conformist: 'I wish I could have a little garden and grow potatoes.'[50]

There is no doubt that licence and authority, freedom and social control, are recurring, intertwined motifs in Potter's world, but it is not easy to disentangle them. Carnivalesque effects usually rely on an established hierarchy, which can then be overturned or restored. Unlike most of the animal stories I have discussed, Potter's world does not seem to have a consistent hierarchy, or even an evolutionary ladder, only a food-chain: frogs eat butterflies and trout eat frogs, and humans eat rabbits and pigs. Occasionally rats try to eat kittens. Certain animal characters are identified with certain human social classes through clothes and speech: the upper-class fox, the humble washerwoman Mrs Tiggy-winkle, the respectable middle-class Tabitha Twitchett, the disreputable and vulgar Tommy Brock. But there is no sense that any of these are better than any others, as there is in *The Wind in the Willows*, with its demonisation of the working-class weasels and ferrets. Their takeover of Toad

---

50 Potter, *Complete Tales*, p. 291.

Hall is useful to compare with the Bad Mice's invasion of the dolls' house, where sympathy is with the mice, and the house is not worth having. Humans are not better or higher than animals in Potter's stories, but neither are animals consistently better than humans. Property-owners like Mr McGregor and Old Brown the owl have great power, which is not disputed but not admired either. Peter Rabbit ends up keeping a nursery garden, like Mr McGregor. Both the human narrator and Aunt Pettitoes the sow act as farmers and as advisers to the young pigs.

Is there a gender hierarchy in Potter's world? While Kipling's animal world is aggressively masculine, is hers correspondingly feminine? Does she subscribe to the superiority of the male? I have mentioned suffocating mothers, but these are balanced by violent male power figures – Mr McGregor, Old Brown, Old Mr Benjamin Bunny, Mr Tod, Tommy Brock, Mr Piperson. Power is differently exercised by male and female adults, but both can threaten the freedom of child animals. But other adult animals act against authority – the Flopsy bunnies' parents co-operate in outwitting Mr McGregor, Hunca Munca and Tom Thumb sack the dolls' house together. There are also innocent and simple-minded adult animals of both sexes, like Jemima, Jeremy Fisher and Duchess. It is true that the disobedient child heroes of the tales are often male – Peter, Benjamin, Nutkin, Tom. Peter's good little siblings are sisters. But Tom's sisters join in his riot, and while he ends up afraid of mice, they become champion rat catchers, who 'charge so much a dozen, and earn their living very comfortably'.[51] A picture shows them nailing up the rats' tails on the barn door: they have become enforcers of order. Pigling Bland and Pig-wig share the rebellious role between them, with Pig-wig doing much to encourage Pigling.

The question of hierarchy involves the question of values. Several critics have pointed out that Potter's tales, unlike traditional fables, have no moral. While *Peter Rabbit* seems to be enforcing the moral that children should obey their parents, it also subversively suggests that the disobedient Peter has a more exciting time than his obedient sisters. Potter's original manuscript opening to *Mr Tod*, makes it even clearer than the book that 'disagreeable' people make better stories: 'I am quite tired of making goody goody books about nice people. I will make a story about two disagreeable people, called Tommy Brock and Mr Tod.'[52] Her publishers rejected this opening as too unpleasant. In some ways, the Potter world is similar to the traditional fairy-tale world, with its lack of consistent morals. As I have said, the pattern of Red Riding Hood can be detected in several of the tales: in *Peter Rabbit* the illustration of Mrs Rabbit going through the wood to the baker's with her basket likens her to Red Riding Hood, and Peter's story of disobedience is also a reference to the fairy-tale. Jemima Puddle-duck and the fox re-enact the story in a different way, as do Lucie and Mrs Tiggy-winkle – these two stories depend on animals disguised by their clothes. In Jemima's story, the dogs play the part of the rescuing woodcutter. It is interesting that Potter's own retelling of the fairy-tale allows no rescue: '"But Granny, Granny – what big white teeth – " And that was the end of little Red Riding

---

51 Ibid., p. 195.
52 Linder, p. 210.

Hood.'[53] Red Riding Hood, unlike Peter but like Jemima, has not been warned of danger, so there is no moral point to her being eaten.

In substituting animals and science for fairy-tales and magic, Potter is carrying on the tradition of Enlightenment children's stories. Peter Hollindale quotes a revealing passage from her journal:

> I remember I used to half believe and wholly play with fairies when I was a child. What heaven can be more real than to retain the spirit-world of childhood. Tempered and balanced by knowledge and common-sense, to fear no longer the terror that flieth by night, yet to feel truly and understand a little, a very little, of the story of life.[54]

This passage also bears a resemblance to Seton's aspirations, as told in his story 'The Kangaroo Rat'. When he first sees the rats' little footprints, he speculates that 'any peasant could have explained it offhand – invisible pairs of tiny, furry boots, dancing in the moonlight – why, the veriest idiot knows that – *fairies*, of course.' But he has forsworn such beliefs: 'for long ago, when my soul came to the fork in the trail marked on the left "To Arcadie," on the right "To Scientia," I took the flinty, upland right-hand path. I had given my fairyland eyes for – for I do not know what.' By the end of the story, however, he realises how remarkable the Kangaroo Rat is: 'I had been willing to find an impossible mystery, but I had found a delightful story from Nature's wonderland.'[55] Like Seton, Potter is able to play with the fairy-tale implication of tiny footprints, which yet have an animal cause: 'It looked as though some person had been walking all over the garden in a pair of clogs – only the foot-marks were too ridiculously little!'[56] Unlike Seton's rat, her animal does wear clogs, while his 'tiny, furry boots' are only a metaphor. Belief in fairies is attributed by one writer to children, and the other to peasants: childhood again corresponds to a more 'primitive', superstitious phase of human history. Potter, like Kipling, is more willing to retain some aspects of this phase, tempered and balanced by knowledge, and not renounced entirely for the 'flinty' path of science.

It is interesting that for both Seton and Potter, the 'magic' element is to do with miniaturisation, while for Kipling it is more to do with the foreign and exotic. While Potter's small creatures and their homes may not provide the comfort of Bachelard's 'nests and shells', there is a fascination with the miniature in her stories. In *Mrs Tiggy-winkle*, Lucie comes upon a 'can no bigger than an egg-cup! And where the sand upon the path was wet – there were foot-marks of a *very* small person … there were clothes-props cut from bracken stems, with lines of plaited rushes, and a heap of tiny clothes pins.'[57] Once again, we have the mysterious, fairy-like footprints. The perspectives of small animals also casts human beings as giants, as in the illustrations that show Mr McGregor only as a large pair of hands or a large boot at the edge of a

---

53 Ibid., p. 363.
54 Hollindale, pp. 131–2, quoting Beatrix Potter's *Journal*, 17 November 1896.
55 Seton, *Lives of the Hunted*, pp. 236, 239, 256.
56 Potter, *Complete Tales*, p. 67.
57 Potter, *Tiggy-winkle*, pp. 17–18.

picture of Peter trying to escape. Seton too sees himself as playing the part of a fairy-tale 'Giant' to the kangaroo rats. We have something here of the insects' or birds'-eye views of Trimmer and Barbauld's stories, which defamiliarise the human world (see pp. 35, 47 above). But Potter is not using this device in order to recommend kindness to animals. The dedication to her *Tale of Samuel Whiskers* sounds at first as if the story carries the same message as the autobiographical *Rambles of a Rat*, by Charlotte Tucker (1857), whose Preface asserts: 'there is so much to interest and admire even in those animals which we usually regard with contempt and disgust.'[58] But these are Potter's words: 'In remembrance of Sammy, the intelligent pink-eyed representative of a persecuted (but irrepressible) race. An affectionate little friend and most accomplished thief.'[59] Potter alludes ironically to a whole tradition which used oppressed peoples as metaphors for animals, and vice versa.

Potter does not then directly urge kindness to or admiration for animals, and nor does she overtly relay a conservationist message, as Seton did. Nevertheless, outside her books she gave her land in the Lake District to the National Trust, with a conservationist aim. Her writings and her 'world' are firmly associated with a particular landscape and location, which draws tourists to Hill Top, her house in Sawrey. Most of her illustrations are based on particular places and houses in the Lake District. Readers can visit Lucie's farm at New Town, the bay from which Nutkin and the other squirrels sailed on Derwentwater, the house in which Tabitha Twitchett and Samuel Whiskers lived. Leslie Linder in *A History of the Writings of Beatrix Potter* recounts his stay in Sawrey, at 'Ginger and Pickles'. The response of readers transforms life into art, as they read Potter's stories into the existing landscape. If there is an 'autobiographical pact' made by the texts, it is largely through the illustrations that portray specific, identifiable places. This intense identification with particular locations is rather different from the way Kipling apparently changed the location of his Jungle to an area he knew little of, and transposed the details of different places.[60] Seton, however, does set his stories in particular landscapes and places such as New Mexico, or Yellowstone Park. The latter preserves his wilderness, as the National Trust preserves Potter's countryside. Her Lake District already carries the weight of Wordsworthian significance, as a place of special closeness to Nature, where ancient ways of life are still preserved, a place of pilgrimage and recreation for those who did not live there. Unlike the (ideal) wilderness, this area always includes human beings and their effect on the landscape.

While the word critics use to describe Beatrix Potter's technique is 'seamless', their evaluations of Kenneth Grahame's *The Wind in the Willows* use phrases such as 'densely layered', 'fragmented', 'pasted together', and 'swerv[ing] unsteadily, even wildly'.[61] Other critics feel called upon to defend the structural integrity of the book,

---

58 Tucker, p. vi.

59 Potter, *Complete Tales*, p. 174.

60 Roger Lancelyn Green, 'Mowgli's Jungle', *Kipling Journal*, 57/227 (1983): 29–35.

61 Peter Hunt, *The Wind in the Willows: A Fragmented Arcadia* (New York, 1994), pp. 9, iii, 26, 97; Neil Philip, 'Kenneth Grahame's *The Wind in the Willows*: A Companionable

pointing to repeated themes of adventure and return, home and away, which unite its various parts: Mole's *Bildungsroman*, Toad's adventures, the semi-religious vision of the god Pan, and Rat's temptation by the wandering Sea-Rat. The uncertainty that surrounds the text extends to the question of whether it is a children's book at all, Carpenter asserting that '*The Wind in the Willows* has nothing to do with childhood or children', while Kathryn Graham sees it as a school story addressed to Grahame's son, Alastair, and Bonnie Gaarden privileges her reading of the text as a nine-year-old over the interpretations of adult critics.[62]

The text rarely addresses a reader: Mole, discovering the river, 'trots, as one trots, when very small, by the side of a man, who holds one spellbound by exciting stories'. This 'one' is clearly an adult narrator, appealing to an adult reader to join him in remembering childhood, as Margaret Gatty does at the beginning of 'Inferior Animals'. In its romanticising of both childhood and nature, *The Wind in the Willows* is similar to both Gatty's and Kingsley's works, though without their interest in science or their religious framework. Later in the text there is also an isolated address to a child reader: Badger doesn't mind his guests ignoring their table manners, and the narrator comments, 'We know of course that he was wrong, and took too narrow a view; because they do matter very much, though it would take too long to explain why.'[63] The 'we' is the cajoling, didactic plural of an adult addressing a child, while the final clause seems to send up the inadequacy of adult explanations. The varying address, and the book's status somewhere between adults' and children's literature can be paralleled by the earlier *Parables from Nature*, and the papillonades: recent critics have become used to a more rigid division between adult and children's literature.

The disjunctive nature of the text enables and is partly caused by the multi-layered, ambiguous status of its animal protagonists and their relation to the human world. As A. A. Milne puts it, 'it is necessary to think of Mole, for instance, sometimes as an actual mole, sometimes as a mole in human clothes, sometimes as a mole grown to human size, sometimes walking on two legs, sometimes on four.'[64] The comparable changes in size of Beatrix Potter's animals were either subtly managed, or openly remarked on, as with Mrs Tiggy-winkle's sudden 'shrinking' as she sheds her clothes and reverts back to hedgehog size. There is no such subtlety in Grahame's treatment: his animals veer between natural and human size without comment. Rat can walk among a forest of corn-stalks that wave over his head; he and Mole can also enter a human village in search of an inn, and put Toad on a train, tipping the Porter.

Vitality', in Perry Nodelman (ed.), *Touchstones*, vol. 1 (West Lafayette, IN, 1985), p. 104; Jay Williams, 'Reflections on *The Wind in the Willows*', *Signal*, 21 (1976): 104.

62 Carpenter, p. 168; Kathryn V.Graham, 'Of School and the River: *The Wind in the Willows* and its Immediate Audience', *Children's Literature Association Quarterly*, 23/4 (1998–99): 181–6; Bonnie Gaarden, 'The Inner Family of *The Wind in the Willows*', *Children's Literature*, 22 (1994): 43–57.

63 Grahame, pp. 10, 79.

64 Hunt, p. 52.

Mole and Toad ride horses, and Toad famously drives cars, and passes as a human washerwoman. But later he is recognised as a toad and flung in the canal.

The changes in size are paralleled by wildly fluctuating degrees of anthropomorphism, perhaps most obviously when Toad is in gaol. The gaoler's daughter is full of sympathy with him as a small animal which she hopes to make into a pet. Toad, on the other hand, is regretting that their social positions are too widely apart for him to consider marrying her. Next she is proposing he dress up as her aunt, the washerwoman. Elsewhere, the 'wild' animal heroes incongruously make use of domestic animals. So Mole, Rat and Toad drive or ride horses, and 'hams' hang in Badger's kitchen. While Jeremy Fisher eats a 'butterfly sandwich', Rat and Mole have a picnic basket full of 'coldtonguecoldhamcoldbeef pickledgher-kinssaladfrenchrollscresssandwidgespottedmeatgingerbeerlemonadesodawater'.[65]

Beatrix Potter objected to this excessive humanisation of Grahame's animals:

> Yes – Kenneth Grahame ought to have been an artist – at least all writers for children ought to have a sufficient recognition of what things look like – did he not describe 'Toad' as combing his *hair*? A mistake to fly in the face of nature – A frog may wear goloshes; but I don't hold with toads having beards or wigs! So I prefer Badger.[66]

But it is important to bear in mind that Grahame was originally opposed to the idea of illustrating the text.[67] E. H. Shepard's famous illustrations were not added until 1930. In the same year, A. A. Milne's stage adaptation, *Toad of Toad Hall*, began the convention that the animals would be played by human actors with minimal animal disguise (tails, ears, colouring). Shepard and Milne have thus established two fixed visual interpretations of the characters: as animals in clothes, and as humans in animal costume. What the unillustrated 1908 text would have done is to leave both these possibilities open, and allow for their merging and transforming one into the other. Grahame's effect is very different from the precise visual detail and natural historical accuracy of Potter. Famously, an early reviewer of *Wind in the Willows*, influenced perhaps by the tradition stretching from Trimmer to Potter, remarked that 'as a contribution to natural history, the work is negligible.'[68]

Nevertheless, as Jane Darcy points out, 'in *The Wind in the Willows* Grahame's knowledge of the flora and fauna of the Riverbank and the habits of the small animals who live there is extensive.'[69] The animal-ness of the protagonists and the natural setting, though much less important than in Potter's tales, contribute to the overall effect. As animals, the characters have different habits and abilities from humans. For instance, they hibernate:

---

65 Grahame, p. 13.

66 Linder, p. 175.

67 Cynthia Marshall, 'Bodies and Pleasures in *The Wind in the Willows*', *Children's Literature*, 22 (1994): 58.

68 Hunt, p. 14.

69 Jane Darcy, 'The Representation of Nature in *The Wind in the Willows* and *The Secret Garden*', *The Lion and the Unicorn*, 19/2 (1995): 216.

No animal, according to the rules of animal etiquette, is ever expected to do anything strenuous, or heroic, or even moderately active during the off-season of winter. All are sleepy – some actually asleep. All are weather-bound, more or less; and all are resting from arduous days and nights, during which every muscle in them has been severely tested, and every energy kept at full stretch.[70]

Here, animal instinct is humorously recast as 'etiquette' (a milder form of Kipling's 'Jungle Law'). The physical reality of being an animal is insisted on, and at the same time a way is found to talk about it in a human way. 'Etiquette' is also invoked in a light reminder of the grimmer realities of animals' lives: 'the Rat hummed a tune, and the Mole recollected that animal-etiquette forbade any sort of comment on the sudden disappearance of one's friends at any moment, for any reason or no reason whatever.' Otter, a peripheral character who behaves in a more animal-like way than the others, has just disappeared to eat a May-fly, we assume: 'A swirl of water and a "cloop!" and the May-fly was visible no more. Neither was the Otter.'[71] Equally, 'any reason' could include being eaten, though this is not allowed to happen to any of the characters in the book. Grahame simultaneously alludes to and covers up this intrusion of the 'red-in-tooth-and-claw' side of animal life. This is quite different from Potter's 'matter-of-fact' openness about the dangers of animal life.

Grahame is more explicit about animal instinct elsewhere, when Mole is drawn to his nearby but invisible home:

We others, who have long lost the more subtle of the physical senses, have not even proper terms to express an animal's inter-communications with his surroundings, living or otherwise, and have only the word 'smell', for instance, to include the whole range of delicate thrills which murmur in the nose of the animal night and day, summoning, warning, inciting, repelling. It was one of these mysterious fairy calls from out the void that suddenly reached Mole in the darkness, making him tingle through and through with its very familiar appeal, even while as yet he could not clearly remember what it was.[72]

This sort of celebration of animals' supra-human senses was also in evidence in the animal autobiographies. While Grahame here contrasts human ('we others') and animal, he also creates a continuum: 'we' used to possess these senses, and Grahame ends by describing Mole's feelings in very human terms: 'Shabby indeed, and small and poorly furnished, and yet his, the home he had made for himself, the home he had been so happy to get back to after his day's work.'[73] The implication is that humans retain traces of these sensory calls – like the call of Spring that initially draws Mole up from his cleaning underground. One of the book's most sensuous moments is evoked in terms of smell: the bubble and squeak, and then the hot buttered toast that the gaoler's daughter tempts Toad with:

---

70 Grahame, p. 71.
71 Ibid., p. 21.
72 Ibid., pp. 87–8.
73 Ibid., pp. 88–9.

> The smell of that buttered toast simply talked to Toad, and with no uncertain voice; talked of warm kitchens, of breakfasts on bright frosty mornings, of cosy parlour firesides on winter evenings, when one's ramble was over and slippered feet were propped on the fender; the purring of contented cats, and the twitter of sleepy canaries.[74]

The basic physical pleasures called up here – home, warmth, food – are those a child would understand, a child who is seen as 'nearer' to our animal origins. At the same time, adult nostalgia for such a simplified, physically alive, 'child-like' or 'animal' world is played upon. The animal trace in the human is not a matter of violent 'beastly' instincts, but of direct, physical, sensory pleasure – though excluding sex.

The protagonists, then, exist between the animal and human, and also between the adult and child. As humans, they can be identified as members of a leisured, masculine elite. But their protected, irresponsible, sexless existence also corresponds to a version of childhood. Keeping their distance from humans, the animals function like the children-only world, separate from adults, that we find in children's books by Edith Nesbit or Arthur Ransome. The animals also fall into child and adult roles, though they are all ostensibly adult. Mole and Toad are the principal children, the good child and the (lovable) bad child. Rat is an older child friend, initiating Mole into the ways of the Riverbank, or, in some interpretations, he is the mother. Badger acts as a father, protective but stern, or even a headmaster, when he takes Toad off to his study for an impressive telling-off. Mole is the child who grows and learns, earning adult approval from Badger at the end. Toad is the irrepressible, anarchic, rule-breaking child. When he is prevented from driving cars, he arranges the chairs in his room 'in rude resemblance of a motor-car and would crouch on the foremost of them, bent forward and staring fixedly ahead, making uncouth and ghastly noises'.[75] He is like a child playing a pretend game. The adult humans who punish and pursue him are rendered ridiculous. He has a childish self-centredness, boastfulness and amorality, and a short attention-span.

The indeterminacy of the animals' age and humanity also extends to their gender. On the one hand, they can easily be recognised as a group of 'bachelors', and the text excludes most female animals, and casts most human women as large and threatening. Otter's wife is mentioned but never appears; and at the very end some properly subservient weasel mothers speak. The bargewoman is seen by Toad as a representing 'fat women with mottled arms who couldn't tell a real gentleman when they saw one'.[76] Mole threatens Toad with another stay in hospital, being ordered about by female nurses. The helpful gaoler's daughter is an exception, but Peter Hunt has pointed out that it is the women who are able to recognise Toad as an animal, and consequently demean him.[77] But Toad's bumptiousness requires demeaning: it is notable that none of the other animals are seen through human or female eyes. Toad is the Peter Rabbit of the story, who ventures out into human-controlled space. The

---

74 Ibid., p. 146.
75 Ibid., p. 116.
76 Ibid., p. 311.
77 Hunt, p. 85.

absence of female animals in the animal-controlled space is a different matter, and reminiscent of Mowgli's masculine Jungle. The way the chief protagonists are named partially conceals this absence – the Mole, the Rat, the Badger, the Toad. There is only one of each, and that one is referred to by male pronouns. This is, of course, not an unusual procedure in natural histories, and also earlier in bestiaries and fables. It is also widespread in contemporary children's books that feature groups of animals, where, as in *The Wind in the Willows*, the species name then becomes the proper name: Mole, Rat, Badger, Toad.

These characters have been identified as types of human males of a certain class and era. But Gaarden objects to these adult identifications, remembering instead her reading of the text as a nine-year-old, in which the characters were 'ageless, timeless, genderless'. She contends that 'Grahame's refusal to so much as name any female animal until the very last page of the book does not obliterate the feminine. Rather, it circumvents the reader's habit of classifying individuals primarily by sex, and leads us to differentiate, instead, by species.'[78] It has been recognised that the animal protagonists have many 'feminine' characteristics. They are certainly very different from the large, aggressively masculine carnivores who inhabit Mowgli's forest. Although Grahame's story does end with a fight, there is no killing involved. Not only are his animals small herbivores (though they do eat ham sandwiches), they are also overwhelmingly domestic, living in cosy holes and burrows (Toad is an exception here). Though there are hints of off-stage servants, Rat, Mole and Badger engage in domestic tasks, and nurture and support each other emotionally. Rat is full of emotional tact when he praises and revivifies Mole's home, finding food and comfort; Mole in return just as tactfully brings Rat back from the trance induced by the Sea Rat's tales of adventure, by telling him of the joys of home-life.

Kuznets, while noting this androgyny, points out that it is not available to females in the text, but Marshall argues that a more performative notion of gender gives a more positive feminist reading.[79] The very lack of visual specificity and detailed embodiment of the characters, means that their gender can be unfixed. Toad's and Mole's convincing performances in the washerwoman's dress show that gender is external and inessential. There is an interesting contrast with Potter here. 'Miss Potter's' role as woman farmer, and Moppet and Mitten's careers as champion rat-catchers suggest a positive female androgyny. Strong women are not seen as coarse, fat bargewomen; the dangerous women are suffocating mothers who impose domestic ideals. A violent male character like Mr Tod who also displays a feminine concern with the domestic is ridiculed. Despite the importance of clothes in Potter's stories, there is no cross-dressing between the sexes, only between animal and human.

What kind of language, then, do the animals talk in The Wind in the Willows? Not surprisingly, it varies wildly, from the witty to the poetic, from the 'impoverished'

---

78 Gaarden, pp. 43–4.

79 Lois Kuznets, 'Kenneth Grahame and Father Nature', *Children's Literature*, 16 (1988): 175–81; Marshall, pp. 59, 67.

slang and invective of schoolboys to the awe-struck language of dream and trance.80 Here is Rat talking to Mole in Mole's house: 'Mole, old chap, I'm ready to drop. Sleepy is simply not the word ... What a ripping little house this is! Everything so handy!' Here is the same Rat on Pan's island: 'This is the place of my song-dream, the place the music played to me ... Here, in this holy place, here if anywhere, surely we shall find Him!' Rat is a poet: when Mole too becomes poetic, indirect speech partly conceals the incongruity: 'the Mole turned his talk to the harvest that was being gathered in, the towering wagons and their straining teams, the growing ricks, and the large moon rising over bare acres dotted with sheaves. He talked of the reddening apples around, of the browning nuts, of jams and preserves and the distilling of cordials.'81 This is a Keatsian description, and Rat, mesmerised by the Sea Rat's tale, is described like the wedding-guest in Coleridge's 'Ancient Mariner'. The influence of the Romantic poets on Grahame's book has often been remarked.82 His talking animals inhabit and emerge from a Wordsworthian talking landscape. The River, when first encountered, 'chattered on' to Mole, 'a babbling procession of the best stories in the world'. When Otter and Rat talk 'river-shop' at Badger's, it is 'talk that is endless, running on like the babbling river itself'.83 The talking, or singing river is a feature of Kingsley's Water Babies, where the stream sings to Tom.

Like the Romantics, Grahame is ambiguous as to whether the sense of a living Nature is an effect of pantheism, or of the perceiving human mind. In an essay entitled 'The Fellow that Goes Alone' (1913), he wrote:

> For Nature's particular gift to the walker ... is to set the mind jogging, to make it garrulous, exalted, a little mad maybe – certainly creative and suprasensitive, until at last it really seems to be outside of you and as if it were talking to you while you are talking back to it. Then everything gradually seems to join in, sun and the wind, the white road and the dusty hedges, the spirit of the season ... till you walk in the middle of a blessed company, immersed in a dream-talk far transcending any possible human conversation.[84]

'Dream' mediates between outward symbol and inner state. It is his 'dream-song' that Rat finds on the island. Some critics have read the book's landscapes as symbolic of states of mind, and the animals themselves as actors in a psychodrama. So Maureen Thum for instance reads Mole's visit to the Wild Woods as 'a description of the mind's troubling disorientation' when entering 'uncharted psychological territory',

80 Graham, p. 184.

81 Grahame, pp. 105, 134, 225.

82 Lesley Willis, '"A Sadder and a Wiser Rat/He Rose the Morrow Morn": Echoes of the Romantics in Kenneth Grahame's *The Wind in the Willows*', *Children's Literature Association Quarterly*, 13/3 (1988): 108-11; Richard Gillin, 'Romantic Echoes in the Willows', *Children's Literature*, 16 (1988): 169–74.

83 Grahame, pp. 4–5, 89.

84 Grahame, 'The Fellow that Goes Alone', *St Edward's School Chronicle*, 12/321 (1913), reprinted in Peter Green, *Kenneth Grahame, A Biography* (London, 1959), pp. 4–6.

while for Carpenter, the Wood symbolises 'the unpleasant possibilities of one's personal psychology', while Toad 'represents the threat to the individual from the excesses of his own nature'.[85] Gaarden assigns Jungian archetypes to the different characters. These readings become plausible since Grahame is not operating in the secure religious framework of Gatty or Kingsley, who also give inanimate Nature speech and meaning. Psychology takes over from theology.

'Talk', 'voice', 'song', 'story' are key words in Grahame's animation of his landscape. Even the smell of the buttered toast 'talks' to Toad. The moon comes out to 'listen' to the talk of the animals. Behind the 'voices' of the River is the almost inarticulate whispering of the wind in the willows. These hints of the numinous culminate in the appearance of the god Pan, whose presence is heralded by music in the chapter 'The Piper at the Gates of Dawn'. While Rat hears piping, Mole at first hears only 'the wind playing in the reeds and rushes and osiers'. After the god's appearance, the music mutates into words, which only Rat can catch: 'Dance-music – the lilting sort that runs on without a stop – but with words in it too – it passes into words and out of them again – I catch them at intervals – then it is dance-music once more, and then nothing but the reeds' whispering.'[86] Finally the song dies away into 'reed-talk' – the 'talking' landscape that underlies the varied speech of the animal characters.

The god himself is described in a surprisingly visual way, given the 'unbodied' nature of the animal characters. We are given a list of separate body-parts: 'the curved horns', 'the stern, hooked nose between the kindly eyes', 'the bearded mouth', 'the rippling muscles', 'the long supple hand', 'the parted lips', 'the splendid curves of the shaggy limbs'.[87] Pan appeared often in neo-pagan texts of the *fin de siècle* and the Edwardian era – Grahame is of his time here – but what is original is to have thought of a religion appropriate to animal protagonists.[88] There are signs of such a development in the *Jungle Books*, where the animals have their own creation myth, and, unexpectedly, in Seton's 'realist' work. In 'Lobo', a (perhaps metaphorical) 'Angel of the wild' protects the wolf; in 'Raggylug', 'the good Angel' leads pursued and exhausted animals to the safety of running water; in 'Krag', the ram is protected by another power: 'Oh Chinook! Mother West Wind! … are you only a puff of air, or are you, as Greek and Indian both alike have taught, a something better, a living, thinking thing, that first creates, then loves and guards its own?'[89] The Chinook even sings:

---

85 Maureen Thum, 'Exploring the Country of the Mind: Mental Dimensions of Landscape in Kenneth Grahame's *The Wind in the Willows*', *Children's Literature Association Quarterly*, 17/3 (1992): 29; Carpenter, pp. 157–8.

86 Grahame, pp. 39, 26, 158–9, 168.

87 Ibid., p. 163.

88 William Greenslade, '"Pan" and the Open Road: Critical Paganism in R. L. Stevenson, K. Grahame, E. Thomas and E. M. Forster', in Lynne Hapgood and Nancy L. Paxton (eds), *Outside Modernism: In Pursuit of the English Novel, 1900–30* (London, 2000), pp. 145–61.

89 Seton, *Wild Animals*, pp. 33, 85; *Lives of the Hunted*, p. 86.

I am the mothering White Wind;
    This is my hour of might.
The hills and the snow are my children;
    My service they do tonight.[90]

In 'Tito', the 'All-mother' is invoked, and 'Mother Carey' makes an appearance in 'The Chickadee'.[91] These nature deities owe something to Kingsley's mother-goddesses, something to classical myth, and something to Native American lore. Like Grahame's Pan, they are protective of animals – Pan is 'the Friend and Helper', and his song is partly about rescuing animals: '*I spring the trap that is set – As I loose the snare you may glimpse me there ... I cheer – Small waifs in the woodland wet – Strays I find in it, wounds I bind in it.*'[92] The purpose of the god's appearance in this chapter is to find the lost Otter child, Portly. Seton's and Grahame's animal religion hovers ambiguously between the metaphorical and the spiritual. Their works do not have either the assured framework of the Christian tradition, or the bracing secularism of Beatrix Potter's world.

As well as symbolic or spiritual readings, *The Wind in the Willows* has lent itself also to interpretations in terms of political and social allegory. As in the *Jungle Books*, we are presented with a community of animals, living according to their own social code, and defending their way of life. Grahame's characters represent a particular social hierarchy. Badger is the Squire, Toad the aristocrat, though also with a hint of the *nouveau riche*, Rat the leisured upper-middle-class gentleman, Mole a shabby-genteel Pooterish clerk, or a grammar-school boy. The weasels and stoats can be read as the lower classes. They are feared and despised in the same way that the monkeys are in the Jungle. Their invasion of Toad Hall is a revolution of sorts, and good order is only restored when they return to their woods and to proper deference. In both Kipling's and Grahame's stories, the animal/human hierarchy has to some extent been overturned: Kipling's animals are nobler than the human villagers, and Grahame's 'good' animals shun human society and its inventions, while Toad comes to grief by mixing with the human. But any carnivalesque tendencies are checked by the hierarchy *within* the animal world. Toad's carnivalesque excesses lead to the unpleasant overturning of authority and hierarchy represented by the weasels' takeover of Toad Hall.

This kind of interpretation is, however, somewhat undercut by the way the Chief Weasel speaks: '"Well, I do not propose to detain you much longer" – (great applause) – "but before I resume my seat" (renewed cheering) – "I should like to say one word about our kind host, Mr Toad. We all know Toad!" – (great laughter) ... .'[93] As Carpenter points out, this speech is 'not rabble-rousing by a mob leader, but a typical piece of after-dinner oratory at a banquet'.[94] But is the Chief Weasel *imitating*

---

90 Ibid., p. 102.
91 Ibid., pp. 318, 355.
92 Grahame, p. 169.
93 Ibid., p. 239.
94 Carpenter, p. 165.

an upper-class speaker, in the same way that Toad is so easily able to impersonate a lower-class washerwoman: '"Never so happy as when I've got both arms in the wash-tub! But, then, it comes so easy to me! No trouble at all! A real pleasure, I assure you, ma'am"'?[95] Is class as well as gender a matter of performance? Toad's adventures are full of his anxieties at not being seen as a 'gentleman'. The scene at the railway station, when Toad is wearing the washerwoman's clothes, suggests both gender and class are a matter of dress:

> To his horror he recollected that he had left both coat and waistcoat behind him in his cell, and with them his pocket-book, money, keys, watch, matches, pencil-case – all that makes life worth living, all that distinguishes the many-pocketed animal, the lord of creation, from the inferior one-pocketed or no-pocketed productions that hop or trip about permissively, unequipped for the real contest.[96]

But, despite his volatile character and his disguises, Toad is restored to his rightful place in Toad Hall at the end, and the weasels are sent back to the wood.

The world of *The Wind in the Willows*, then, is a hierarchical one. It is also a protected world, insulated from the 'Wide World'. Rat explains its dimensions: 'O, that's just the Wild Wood ... we don't go there very much, we river-bankers ... Beyond the Wild Wood comes the Wide World ... and that's something that doesn't matter, either to you or to me.'[97] Once Toad returns to the river-bank, he is safe from human pursuit. This safe, idyllic world is both the holiday playground of an Edwardian gentleman from the suburbs, and the image of a certain kind of childhood. Cosy domesticity is celebrated, nowhere more so than in the description of Badger's kitchen, a refuge from the hostile wood outside. This celebration of domesticity is quite different from the dangers it poses in Potter's works. The cosy womb-like homes of the animals echo Bachelard's 'nests and shells' (see p. 165 above). Watkins has drawn attention to the way the world of the book has been used as a nostalgic symbol of Englishness, though he also points out that nostalgia can be read as a radical critique of modernity.[98] Greenslade expands this point, seeing Grahame and his fellow artists as celebrating idleness and 'sheer uselessness' in opposition to the industrialism of the modern world and its obsession with clock-time.[99] Grahame's recourse to nature is very different from the strenuous imperialistic romanticism that produced the Boy Scout movement.

Animals, then, for Grahame are used to figure leisure and recreation, not work or struggle. They potter, they dawdle, they live in a timeless and ageless present, as Badger explains when he contrasts the animal inhabitants of the Wild Wood with

---

95 Grahame, p. 232.

96 Ibid., p. 186.

97 Ibid., pp. 13–14.

98 Tony Watkins, 'Reconstructing the Homeland: Loss and Hope in the English Landscape', in Maria Nikolajeva (ed.), *Aspects and Issues in the History of Children's Literature* (Westport, CT, 1995), p. 168.

99 Greenslade, p. 145.

the ruins left by their human predecessors. Like the Cold Lairs in the *Jungle Book*, these ruins serve to show the vanity of human pretensions. There is an implicit conservationist message in the book, in that humans and their technology – Toad's motor cars – threaten the balance of the natural world. The recent Terry Jones film of *The Wind in the Willows* emphasises this message: Mole's home is destroyed by a bulldozer driven by the weasels, who plan to build a dog-food factory on the meadow above. The meadow has been sold to the weasels by Toad, who needs the money for his crazes. The weasels are transformed from lower-class rioters to gangsters, entrepreneurs and salesmen. The good animals are not only saving Toad from his extravagances, and the aristocracy from the masses, they are saving the English countryside from the forces of industrialisation and exploitation.

Afterword

Throughout this study, I have occasionally pointed forward to later texts that share in the nineteenth-century tradition of animal stories, or take it in new directions. Examples would be Hugh Lofting's *Dr Dolittle* books, P. L. Travers' *Mary Poppins* series, Roald Dahl's *Magic Finger* and *Dirty Beasts*, and Richard Adams' *Watership Down* (see pp. 42, 59, 130, 152 above). *Watership Down,* read in this context, seems almost like a throwback to an earlier mode of writing about animals, intimately related to the *Jungle Books*, *The Wind in the Willows*, and even, as has recently been argued, to *Peter Rabbit*.[1] It presents a hierarchical society of all-male animals, who have their own myths and language. The narrator, like Kipling's 'editor', intervenes via footnotes to explain and translate elements of that language to us. Other footnotes refer us to a natural historical guide to rabbit behaviour, *The Private Life of the Rabbit* by R. M. Lockley. It is symptomatic of the way we read animal stories today, that when I taught this text my students raised the idea that Lockley and his book had been made up by Adams, and I found this quite an attractive idea. But further research revealed that Lockley's book really existed. Like nineteenth-century talking animal stories, Adams' book has a dual allegiance to the factual and to the fabular.

The history and characteristics of these stories can easily be reduced, simplified and dismissed by generalising critics. For instance, Harriet Ritvo in her book on the nineteenth-century 'Animal Estate' finds no connection to 'real creatures' in 'the large literature of animal fable and fantasy'.[2] On the other hand, John Berger looks back to the 'authentic', pre-Enlightenment symbolic relation between peasant and animal, which, in his account, was replaced by a new urban realism. One sign of this change was a new 'demand for verisimilitude in animal toys'. The implication is that realism in the representation of animals is inauthentic and reductive, and that this is only what we will find in the ways animals are presented to children in the nineteenth century. Steve Baker, explicating Berger, gives as examples of the way animals have been co-opted into family relations 'Pets, Beatrix Potter books and Disney films', as if these were all alike.[3] Beatrix Potter's *Tales* are very different from the received image of 'Beatrix Potter', and can give the twenty-first-century parent a nasty shock, as can the realities of pet-keeping.

Baker is one of the few recent critics to have addressed the talking animal story as such, and interestingly he is concerned to counter what he sees as a 'denial of the animal' in these stories. Significantly, his main example is from the 'Rupert' books, stories in which the characters are human beings with animal heads. This is not the

---

1   Pennington.

2   Ritvo, *Animal Estate*, p.

3   Steve Baker, Picturing the Beast (Manchester, 1993), pp. 12–14, explicating John Berger, 'Why Look at Animals?' in About Looking (London, 1980) pp. 1–26.

norm in the stories I have been dealing with, nor is it generally true that 'it goes
without saying that talking animals lead thoroughly human lives. This is why they
wear clothes, why they drive or ride in cars, why they eat the food they do.' Baker's
examples here are *The Wind in the Willows*, and *Rupert*. He is interested in a moment
in a Rupert story when the hero has to differentiate himself from a 'real' bear, in
order to avoid being imprisoned on Noah's Ark. Here, the denied animal becomes
suddenly visible and embarrassing. It is the subversiveness of such moments that
Baker values: 'it is precisely this denial of the animal, this edgy avoidance of
embarrassment, of contamination, which the talking animal story has the potential
to subvert ... in narrative, the animal might be a spanner in the workings and self-
identifications of the dominant culture.' What Baker wants to resist is 'the notion that
talking animal narratives are not really about animals – that the worthwhile ones,
at least, must surely be about something more important than mere animals'. Such
an interpretation would be 'consistent with the far wider cultural trivialisation and
marginalisation of the animal'.[4]

The strength of the stories I have been dealing with in this book is that they
are manifestly 'about' animals. Sarah Trimmer's warning to her audience that
animals can't really talk is the reverse of the 'Rupert' incident in which he insists,
'I'm not that sort of bear!'[5] The same could be said of the unclothing of Potter's
characters, the footnotes to the papillonades, the inability of human characters
to understand the animal autobiographers, and all the other devices by which the
animality of the protagonists is maintained. The animal characters in the stories
may be metaphors for slaves, women or children, but they are also metaphors for
animals. The books insist, or at least take for granted that their stories are related
to their readers' understanding and/or treatment of animals in the world beyond the
book. Because of identifications with animal protagonists, and an address to child
readers, the subversion of hierarchy and of human dominance is always at least part
of their effect. At the end of his book, Baker looks forward to animal stories that will
change things 'to the advantage of animals'.[6] Two strategies that he recommends
are therianthropism and anthropomorphism, which blur the distinction between
the human and animal bodies, and question the illusion of human superiority. As
I suggested in the Introduction, animal-like children meet human-like animals in
nineteenth-century children's talking animal stories, frequently blurring the animal/
human distinction.

Baker is in the mould of the nineteenth-century animal advocates. The strategies
he recommends are different, involving postmodern ironies and indirectness, but
like those earlier reformers he is concerned with the effects of representation on
the treatment of animals. The animal story as an educational tool is also making
a comeback. A recent article in *Science Education* is significantly titled 'Lifting
the Taboo Regarding Teleology and Anthropomorphism in Biology Education

---

4   Baker, pp. 152, 125, 138.
5   *1999 Rupert Annual* (London: 1988), p. 83.
6   Ibid., p. 187.

– Heretical Suggestions'.[7] The authors are concerned to show the educational advantages of anthropomorphic and narrative accounts, and also to demonstrate that students understand these formulations as metaphors, and are not deluded as to their explanatory value. Again, I am reminded of Trimmer and her insistence that her anthropomorphism should not be taken literally. At the same time, the study of animal behaviour is revaluing anthropomorphism as an explanatory tool, not merely a metaphor, blurring the human/animal divide in the way that many nineteenth-century animal stories, deliberately or unconsciously, also do (see p. 147 above). In an article entitled 'Scientists Rethink Anthropomorphism' in the *Chronicle of Higher Education*, we are told about a researcher who solved a problem about snake behaviour by imagining himself as the snake, reviving the reversal strategy recommended by Trimmer.[8] When this strategy appears in children's books, it is usually has an ethical purpose. At the end of the article, there is agreement that the new anthropomorphic approach should and will lead to a concern over the welfare of laboratory animals. In both science and art, anthropomorphism is making a comeback as a useful tool in the understanding, representation and defence of animals.

---

7   Anat Zohar and Shlomit Ginossar, 'Lifting the Taboo Regarding Teleology and Anthropomorphism', Science Education, 82/6 (1998): 679–99.

8   McDonald, p. A8.

Bibliography

Achar, Radha, 'The Child in Kipling's Fiction', *The Literary Criterion*, 2/4 (1987): 46–53.

Adams, Carol J. and Josephine Donovan (eds), *Animals and Women* (Durham, NC: Duke University Press, 1995).

Adams, James Eli, 'Woman Red in Tooth and Claw', *Victorian Studies*, 33/1 (1989): 7–27.

Adams, Richard, *Watership Down* (London: Rex Collings, 1972).

Agamben, Giorgio, *The Open: Man and Animal* (Stanford, CA: Stanford University Press, 2004).

Allen, David, 'Tastes and Crazes', in N. Jardine, J. A. Secord and E. C. Spary (eds), *The Cultures of Natural History* (Cambridge: Cambridge University Press, 1995).

Anderson, Celia Catlett, 'The Ancient Lineage of Beatrix Potter's Mr Tod', in Perry Nodelman and Jill May (eds), *Festschrift: A Ten Year Retrospective* (West Lafayette, IN: Children's Literature Association, 1983).

Anderson, H. Allen, *The Chief* (College Station: Texas A&M Press, 1986).

Ankers, Arthur R., *The Pater: John Lockwood Kipling* (Oxford: Pond View Books, 1988)

Argus, Arabella, *Further Adventures of Jemmy Donkey* (W. Darton, 1821).

——, *The Adventures of a Donkey* (W. Darton, 1815).

Asquith, Pamela J., 'Why Anthropomorphism is *Not* Metaphor', in Robert W. Mitchell, Nicholas S. Thompson and H. Lyn Miles (eds), *Anthropomorphism, Anecdotes, and Animals* (New York: State University of New York Press, 1997).

Autobiography of a Cat (London: Emily Faithfull, 1864).

Avery, Gillian, 'The Children's Writer', in John Gross (ed.), *Rudyard Kipling* (London: Weidenfeld and Nicholson, 1972).

——, *Childhood's Pattern* (London: Hodder and Stoughton, 1975).

Axtell, James L. (ed.), *The Educational Writings of John Locke* (Cambridge: Cambridge University Press, 1968).

Bachelard, Gaston, *The Poetics of Space*, trans. Maria Jolas (Boston, MA: Beacon Press, 1969).

Baker, Steve, *Picturing the Beast* (Manchester: Manchester University Press, 1993).

Ballantyne, R, *The Dog Crusoe* (London: Dent, 1966).

Barbauld, Anna, and J. Aikin, *Evenings at Home* [1792–96] (Edinburgh: William P. Nimmo, n.d.).

——, *Poems* (London: Joseph Johnson, 1773).

Barker-Benfield, G. J., *The Culture of Sensibility* (Chicago, IL: University of Chicago Press, 1992).

Beer, Gillian, *Darwin's Plots* (London: Routledge and Kegan Paul, 1985).

——, *Open Fields: Science in Cultural Encounter* (Oxford: Clarendon Press, 1996).

Benjamin, Marina, *Science and Sensibility* (Oxford: Blackwell, 1991).

Berger, John, 'Why Look at Animals?' in *About Looking* (London: Writers and Readers, 1980).

Bewick, *A General History of Quadrupeds* (Newcastle: Beilby and Bewick, 1790).

——, *History of British Birds* (Newcastle: Beilby and Bewick, 1797).

Blount, Margaret, *Animal Land* (London: Hutchinson, 1974).

Boakes, Robert, *From Darwin to Behaviourism* (Cambridge: Cambridge University Press), 1984.

Brantlinger, Patrick, *Rule of Darkness* (Ithaca, NY: Cornell University Press, 1988).

Bratton, J. S. *The Impact of Victorian Children's Fiction* (London: Croom Helm, 1981).

Brock, W. H., '*Glaucus*: Kingsley and the Seaside Naturalists', *Cahiers Victoriens et Edouardiens* (1976): 25–36.

Brogan, Hugh, *Mowgli's Sons* (London: Jonathan Cape, 1987).

Browning, Robert, *Complete Works*, ed. John Pettigrew (Harmondsworth: Penguin, 1981).

Burroughs, John, 'Real and Sham Natural History', in Ralph H. Lutts (ed.), *The Wild Animal Story* (Philadelphia, PA: Temple University Press, 1998).

Burrows, E., *Neptune* (London: Griffith and Farran, 1869).

——, *Tuppy* (London: Griffith and Farran, 1859).

Butler, Joseph, *The Analogy of Religion* (London: James, John and Paul Knapton, 1736).

Carpenter, Humphrey, *Secret Gardens* (Boston, MA: Houghton Mifflin, 1985).

Castle, Terry, *Masquerade and Civilisation* (London: Methuen, 1986).

Cato, or Interesting Adventures of A Dog of Sentiment (London: J. Harris, 1816).

Chitty, Susan, *The Woman Who Wrote Black Beauty* (London: Hodder and Stoughton, 1971).

Clarke, Norma, 'The Cursed Barbauld Crew', in Mary Hilton and Morag Styles (eds), *Opening the Nursery Door* (London: Routledge, 1997).

Clausen, Christopher, 'Home and Away in Children's Fiction', *Children's Literature*, 10 (1982): 141–52.

Cobbe, Frances Power, 'The Rights of Man and the Claims of Brutes', in *Studies New and Old of Ethical and Social Subjects* (London: Trubner, 1865).

——, *The Confessions of a Lost Dog* (London: Griffith and Farran, 1867).

Cockle, Mrs, *The Fishes Grand Gala* (London: J. Harris, 1808).

Coleman, William, *Biology in the Nineteenth Century* (London: John Wiley and Sons, 1971).

Cosslett, Tess, '"Animals Under Man"? Margaret Gatty's *Parables from Nature*', *Women's Writing*, 10/1 (2003): 137–52.

——, 'Child's Place in Nature', *Nineteenth Century Contexts*, 23 (2002): 475–95.

——, *Science and Religion in the Nineteenth Century* (Cambridge: Cambridge University Press, 1984).

Coventry, Francis, *The History of Pompey the Little* (London: M. Cooper, 1751).

Crichton-Browne, James, 'Education and the Nervous System', in M. A. Morris (ed.), *The Book of Health* (London: Cassell, 1883).

Crist, Eileen, *Images of Animals: Anthropomorphism and the Animal Mind* (Philadelphia, PA: Temple University Press, 1999).

Cunningham, Hugh, *Children and Childhood in Western Society Since 1500* (London: Longman, 1995).

Cunningham, Valentine, 'Soiled Fairy: The Water Babies in Its Time', *Essays in Criticism* 35/2 (April 1985): 121–48.

Dahl, Roald, *Dirty Beasts* (London: J. Cape, 1983).

——, *The Magic Finger* (London: HarperCollins, 1966).

Darcy, Jane, 'The Representation of Nature in *The Wind in the Willows* and *The Secret Garden*', *The Lion and the Unicorn*, 19/2 (1995): 211–22.

Darton, Harvey, *Children's Books in England* (Cambridge: Cambridge University Press, 1958).

Darwin, Charles, 'Biographical Sketch of an Infant', *Mind* 2/7 (1877): 285–94.

——, *The Expression of the Emotions in Man and Animals* [1872] (London: John Murray, 1904).

——, *The Descent of Man* (London: John Murray, 1871).

——, *The Origin of Species* [1859] (Harmondsworth: Penguin, 1982).

Darwin, Erasmus, *The Botanic Garden* (London: J. Johnson, 1791).

——, *The Temple of Nature* (London: J. Johnson, 1803).

——, *Zoonomia* (London: J. Johnson, 1794–96).

Davis, Karen, 'Thinking like a Chicken', in Carol J. Adams and Josephine Donovan (eds), *Animals and Women* (Durham, NC: Duke University Press, 1995).

Day, Thomas, *The History of Sandford and Merton* [1783] (London: The Standard Library Company, n.d.).

——, 'The Story of Little Jack', in *The Children's Miscellany* (London: John Stockdale, 1788).

Deforest, Mary, '*The Wind in the Willows*: A Tale for Two Readers', *Classical and Modern Literature*, 10/1 (1989): 81–7.

Demers, Patricia, *Heaven Upon Earth* (Knoxville: University of Tennessee Press, 1993).

Dickens, Charles, *Hard Times* [1854] (Harmondsworth: Penguin, 1969).

Dorset, Catherine, *The Lion's Masquerade* (London: J. Harris, 1807).

——, *The Lioness's Rout* (London: B. Tabart, n.d).

——, *The Peacock At Home* (London: J. Harris, 1807).

——, *The Peacock At Home, and Other Poems* (London: John Murray, 1809).

Douthwaite, Julia V., *The Wild Girl, Natural Man and the Monster* (Chicago, IL: University of Chicago Press, 2002).

Dunae, Patrick A., 'Boys' Literature and the Idea of Empire', *Victorian Studies*, 24 (1980): 105–21.

Dunlap, Thomas R., 'The Realistic Animal Story', in Ralph H. Lutts (ed.), *The Wild Animal Story* (Philadelphia, PA: Temple University Press, 1998).

Eastman, Jackie F., 'Beatrix Potter's *The Tale of Peter Rabbit*', in Perry Nodelman (ed.), *Touchstones* (West Lafayette, TX: ChLA Publishers, 1987).

Ellegard, Alvar, *Darwin and the General Reader* (Chicago, IL: University of Chicago Press, 1990).

Ellis, Markman, *The Politics of Sensibility* (Cambridge: Cambridge University Press, 1996).

Elston, Mary Ann, 'Women and Anti-Vivisection in Victorian England', in Nicholaas A. Rupke (ed.), *Vivisection in Historical Perspective* (London: Croom Helm, 1987).

Elwes, Alfred, *Adventures of a Dog* (London, 1857).

Fenn, Lady Eleanor, *Fables in Monosyllables by Mrs Teachwell* (London: John Marshall, 1783).

Ferguson, Moira, *Animal Advocacy and the Englishwoman* (Ann Arbor: University of Michigan Press, 1998).

——, 'Breaking in Englishness', *Women: A Cultural Review*, 5/1 (Spring 1994): 34–52.

——, 'Sarah Trimmer's Warring Worlds', *Children's Literature Association Quarterly*, 21/3 (1996): 105–10.

Fletcher, Lorraine, *Charlotte Smith* (Basingstoke: Macmillan, 1998).

Flynn, Richard, 'Kipling and Scouting', *Children's Literature Association Quarterly*, 16/2 (1991): 55–8.

French, Richard D., *Antivivisection and Medical Science in Victorian Society* (Princeton, NJ: Princeton University Press, 1975).

Frey, Charles, 'Victors and Victims in the Tales of *Peter Rabbit* and *Squirrel Nutkin*', *Children's Literature in Education*, 18/2 (1987): 105–11.

Fudge, Erica, *Perceiving Animals* (Houndmills: Macmillan, 2000).

——, (ed.), *Renaissance Beasts* (Urbana and Chicago: University of Illinois Press, 2004).

——, Ruth Gilbert, and Susan Wiseman (eds), *At the Borders of the Human* (Houndmills: Palgrave, 1999).

Gaard, Greta, *Ecofeminism* (Philadelphia, PA: Temple University Press, 1993).

Gaarden, Bonnie, 'The Inner Family of *The Wind in the Willows*', *Children's Literature*, 22 (1994): 43–57.

Gates, Barbara T., *Kindred Nature* (Chicago, IL: University of Chicago Press, 1998).

——, 'Revisioning Darwin with Sympathy', in Barbara T. Gates and Ann B. Schteir (eds), *Natural Eloquence* (Madison: University of Wisconsin Press, 1997).

Gatty, Margaret, *Parables from Nature* (London: J. M. Dent and Co., 1907).

Gaull, Marilyn, *English Romanticism* (New York and London: W. W. Norton and Co., 1988).

Gilead, Sarah, 'The Undoing of Idyll in *The Wind in the Willows*', *Children's Literature*, 16 (1988): 145–57.

Gillin, Richard, 'Romantic Echoes in the Willows', *Children's Literature*, 16 (1988): 169–74.

Golden, Catherine, 'Beatrix Potter: Naturalist Artist', in Bill Katz (ed.), *A History of Book Illustration* (London: Scarecrow Press, 1994).

Goldstone, Bette, *Lessons to be Learned* (New York: Peter Lang, 1984).

Gould, Stephen Jay, 'The Invisible Woman', in Barbara T. Gates and Ann B. Schteir (eds), *Natural Eloquence* (Madison: University of Wisconsin Press, 1997).

Graham, Kathryn V., 'Of School and the River', *Children's Literature Association Quarterly*, 23/4 (1998-99): 181–6.

Grahame, Kenneth, *The Wind in the Willows* [1908] (London: Methuen, 1969).

Green, Martin, *Dreams of Adventure, Deeds of Empire* (New York: Basic Books, 1979).

Green, Peter, *Kenneth Grahame* (London: John Murray, 1959).

Green, Roger Lancelyn, 'Mowgli's Jungle', *Kipling Journal*, 57/227 (1983): 29–35.

Greenleaf, Sarah, 'The Beast Within', *Children's Literature in Education*, 23 (1992): 49–57.

Greenslade, William, '"Pan" and the Open Road', in Lynne Hapgood and Nancy L. Paxton (eds), *Outside Modernism* (London: Macmillan, 2000).

Grenby, Matthew, *The Hockliffe Project Website.*

Gross, John (ed.), *Rudyard Kipling* (London: Weidenfeld and Nicolson, 1972).

Hall, G. Stanley, *Adolescence* (New York: Appleton, 1904).

Harris, J., (ed.) *Harris's Cabinet of Amusement and Instruction* (London: J. Harris, 1809).

Harrison, Brian, *Peaceable Kingdom* (Oxford: Clarendon, 1982).

Hawley, John C., '*The Water-Babies* as Catechetical Paradigm', *Children's Literature Association Quarterly*, 14/1 (1989): 19–21.

Hearne, Vicki, *Adam's Task* (London: Heinemann, 1987).

Hollindale, Peter, 'Aesop in the Shadows', *Signal*, 89 (May 1999): 115–32.

——, 'Humans are so Rabbit', in Margaret Mackey (ed.), *Beatrix Potter's Peter Rabbit* (London: Scarecrow Press, 2002).

Hotchkiss, Jane, 'The Jungle of Eden', *Victorian Literature and Culture*, 29/2 (2001): 435–49.

Hunt, Peter, *The Wind in the Willows* (New York: Twayne, 1994).

Huxley, Thomas Henry, *Collected Essays* (London, Macmillan, 1893–94).

Jackson, Mary V., *Engines of Instruction, Mischief, and Magic* (Lincoln: University of Nebraska Press, 1989).

Jacobs, Harriet, *Incidents in the Life of a Slave Girl* [1861] (New York: Norton, 2001).

Katz, Wendy, *The Emblems of Margaret Gatty* (New York: AMS Press, 1993).

Kean, Hilda, *Animals Rights* (London: Reaktion, 1998).

Keller, Betty, *Blackwolf* (Vancouver: Douglas and McIntyre, 1984).

Kemp, Sandra, *Kipling's Hidden Narratives* (Oxford: Basil Blackwell, 1988).

Kendall, Edward Augustus, *Keeper's Travels in Search of His Master* [1798] (Boston, MA: T. H. Carter and Co., 1844).

Kennedy, J. S., *The New Anthropomorphism* (Cambridge: Cambridge University Press), 1992.

Kenyon-Jones, *Kindred Brutes* (London: Ashgate, 2001).

Kilner, Dorothy, *The Adventures of a Whipping Top* (London: John Marshall, 1784)

——, *The Life and Perambulations of a Mouse* (London: John Marshall, 1783).

Kilner, Mary Ann, *The Adventures of a Pincushion* (London: John Marshall, 1783).

——, *Memoirs of a Peg-Top* (London: John Marshall, 1783).

Kingsley, Charles, *Glaucus* [1855] (Boston, MA: IndyPublish.com, n.d.).

——, *Madam How and Lady Why* (London: Macmillan, 1890).

——, *The Water Babies* [1863] (London: Penguin, 1995).

Kipling, John Lockwood, *Beast and Man in India* (London: Macmillan, 1891).

Kipling, Rudyard, 'In the Rukh', in *Many Inventions* (London: Macmillan, 1893).

——, *Something of Myself* [1937] (London: Macmillan, 1964).

——, *The Jungle Book* [1894] (London: Macmillan, 1962).

——, *The Second Jungle Book* [1895] (London: Macmillan, 1962).

——, 'Thy Servant a Dog' [1930] in *Thy Servant a Dog and Other Stories* (London: Macmillan, 1965).

Knoepflmacher, U. C., 'Female Power and Male Self-Assertion', *Children's Literature*, 20 (1992): 15–51.

——, 'Kipling's Just-So Partner', *Children's Literature*, 25 (1997): 24–49.

——, 'The Balancing of Child and Adult', *Nineteenth Century Literature*, 37/4 (March 1983): 497–530.

Kutzer, M. Daphne, 'A Wilderness Inside: Domestic Space in the Work of Beatrix Potter', *The Lion and the Unicorn*, 21 (1997): 204–14.

——, *Beatrix Potter, Writing in Code* (London: Routledge, 2003).

Kuznets, Lois, 'Kenneth Grahame and Father Nature', *Children's Literature*, 16 (1988): 175–81.

——, 'Toad Hall Revisited', *Children's Literature*, 7 (1978): 115–28.

Lamb, Charles and Mary Lamb, *Letters*, ed. Edward W. Marrs (Ithaca, NY: Cornell University Press, 1976).

Landow, George, *Victorian Types, Victorian Shadows* (London: Routledge and Kegan Paul, 1980).

Landry, Donna, 'Green Languages? Women Poets as Naturalists in 1653 and 1807', *Huntingdon Library Quarterly*, 63 (2000): 467–89.

——, *The Invention of the Countryside* (Houndmills: Palgrave, 2001).

Lansbury, Coral, *The Old Brown Dog* (Madison: University of Wisconsin Press, 1985).

Lejeune, Philippe, *On Autobiography*, ed. Paul John Eakin, trans. Katherine Leary (Minneapolis: University of Minnesota Press, 1989).

Lesnik-Oberstein, Karin, 'Children's Literature and the Environment', in Richard Kerridge and Neil Sammells (eds), *Writing the Environment* (London: Zed Books, 1998).

Lightman, Bernard, '"The Voices of Nature"', in Bernard Lightman (ed.), *Victorian Science in Context* (Chicago, IL: University of Chicago Press, 1997).

Linder, Leslie, *A History of the Writings of Beatrix Potter* (London: Frederick Warne, 1971).

Lockley, R. M., *The Private Life of the Rabbit* (London: A. Deutsch, 1964).

London, Jack, 'The Other Animals', in Ralph H. Lutts (ed.), *The Wild Animal Story* (Philadelphia, PA: Temple University Press, 1998).

Longfellow, Henry Wadsworth, *Poetical Works* (Oxford: Oxford University Press, 1961).

Lurie, Alison, *Not in Front of the Grown-Ups* (London: Sphere Books, 1991).

Lutts, Ralph H., *The Nature Fakers* (Golden, CO: Fulcrum, 1990).

—— (ed.), *The Wild Animal Story* (Philadelphia, PA: Temple University Press, 1998).

MacDonald, Robert H., *Sons of the Empire* (Toronto: University of Toronto Press, 1993).

——, 'The Revolt Against Instinct', in Ralph H. Lutts (ed.), *The Wild Animal Story* (Philadelphia, PA: Temple University Press, 1998).

Macdonald, Ruth, 'Narrative Voice and Narrative View in Beatrix Potter's Books', in Charlotte F. Otten and Gary D. Schmidt (eds), *The Voice of the Narrator in Children's Literature* (New York: Greenwood Press, 1989).

——, 'Why This is Still 1893', *Children's Literature Association Quarterly*, 10/4 (1986): 185–7.

Mackey, Margaret (ed.), *Beatrix Potter's Peter Rabbit* (London: Scarecrow Press, 2002).

Madame Grimalkin's Party (London: Didier and Tebbit, 1808).

Maitland, Edward, *The Life of Anna Kingsford* (London: Macmillan, 1913).

Mallett, Philip, *Rudyard Kipling* (Houndmills: Palgrave, 2003).

Mangum, Teresa, 'Dog years, Human fears', in Nigel Rothfels (ed.), *Representing Animals* (Bloomington: Indiana University Press, 2002).

Marcet, Jane, *Conversations on Chemistry* (London: Longman, 1806).

——, *Conversations on Natural Philosophy* (London: Longman, 1819).

Marshall, Cynthia, 'Bodies and Pleasures in *The Wind in the Willows*', *Children's Literature*, 22 (1994): 58–69.

Maxwell, Christabel, *Mrs Gatty and Mrs Ewing* (London: Constable, 1949).

McBratney, John, 'Imperial Subjects, Imperial Space', *Victorian Studies*, 35/3 (Spring 1992): 277–93.

McBride, Dwight A., *Impossible Witnesses* (New York: New York University Press, 2001).

McClure, John A., *Kipling and Conrad* (Cambridge, MA: Harvard University Press, 1981).

McDonald, Kim A., 'Scientists Rethink Anthropomorphism', *Chronicle of Higher Education*, 41/24 (1995): A8–A9, A14.

McMaster, Juliet, 'The Trinity Archetype in *The Jungle Books* and *The Wizard of Oz*' *Children's Literature*, 20 (1992): 90–110.

Memoirs of Dick the Poney (London: J. Harris, 1799).

Mendelson, Michael, '*The Wind in the Willows* and the Plotting of Contrast', *Children's Literature*, 16 (1988): 127–44.

Milne, A. A., *Toad of Toad Hall* (London: Methuen, 1929).

Mitchell, Robert W., Nicholas S. Thompson and H. Lyn Miles (eds), *Anthropomorphism, Anecdotes, and Animals* (New York: State University of New York Press, 1997).

Mohanty, Satya P., 'Drawing the Color Line', in Dominick LaCapra (ed.), *The Bounds of Race* (Ithaca, NY: Cornell University Press, 1991).

Moore, John David, 'Pottering about in the Garden', *Journal of the Midwest Modern Language Association* 23/1 (1990): 45–60.

Morgan, C. Lloyd, *Animal Behaviour* (London: Edward Arnold, 1900).

Morris, Paul, Margaret Fidler and Alan Costall, 'Beyond Anecdotes: An Empirical Study of "Anthropomorphism"', *Society and Animals*, 8/2 (2000): 151–65.

Morris, Timothy, *You're Only Young Twice* (Urbana: University of Illinois Press, 2000).

Mullan, John, *Sentiment and Sociability* (Oxford: Oxford University Press, 1988).

Muller, Charles H., 'Spiritual Evolution and Muscular Theology', *University of Capetown Studies in English*, 15 (1986): 24–34.

Murray, John, 'The Law of *The Jungle Books*', *Children's Literature*, 20 (1992): 1–14.

Myers, Mitzi, 'Impeccable Governesses, Rational Dames and Moral Mothers', *Children's Literature*, 14 (1986): 31–59.

——, 'Little Girls Lost: Rewriting Romantic Childhoods', in Glenn Edward Sadlier (ed.), *Teaching Children's Literature* (New York: Modern Language Association of America, 1992)

——, 'Of Mice and Mothers', in Louise Weatherbee Phelps and Janet Emig (eds), *Feminine Principles and Women's Experience in American Composition and Rhetoric* (Pittsburgh, PA: University of Pittsburgh Press, 1995).

——, 'Portrait of the Female Artist as a Young Robin', *The Lion and the Unicorn*, 20/2 (1996): 230–63.

——, 'Reading Rosamond Reading' in Elizabeth Goodenough, Mark Heberle and Naomi Sokoloff (eds), *Infant Tongues* (Detroit, MI: Wayne State University Press, 1994).

——, 'The Erotics of Pedagogy', *Children's Literature*, 23 (1995): 1–30.

Nelson, Claudia, *Boys Will Be Girls* (New Brunswick, NJ: Rutgers University Press, 1991).

Newbery, John, *Fables in Verse for the Improvement of the Young and the Old* (London: Newbery, 1758).

Newman, John Henry, *Apologia Pro Vita Sua*, ed. Martin Svaglic (Oxford, 1967).

——, *The Idea of a University*, ed. I. T. Ker (Oxford, 1976).

Newton, Michael, 'Kipling and the Savage Child', *Commonwealth Essays and Studies*, 15/1 (1992): 12–18.

Nikolajeva, Maria (ed.), *Aspects and Issues in the History of Children's Literature* (Westport, CT: Greenwood Press, 1995).

Ouida, *Puck* [1870] (London: Chapman and Hall, n.d).

Pafford, Mark, *Kipling's Indian Fiction* (Houndmills: Macmillan, 1989).

Parkes, Bessie Rayner, *The History of Our Cat, Aspasia* (London, 1856).

Passmore, John, 'The Treatment of Animals', *Journal of the History of Ideas*, 36 (1975): 196–8.

Patteson, S. Louise, *Pussy Meow* (Philadelphia, PA: George W. Jacobs, 1901).

Pennington, John, 'From Peter Rabbit to *Watership Down*', *Journal of the Fantastic in the Arts*, 10/2 (1991): 66–80.

Perkins, David, *Romanticism and Animal Rights* (Cambridge: Cambridge University Press, 2003).

Petzold, Dieter, 'Fantasy out of Myth and Fable: Animal Stories in Rudyard Kipling and Richard Adams', *Children's Literature Association Quarterly*, 12/1 (1987): 15–19.

Philip, Neil, 'Kenneth Grahame's *The Wind in the Willows*', in Perry Nodelman (ed.), *Touchstones* (West Lafayette, IN: Children's Literature Association, 1985).

Pickering, Samuel F., *John Locke and Children's Books in Eighteenth-Century England* (Knoxville: University of Tennessee Press, 1981).

Pilkington, Mary, *Marvellous Adventures* (London: J. Harris, 1802).

——, *The Sorrows of Caesar* (London: G. and S. Robinson, 1813).

Pitts, Deidre Owen, 'Discerning the Animal of a Thousand Faces', *Children's Literature*, 3 (1974): 169–72.

Plumb, J. H. 'The New World of Children in Eighteenth-Century England', *Past and Present*, 67 (1975): 64–95.

Poss, Geraldine, 'An Epic in Arcadia', *Children's Literature*, 4 (1975): 80–89.

Potter, Beatrix, *The Complete Tales* (London: Frederick Warne, 2002).

——, *The Tale of Jemima Puddle-duck* (London: Frederick Warne, 1908).

——, *The Tale of Mr Jeremy Fisher* (London: Frederick Warne, 1906).

——, *The Tale of Mrs Tiggy-winkle* (London: Frederick Warne, 1905).

——, *The Tale of Mr Tod* (London: Frederick Warne, 1912).

——, *The Tale of Peter Rabbit* (London: Frederick Warne, 1902).

——, *The Tale of Squirrel Nutkin* (London: Frederick Warne, 1903).

——, *The Tale of Two Bad Mice* (London: Frederick Warne, 1904).

Povinelli, Daniel J., '*Pan*morphism', in Mitchell, Robert W., Nicholas S. Thompson and H. Lyn Miles (eds), *Anthropomorphism, Anecdotes, and Animals* (New York: State University of New York Press, 1997).

Pratt, Samuel, *Pity's Gift* (London: Longman and Newbery, 1798).

Primatt, Humphrey, D. D., *A Dissertation on the Duty of Mercy and Sin of Cruelty to Brute Animals* (London: R. Hett, 1776).

Quarles, Francis, *Emblems Divine and Moral* (London: H. Trapp, 1777).

Rahn, Suzanne, 'Tailpiece: The Tale of Two Bad Mice', *Children's Literature*, 12 (1984): 78–91.

Randall, Don, *Kipling's Imperial Boy* (Houndmills: Palgrave, 2000).

Rauch, Alan, 'A World of Faith on a Foundation of Science', *Children's Literature Association Quarterly*, 14/1 (1989): 13–19.

——, 'Parables and Parodies', *Children's Literature*, 25 (1997): 137–52.

Ray, Laura Krugman, 'Kenneth Grahame and the Literature of Childhood', *English Literature in Transition*, 20 (1977): 3–12.

Richards, Robert J., 'Instinct and Intelligence in British Natural Theology', *Journal of the History of Biology*, 14 (1981): 193–230.

Richardson, Alan, 'Wordsworth, Fairy Tales, and the Politics of Children's Reading', in James Holt McGavran (ed.), *Romanticism and Children's Literature in Nineteenth-Century England* (Athens: University of Georgia Press, 1991).

Ricketts, Harry, *The Unforgiving Minute* (London: Chatto and Windus, 1999).

Ricks, Christopher (ed.), *The Poems of Tennyson* (London: Longmans, 1969).

Ritvo, Harriet, 'Learning from Animals', *Children's Literature*, 13 (1985): 72–93.

——, *The Platypus and the Mermaid* (Cambridge, MA: Harvard University Press, 1997).

——, *The Animal Estate* (Harmondsworth: Penguin, 1987).

Rollin, Bernard E., 'Anecdote, Anthropomorphism, and Animal Behavior', in Mitchell, Robert W., Nicholas S. Thompson and H. Lyn Miles (eds), *Anthropomorphism, Anecdotes, and Animals* (New York: State University of New York Press, 1997).

Romanes, George J., *Animal Intelligence* (London: Kegan Paul, Trench, and Co, 1883).

Roscoe, William, *The Butterfly's Ball and the Grasshopper's Feast* (London: J. Harris, 1807).

Rothfels, Nigel (ed.), *Representing Animals* (Bloomington: Indiana University Press, 2002).

Rousseau, Jean Jacques, *His Educational Theories Selected From Emile, Julie and Other Writings*, ed. R. L. Archer (New York: Barron's Educational Series, 1964).

Ruwe, Donelle, 'Guarding the British Bible from Rousseau: Sarah Trimmer, William Godwin, and the Pedagogical Periodical', *Children's Literature*, 29 (2001): 1–17.

Sandham, Elizabeth, *The Adventures of Poor Puss* (London: J. Harris, 1809).

Saunders, Julia, '"The Mouse's Petition": Anna Laetitia Barbauld and the Scientific Revolution', *Review of English Studies*, 53/212 (2002): 500–16.

Saunders, Marshall, *Beautiful Joe* (London: Jarrold, 1901).

Sendak, Maurice, *Where the Wild Things Are* (New York: Harper and Row, 1963).

Schlobin, Roger C., 'Danger and Compulsion in the *Wind in the Willows*', *Journal of the Fantastic in the Arts*, 8/1 (1997): 34–41.

Scholtmeijer, Marian. 'The Power of Otherness', in Carol J. Adams and Josephine Donovan (eds), *Animals and Women* (Durham, NC: Duke University Press, 1995).

Schramm, Jan-Melissa, *Testimony and Advocacy in Victorian Law, Literature and Theology* (Cambridge: Cambridge University Press, 2000).

Scott, Carole, 'An Unusual Hero', in Margaret Mackey (ed.), *Beatrix Potter's Peter Rabbit* (London: Scarecrow Press, 2002).

——, 'Between Me and the World', *The Lion and the Unicorn* 16 (1992): 192–8.

——, 'Kipling's Combat Zones', *Children's Literature*, 20 (1992): 52–68.

——, 'Clothed in Nature or Nature Clothed', *Children's Literature*, 22 (1994): 70–89

Seton, Ernest Thompson, *Lives of the Hunted* [1901] (London: Hodder and Stoughton, 1924).

——, *Wild Animals I have Known* [1898] (Toronto: McClelland and Stewart, 1991).

Sewell, Anna, *Black Beauty* [1877] (London: Puffin, 1994).

Sherwood, Martha, *The Little Woodman, and his Dog Caesar* [1818] (Wellington, Salop: F. Houlston and Son, c.1825).

Shteir, Ann B., *Cultivating Women, Cultivating Science* (Baltimore, MD: Johns Hopkins University Press, 1996).

Shuttleworth, Sally and Jenny Bourne Taylor (eds), *Embodied Selves* (Oxford: Clarendon, 1998).

Smith, Charlotte, *Conversations, Introducing Poetry* (London: Joseph Johnson, 1804).

——, *Poems*, ed. Stuart Curran (Oxford: Oxford University Press, 1993).

Spiegel, Marjorie, *The Dreaded Comparison* (London: Heretic Books, 1988).

Stables, Gordon, *Sable and White* (London: Jarrold, 1894).

Steedman, Carolyn, 'Enforced narratives: stories of another self', in Tess Cosslett, Celia Lury and Penny Summerfield (eds), *Feminism and Autobiography* (London: Routledge, 2000).

Stephens, John, *Language and Ideology in Children's Fiction* (London: Longmans, 1992).

Stocking, George W. Jnr. *Victorian Anthropology* (London: Collier Macmillan, 1987).

Sullivan, Zoreh T., *Narratives of Empire* (Cambridge: Cambridge University Press, 1993).

Sully, James, Introduction to Bernard Perez, *The First Three Years of Childhood* (London: Swan Sonnenschein, 1885).

Swift, Jonathan, *Gulliver's Travels* [1726] (Harmondsworth: Penguin, 2001).

Tabbert, Reinbert, 'National Myths in Three Classical Picture Books', in Maria Nikolajeva (ed.), *Aspects and Issues in the History of Children's Literature* (Westport, CT: Greenwood Press, 1995).

Taine, Hypolite, 'The Acquisition of Language by Children', *Mind* 2: 6 (1877): 252–9.

Taylor, Ann and Jane, *Signor Topsy-Turvy's Wonderful Magic Lantern* (London: Tabart and Co., 1810).

Taylor, Judy, Joyce Irene Whalley, Anne Stevenson Hobbes and Elizabeth M Battrick (eds), *Beatrix Potter* (London: Frederick Warne, 1987).

Taylor, Thomas, *A Vindication of the Rights of Brutes* (London: Edward Jeffery, 1792).

Tennyson, Alfred, *Letters*, eds Cecil Y. Lang and Edgar F. Shannon Jr (Oxford: Clarendon Press 1982)

Tennyson, G. B., 'The Sacramental Imagination', in U. C. Knoepflmacher and G. B. Tennyson (eds), *Nature and the Victorian Imagination* (Berkeley: University of California Press, 1977).

——, *Victorian Devotional Poetry* (Cambridge, MA: Harvard University Press, 1981).

The Cat's Concert (London: C. Chapple, 1808).

The Dog of Knowledge; or, Memoirs of Bob, the Spotted Terrier: Supposed to be written by Himself (London: J. Harris, 1801).

The History of Little Goody Two-Shoes (London: Newbery, 1765).

The Jackdaw 'At Home' (London: Didier and Tebbett, 1808).

The Lion's Parliament, or The Beasts in Debate (London: J. B. Batchelor, 1808).

The Lioness's Ball (London: J. Harris, 1808).

The Lobster's Voyage to the Brazils (London: J. Harris, 1808).

The Mermaid at Home (London: J. Harris, 1809).

The Peacock and Parrot (London: J. Harris, 1816).

The Water-King's Levee (London: W. Lindall, 1808).

Thomas, Keith, *Man and the Natural World* (New York: Pantheon, 1983).

Thorndike, Edward, *Animal Intelligence* (New York: Macmillan, 1898).

Thornton, Lucy D., *The Story of a Poodle by Himself and His Mistress* (London: Sampson Low, Marston, Searle and Rivington, 1889).

Thorpe, W. H. *Animal Nature and Human Nature* (London: Methuen, 1974).

Thum, Maureen, 'Exploring the Country of the Mind', *Children's Literature Association Quarterly*, 17/3 (1992): 27–32.

Todd, Janet, *Sensibility* (London: Methuen, 1986).

Tompkins, J. M. S., *The Art of Rudyard Kipling* (London: Methuen, 1959).

Travers, P. L., *Mary Poppins* (London: G. Howe, 1934).

Trimmer, Sarah, *An Easy Introduction to the Knowledge of Nature* (London: Printed for Author, 1770).

——, *Fabulous Histories* (London: T. Longman, 1786).

——, *The Guardian of Education* (London: J. Hatchard, 1802–06).

——, *The Story of the Robins* (London: Frederick Warne, 1873)

Tucker, Charlotte, *The Rambles of a Rat* (London: T. Nelson and Sons, 1857).

Turner, James, *Reckoning with the Beast* (Baltimore, MD: Johns Hopkins University Press, 1981).

Vance, Linda, 'Beyond Just-So Stories', in Carol J. Adams and Josephine Donovan (eds), *Animals and Women* (Durham, NC: Duke University Press, 1995).

W. B., *The Elephant's Ball* (London: Harris, 1807).

Wall, Barbara, *The Narrator's Voice* (Basingstoke: Macmillan, 1991).

Walsh, Susan, 'Child/Animal', in *Yearbook of English Studies*, (2002): 151–62.

——, 'Untheming the Theme', PhD Thesis, University of Reading, 2001.

Watkins, Tony, 'Making a Break for the Real England', *Children's Literature Association Quarterly*, 9/1 (1984): 34–5.

——, 'Reconstructing the Homeland', in Maria Nikolajeva (ed.), *Aspects and Issues in the History of Children's Literature*, (Westport, CT: Greenwood, 1995).

Whalley, Joyce Irene, 'Beatrix Potter's Art', in Margaret Mackey (ed.), *Beatrix Potter's Peter Rabbit* (London: Scarecrow Press, 2002).

Wheeler, Michael, *Death and the Future Life in Victorian Literature and Theology* (Cambridge: Cambridge University Press, 1990).

White, Lynne Jr., 'The Historical Roots of Our Ecological Crisis', *Science*, 155 (1967): 1203–07.

Whitely, David, 'Samuel Richardson's Aesop', in Mary Hilton and Morag Styles (eds), *Opening the Nursery Door* (London: Routledge, 1997).

Williams, Jay 'Reflections on the *Wind in the Willows*', *Signal*, 21 (1976): 104.

Willis, Lesley, '"A Sadder and a Wiser Rat/He Rose the Morrow Morn"', *Children's Literature Association Quarterly*. 13/3 (1988): 108–11.

Wiseman, Susan, 'Monstrous Perfectibility', in Erica Fudge, Ruth Gilbert, and Susan Wiseman (eds), *At the Borders of the Human* (Houndmills: Palgrave, 1999).

Wollstonecraft, Mary, *Original Stories from Real Life* (London: J. Johnson, 1788).

Wood, Naomi, 'A (Sea) Green Victorian', *The Lion and the Unicorn*, 19 (1995): 233–52.

Worster, Donald, *Nature's Economy*, (Cambridge: Cambridge University Press, 1994).

Wytenbroek, J. R., 'Natural Mysticism in Kenneth Grahame's *The Wind in the Willows*', *Mythlore*, 3/2 (1996): 431–4.

Young, Robert J. C., *Colonial Desire* (London: Routledge, 1995).

Zohar, Anat and Shlomit Ginossar, 'Lifting the Taboo Regarding Teleology and Anthropomorphism', *Science Education* 82/6 (1998): 679–99.

Index

(References to illustrations are in **bold**)

Achar, Radha 127
Adams, Richard, *Watership Down* 152
  hierarchy 181
Aesop's Fables, Locke on 10, 11
Agamben, Giorgio 2
Aikin, John 41
  Evenings at Home (co-author) *see under*
    Barbauld
alphabet books 12
analogical thinking 103
Angell, George T. 74
animal
  advocacy 81
    Tuppy 82
  costumes, masquerades 53
  debates 107–9
animal autobiography 3, 43, 63–92
  authenticity issues 88–9
  didacticism 64
  endings 89–92
  examples 5
  natural history information 64–5
  purpose 63, 64
  slave narratives, similarities 5
animal consciousness 70–73
  Black Beauty 70, 73
  Marvellous Adventures 71
  Sable and White 71, 72 3
animal language 65–70, 109, 130–32, 136,
    144–5, 156, 157–8, 159–61
  The Adventures of a Dog 69, 81–2
  The Adventures of a Donkey 66
  Beautiful Joe 65, 67
  Black Beauty 69
  'Her Majesty's Servants' 130
  as literary device 5
  Sable and White 67, 68–9
  The Story of a Poodle 66
  see also talking animals
animal poems 40–41

footnotes 57–8
  natural history information 57
  patriotism 55–6
  pro-Catholic message 56
  subversiveness 54–5
animal rights 35
  and anthropomorphism 7
animal stories
  Arcadianism 151–2
  gender differences 77–8, 168, 174–6
  origins 1
  see also wild animal stories
animals
  children, analogy 73–5
  cruelty to 10, 58
  death 46
  discussing evolution 60–61
  emotions 145–6
  kindness to 13–14, 17–18, 39
  names, significance 86–8
  naming 143–4
  protection 3
  servants, analogy 83–6
  slaves, analogy 78–81
  as species representatives 86
  women, analogy 75–6
  see also talking animals
  slavery analogy 78–9
Anstey, F., *Vice Versa* 44
anthropomorphism 2, 14, 146, 153–5
  and animal rights 7
  use 42, 110
  value of 147, 182–3
anti-vivisection movement 3, 75
  see also vivisection
Arcadianism, animal stories 151–2
Argus, Arabella
  Further Adventures of Jemmy Donkey
    83, 90
  The Adventures of a Donkey 63, 64
  animal language 66
Autobiography of a Cat 77

Avery, Gillian 149

Bachelard, Gaston 169
   The Poetics of Space 165–6
Baden-Powell, Lord 149, 150
Baker, Steve 181, 182
Ballantyne, R.M., *The Dog Crusoe* 123
Barbauld, Anna 9, 41
   'Council of Quadrupeds' 123
   'The Dog and his Relations' 153
   Evenings at Home (co-author) 4, 26–7,
      28–33, 34, 36
   'The Mouse's Petition' 33–4, 35
   hierarchy in 35
   'The Young Mouse' 153
Barker-Benfield, G.J. 15–16
bearing-rein, abolition, role of *Black Beauty*
   74, 79, 81, 83
Berger, John 181
bestiaries 11–12
Bewick, Thomas 118
Blount, Margaret 59, 164
Boreman, Thomas, *A description of Three*
   Hundred Animals 12
Boy Scout movement 4, 149, 180
Brantlinger, P. 140
Brontë, Anne, *Agnes Grey* 26
Brooke, John Hedley 102–3
Browning, Robert, 'Caliban Upon Setebos'
   106, 137
Brunhoff, Jean de, *The Story of Babar* 152
bull-baiting 23
Burnett, Frances Hodgson, *Secret Garden*
   13
Burroughs, John 146, 147
Burrows, E.
   Neptune 76
   Tuppy 68
   animal advocacy 82
Butler, Joseph, *The Analogy of Religion* 102

carnival, hierarchical reversals 2–3, 5, 6,
   49, 51, 54, 105, 110, 113, 138, 167,
   178–9
Carpenter, Humphrey 152, 164, 171
Castle, Terry 53
Chambers, Robert 96
Chaucer, Geoffrey, *Parliament of Fowles*
   107

children
   evolutionary development 125–6
   language acquisition 125, 126
   literature for, rise of 1
   as 'missing link' 126
   parents, exchange of places 44
   power of belief 94–5
   primitive peoples, comparison 125
   see also wild children
clothing, use of 57, 156–9, 161, 172
Cobbe, Frances Power 3, 77
   Confessions of a Lost Dog 81, 85, 88
Cockle, Mrs, *The Fishes Grand Gala* 54, 55
Coleridge, Samuel Taylor, *Ancient Mariner*
   111
conservationism
   Beatrix Potter 6–7
   Wind in the Willows 180
Cowper, William, *The Task* 22
Crichton-Brown, James 125
Crist, Eileen, *Images of Animals* 147

Dahl, Roald
   Dirty Beasts 181
   The Magic Finger 42, 59, 181
Dann, Colin, *The Animals of Farthing Wood*
   152
Darcy, Jane 172–3
Darwin, Charles
   'Biographical Sketch of an Infant' 125
   The Descent of Man 115, 145
   Expression of the Emotions 43
   The Origin of Species 93, 96, 106, 115
Darwin, Erasmus
   The Temple of Nature 60
   Zoonomia 60
Darwinism 3, 6
   in Kinglsey 115–16
   in Kipling 127, 129, 132, 135, 140
Day, Thomas 9, 41
   'The History of Little Jack' 24
   Sandford and Merton 4, 20–24
Defoe, Daniel, *Robinson Crusoe* 19
Dickens, Charles, *Hard Times* 28, 111
Dingley, Robert 79
Dorset, Catherine,
   Lion's Masquerade 53, 54
   The Peacock at Home 40, 41, 50–51
   anti-cruelty message 58

talking animals 54
Douthwaite, Julia 132

Edgeworth, Maria, 'The Bee and the Cow'
    12
Elwes, Alfred, *The Adventures of a Dog* 151
animal language 69, 81–2
emblem books 12
evolution, animals discussing 60–61

fables, Rousseau on 19–20
Faithfull, Emily 77
Fenn, Eleanor, *Fables in Monosyllables* 11,
    20, 37–8

Gaarden, Bonnie 171, 177
Gates, Barbara 3, 97, 152
Gatty, Alfred 99
Gatty, Margaret 2, 3, 6, 26
    hierarchy 98, 103
    works
        Aunt Judy's Magazine (editor) 95
        British Seaweeds 95
        Parables from Nature 5, 11, 93, 95,
            96–7
            'Inferior Animals' 99, 107, 108–9,
                171
            'Kicking' 98–9
            'A Lesson of Hope' 99, 100, 101
            'Night and Day' 98
            'The Unknown Land' 109–10
            'Whereunto' 103–7
gender differences, animal stories 77–8,
    168, 174–6
Golder, Catherine 153
Goldstone, Betty 37
Gosse, Edmund 110
Graham, Kathryn 171
Grahame, Kenneth 3
    'The Fellow that Goes Alone' 176–7
    Wind in the Willows 6, 7, 150, 151, 162,
        163, 166, 171–80
        animal instinct 173
        archetypes 177
        conservationism 180
        hierarchy 178–9
        illustrations 172
        narratee 171
        religion 177–8

structure 171
Greenslade, William 180
Grenby, Matthew 59, 124

Hallam, Arthur 99, 100, 102
Harris, John
    Alphabet of Goody Two-Shoes 13
    *Harris's Cabinet of Amusement and
        Instruction* 51
Hearne, Vicki 88
hierarchy 98
    carnivalesque reversals 2–3, 5, 6, 49, 51,
        54, 105, 110, 113, 138, 167, 178–9
    children 25
    engagement with 6
    Fabulous Histories 41
    in Kipling 135
    meanings 3
    'The Mouse's Petition' (Barbauld) 35
    in natural histories 41
    notion of 2
    Parables from Nature 103
    Watership Down 181
    The Wind in the Willows 178–9
hippocampus controversy 94
Hollindale, Peter 152, 169
Hotchkiss, Jane 137, 138, 139

Jackson, Mary 11, 28, 39, 40
Jacobs, Harriet, *Incidents in the Life of a
    Slave Girl* 80
'Jungle' 164–5
    as liminal space 139

Kean, Hilda 3, 83
Keble, John, *The Christian Year* 102
Keller, Betty 142
Kemp, Sandra 127
Kendall, Augustus, *Keeper's Travels in
    Search of his Master* 35, 37
Kenyon-Jones, Christine 3, 19, 24, 26–7
Kilner, Dorothy
    The Adventures of a Whipping Top 64
    *The Life and Perambulations of a
        Mouse* 37, 38, 63, 64
Kilner, Mary Ann
    The Adventures of a Pincushion 64
    Memoirs of a Peg-Top 64
Kingsley, Charles 3, 4, 6

Glaucus or, the Wonders of the Shore
    110, 111, 118
Madam How and Lady Why 118
The Water Babies 1, 5, 41, 93, 94–5,
    110–21
    animal imagery 113
    Darwinism 115–16
    influences on 118
    nature, personification of 121–2
    purpose 112
    Rabelais' influence 113
    social criticism 116–17
    talking animals 119–20
Kipling, John Lockwood, *Beast and Man in
    India* 6, 128–9, 132, 140
Kipling, Rudyard
    Darwinism 127, 129, 132, 135, 140
    hierarchy 135
    influences on 124
    masculinity in 140–41
    natives, attitude to 127–30
    talking animals 124, 127, 129–31
    works
        'Her Majesty's Servants' 130, 133
        'How Fear Came' 127, 133, 134–5,
            165
        'In the Rukh' 127, 136
        The Jungle Book 133
        Jungle Books 4, 6, 23, 119, 127,
            128, 129
            allegorical significance 138–9
        Just So Stories 124, 127–8
        Kim 128, 129, 139
        'The King's Ankus' 133
        'Letting in the Jungle' 123, 133
        'The Miracle of Purun Bhagat' 133
        'Quiquern' 130, 133
        'Red Dog' 133
        'Rikki-Tikki-Tavi' 128, 133, 141
        The Second Jungle Book 130, 133,
            136
        'The Spring Running' 133, 135, 136,
            137
        Thy Servant, A Dog 72
        'Tiger, Tiger' 127, 133, 136
        'Toomai of the Elephants' 129, 133
        'The Undertakers' 133
        'The White Seal' 131, 133
Knight, Eric, *Lassie Come Home* 124

Kutzer, M. Daphne 156, 166
Kuznets, Lois 175

Lake District, in Beatrix Potter 170
Lamarck, Jean-Baptiste 96
Lamb, Charles 4, 27–8, 111
Landow, George P. 102
language acquisition, children 125, 126
Lansbury, Coral 75–6
Lejeune, Philippe 86, 88
Lewes, G.H. 110
Lewis, C.S. 112
liminal space, 'Jungle' as 139
Linder, Leslie, *A History of the Writings of
    Beatrix Potter* 170
Locke, John
    on *Aesop's Fables* 10, 11
    on animal cruelty 10
    educational ideas 9–10
    influence 22
    works
        *Essay Concerning Human Under-
            standing* 9
        *Letters to Edward Clarke on Educa-
            tion* 10
        Thoughts Concerning Education 10
Lockley, R.M., *The Private Life of the Rab-
    bit* 181
Lofting, Hugh 130
    Dr Dolittle 181
London, Jack 146
    The Call of the Wild 124
White Fang 124
Longfellow, Henry W. 111
Lurie, Alison 152
Lutts, Ralph H. 146

McBride, Dwight A. 81
McClure, John A. 140
MacDonald, Robert 141, 149, 163
Mangum, Teresa 90
masculinity, in Kipling 140–41
masquerades
    animal costumes 53
    decline 53
    function 54
Memoirs of Bob, the Spotted Terrier 37
Milne, A.A. 171
    Toad of Toad Hall 172

'missing link', children as 126, 137–8
Mohanty, Satya P. 138, 139
monkeys
    allegorical significance 138
    prejudice against 135, 138
Morgan, C. Lloyd, *Animal Behaviour* 145
Morris, Timothy 69
Mulready, William, *The Butterfly's Ball*,
    illustrations **52**
Myers, Mitzi 23, 26, 33, 41–2

narratee
    in *Black Beauty* 69–70
    in *The Wind in the Willows* 171
narrative voice 163–4
natural history
    information, animal autobiographies
      64–5
    marine 110
natural theology 3, 35, 36, 101, 102
    'Caliban Upon Setebos' 106
    In Memoriam 102
    meaning 17
    Newman on 102
    and science 18–19
Newbery, John
    A Little Pretty Pocket Book 12
    Goody Two-Shoes 4, 13, 15, 17
    Pretty Book of Pictures 12
Newman, John Henry, on natural theology
    102

Ouida, *Puck* 64

Pafford, Mark 141
Paley, William, *Natural Theology* 18, 103
Pan 7, 178
    description 177
    Parkes, Bessie Raynor 77
patriotism, in animal poems 55–6
Patteson, S. Louise, *Pussy Meow* 63
    vivisection 75
Perkins, Douglas 3
Petzold, Dieter 127–8
Pickering, Samuel 9, 16, 40
Pilkington, Mary
    Marvellous Adventures 64, 84, 89
      animal consciousness 71
    The Sorrows of Caesar 73

Pitts, Deirdre 164
Plumb, J.H. 12
Potter, Beatrix 3
    animal/human interaction 162
    conservationism 6–7
    Lake District settings 170
    narrative voice 163
    naturalist 152
    space in 165–7
    values 168–9
    works
      Jemima Puddle-duck 158, 162
      Mr Tod 159–60
      Peter Rabbit 37, 57, **154**, **155**, 157,
        165, 168
      The Pie and the Patty-Pan 159
      Pigling Bland 161, 162, 165, 167
      Squirrel Nutkin 154, 157
      The Tailor of Gloucester 152, 158,
        166
      The Tale of Benjamin Bunny 165
      The Tale of Mrs Tiggy-winkle 57,
        153, 159, 169–70
      The Tale of the Pie 154
      Tale of Samuel Whiskers 153, 163,
        166, 167, 170
      The Tale of Two Bad Mice 152–3,
        165, 166
      Tales 5, 6, 150, 151
      Tom Kitten 157, 167
Pratt, Samuel
    'The Brothers and the Blackbird' 35
    Pity's Gift 4, 16–17
Priestley, Joseph, *Disquisitions Relating to
    Matter and Spirit* 34
Primatt, Humphrey, Rev, *Dissertation on the
    Duty of Mercy* 40
Prisoner's Counsel Act (1836) 81

Quakerism, Anna Sewell 83
Quarles, Frances, *Emblems Divine and
    Moral* 11

Randall, Don 138–9
recapitulation theory 125–6, 149
Richardson, Alan 28
Richardson, Samuel 11
Ritvo, Harriet 12, 14–15, 16, 41, 181
Rodger, Mary, *Freaky Friday* 44

Romanes, George 6, 142, 145
Roosevelt, Theodore 146
Roscoe, William, *The Butterfly's Ball* 40, 51,
	52, 53
Rousseau, Jean-Jacques 4, 25
	Emile 19
	on fables 19–20
	influence 19–20, 22, 24, 26–7
RSPCA 3
	endorsement of *Black Beauty* 81
Rupert bear 181, 182

Sandham, Elizabeth, *The Adventures of
	Poor Puss* 64, 68
animal language in 68
Saunders, Julia 34
Saunders, Marshall, *Beautiful Joe* 64, **66**,
	67, 88
	animal language 65, 67
	significance of name 87
Schramm, Jan-Melissa 81, 82, 85
science, and natural theology 18–19
scientific materialism 98, 99
Scott, Carole 57, 156–7
Sellwood, Emily 97
Sendak, Maurice 167
sensibility, cult of 15–16
sentimentality 16
servants, animals, analogy 83–6
Seton, Ernest Thompson 3, 6, 91, 124–5
	animal naming 143–4
	didacticism 148–9
	Woodcraft Indians 149
	works
		'Bingo' 148
		'Johnny Bear' 142
		'The Kangaroo Rat' 142–3, 169
		'Krag, the Kootenay Ram' 143
		Life Histories of Northern Animals
			141
		Lives of the Hunted 141, 148
		'Lobo' 142
		'The Pacing Mustang' 142
		'Raggylug' 144
		'Redruff' 148
		'Silverspot' 142
		Wild Animals I have Known 141–4
		'Wully' 142
Sewell, Anna

Black Beauty 5, 14, 63, 66, 89
	animal consciousness 70, 73
	animal language 69–70
	anti-slavery discourse 78
	bearing-rein abolition 74, 79, 81, 83
	influence 74
	name significance 86
	narratee 69
	RSPCA endorsement 81
	sexual subtext 76
	Quakerism 83
	Uncle Tom's Cabin, comparison 78, 79
Shephard, E.H. 172
Sherwood, Martha, *The Little Woodman*
	123, 124
Shteir, Anne 95
slaves, animals, analogy 78–81
Smith, Charlotte 41
	Conversations 49–50
space, in Beatrix Potter 165–7
SPCA 3
	see also RSPCA
Stables, Gordon, *Sable and White* **67**, 68
	animal consciousness 71, 72–3
	animal language 67, 68–9
	Luath, significance of name 87
	vivisection 75
Steedman, Carolyn 84–5
Sterndale, Robert, *Natural History* 141
Sully, James 125
Swift, Jonathan, *Gulliver's Travels* 32

Taine, Hypolite 126, 127
	'The Acquisition of Language by Chil-
		dren' 125
talking animals
	in Kipling 124, 127, 129–30
	rationale 42–3, 126
	The Peacock at Home 54
	The Water Babies 119–20
	see also animal language
Taylor, Ann & Jane, *Signor Topsy-Turvy's
	Wonderful Magic Lantern* 41, 58–9
Tennyson, Alfred
	In Memoriam 6, 97, 99–100, 100–101,
		102, 104
	The Princess 121
Thorndike, Edward 146–7
Thornton, Lucy, *The Story of a Poodle*

animal language 66
   names, significance 87–8
Thum, Maureen 177
Topsy-Turvey poems 58–60
Tractarian movement 102
transformation trope 108, 112, 114, 132–3
Travers, P.L., *Mary Poppins* 59, 181
Trimmer, Sarah
   Easy Introduction 4, 17, 20
   Fabulous Histories 4, 11, 18, 30, 38–9,
      42–9, 81
      hierarchy in 41
      popularity 37
      xenophobia in 48
   The Guardian of Education 40
   Reading the Holy Scriptures 17
   The Story of the Robins 6, 42, 93–4, 123
Tucker, Charlotte, *Rambles of a Rat* 64–5,
      72, 89, 170
Turner, Brian 3
typological thinking 102

values, in Beatrix Potter 168–9
Victoria League 3
vivisection
   Pussy Meow 75

Sable and White 75
   see also anti-vivisection movement

Walsh, Susan 133
Watts, Isaac, *Treatise on Education* 17
Wells, H.G., *Island of Dr Moreau* 137
Whitley, David 11
wild animal stories, colonial content 123
wild children 132
Wolf Boy of Lucknow 132
Wollstonecraft, Mary 9, 41
   Original Stories from Real Life 4, 24–6,
      28, 40
   Vindication of the Rights of Men 25
   Vindication of the Rights of Women 24
women, animals, analogy 75–6
Woodcraft Indians 149
Wordsworth, William 4
   'Immortality Ode' 94, 114, 120
   'Ode to Duty' 120
Worster, Donald 45–6

xenophobia 48, 56

Young, Robert 139